CONTEMPORARY PAGANISM

GRAHAM HARVEY

Contemporary Paganism

Listening People, Speaking Earth

NEW YORK UNIVERSITY PRESS

Washington Square, New York

First published in the U.S.A in 1997 by
NEW YORK UNIVERSITY PRESS
Washington Square
New York, NY 10003

Library of Congress Cataloging-in-Publication Data

Harvey, Graham.
    Contemporary paganism : listening people, speaking earth / Graham
Harvey.
        p.   cm.
    Includes bibliographical references (p.   ) and index.
    ISBN 0-8147-3549-5
    1. Neopaganism.   I. Title.
    BF1571.H37   1997
    299'. 93--dc21   96-49887
                                                                    CIP

Printed in Hong Kong

Among the stones of the moles,
by salmon pool and heron lake
and in the greenwood of the hedgehogs
I walk with my love,
Molly.

PREFACE AND ACKNOWLEDGEMENTS

Paganism is a religion at home on Earth, an ecological spirituality, a somatic philosophy of life. It is not a preparation for Heaven or a quest for Enlightenment. It does not denigrate the body or the ordinary, mundane, everyday facts of life. It celebrates these things and, in doing so, intersects with many of the most vital interests of the contemporary world.

This book explores this growing religion. It introduces the various traditions and activities which meet under the umbrella term "Paganism". It does not dictate what Paganism *ought* to be, or what Pagans *ought* to do. It is interested in what Pagans actually do, actually believe, actually think, actually say about themselves and their spirituality. It is based on contacts with Pagans of many different sorts in many places. The majority of these contacts have been with British Pagans, but I am grateful also to American, Australian, Breton, Canadian, Finnish, French, German, Irish, Japanese, Norwegian, Swiss and other Pagans whom I have either met or corresponded with. It is these personal contacts which are the source of my celebration of Paganism, not the many books and magazines to which the footnotes draw attention. This literature and the increasing number of web sites on the Internet should not be mistaken for the more typically oral and dramatic presentations of Paganism today. Because humour and Imagination are central to Paganism, I have begun each main chapter with a quotation from Terry Pratchett who probably knows more than anyone about contemporary Paganism. Permission to quote extracts from the Discworld series has been granted by Colin Smythe on behalf of Terry Pratchett—for which I am very grateful.[1]

An increasing number of students are interested in knowing more about Paganism. This book is written with them in mind—without forgetting the lecturers who have the job of teaching them. The small number of researchers engaging with Pagans and Paganism themselves form a community with which I am glad to be associated, from which I have gained much and to which I hope this book will be valuable. I hope too that a broader audience will find the book interesting and useful. Most of all, however, I hope that Pagans—especially those with whom I continue to enjoy celebrating and those who have responded to my questionnaires, letters or email—will be happy to recognise their contribution to the following pages.

My approach within Religious Studies is phenomenological. That

---

[1] At the request of Colin Smythe each quotation that starts a chapter names the novel from which it is taken and refers to both the UK and US publishers—the latter are indicated by *.

vii

means that I take seriously people's self-understanding and self-presentation. While I am not necessarily convinced or enthralled by everything that Pagans do or say, I consider that what they do and say is what Paganism is. This is different to Theology in which the focus of attention is a set of beliefs held by religious people, usually those who claim the authority to define what should be believed. The object for the student of Religion is adequately to understand and describe what actually happens. Understanding is gained by observing and participating—not merely standing on the side spectating but, at some point, trying to experience what others experience. The test of the adequacy of the description comes in the criticism (positive and negative) of the work both by other academics and also, perhaps more important, by those described.

Paganism is a religion in which reciprocal relationships between humans and *all* others with whom we share life on Earth are significant. It is one of the religions of the world in which humans and their mundane deeds, thoughts, desires, intentions and beliefs are important because of the way such things affect and express relationships. Pagans are people who consider the world to be alive; they are listening to a speaking Earth.

I hope that what I have heard, seen and done among Pagans has resulted in a book which will be received as a reciprocation of all the gifts I have received. I am grateful to my publishers for their advice and encouragement. It would be inappropriate to thank by name all those with whom I have enjoyed celebrating or communicating. There are, however, a few who have been particularly helpful in providing encouragement or information. Others have offered invaluable criticism and advice, especially about earlier drafts of particular chapters. It would be wrong not to thank Andy, Asphodel, Barry, Ken, Jymn, Marion, Monica, Philip, Richard, Ronald, Sarasue, Shelley, Tim and Wren. To widen the circle, I cannot possibly repay the debt accrued in sharing the enchantment in Whittle Dean, drumming in Avalon, Newfoundland, walking labyrinths in Wessex and the Wirral, drinking tea in the trees—now destroyed—of Newbury and mead in Avebury, crying Wally in Stonehenge, doing ritual in Castlerigg and joining with blues singers, bodgers and flowerpots far too rarely. Finally, Molly has read all my words, heard all my thoughts, travelled with me to visit the ancestors, deities, dragons, sidhe, herons, hedgehogs and other friends and relations from Glen Carr to Tarxien. If she has not always shared my delight in Pagan gatherings, I am more than ecstatic that she has shared two handfastings and a wedding with me.

October 1996   Graham Harvey

CONTENTS

Preface and Acknowledgements   page vii

Chapters

1. Celebrating the Seasons   1

    Samhain   3
    Midwinter   6
    Imbolc   8
    Spring Equinox   9
    Beltain   10
    Summer Solstice   11
    Lughnasadh or Lammas   12
    Autumn Equinox and the full circle   13
    Lunar rhythms   14
    Star signs   14
    Calendar months   14
    Listening people, speaking Earth   15

2. Druidry   17

    Looking back, looking down   17
    Types and stereotypes   19
    Bards   20
    Ovates   25
    Druids   29
    Grades, hierarchies and Druid time   32
    Stonehenge   33
    Looking forward   33

3. The Craft of Witches   35

    The Charge of the Goddess   36
    Drawing Down the Moon   39
    Polarity and sexuality   40
    Nature   43
    Into the circle   43

Using energy   47
Cakes and wine   48
Types of Wicca   50
Granny Weatherwax, Nanny Ogg and Magrat Garlick   50
New Old Religion   51

4. Heathens   53

Northern cosmology   54
The Nine Worlds now   56
Festivals (time and place)   57
Priests and people   59
Runes: Galdr, Seidr and Taufr   61
Ecology   64
Race   65
Gods and Goddesses   66
Pride and prejudice   68

5. Goddess Spirituality   69

Avalon from the mists   70
History and Herstory   72
Goddess and Goddesses   75
Manifestations of Matriarchy   77
Circles empower   79
Contrary voices   81
Impact on other Pagans   84
Liberation Thealogy   85

6. Magic   87

What is Magic?   87
Esotericism   90
A note on Gnosis   92
What Magic is   92
The Colours of Magic   93
Ceremonial Magic   94
Left-Hand Path Magick   97
Chaos Magick   99

Signs and symbols 101
Natural and Kitchen Magic 101
Eco-magic 102
The Web 103
The ethics of Magic 104
Attentive scepticism 105

7. Shamanism 107

From Siberia with power 107
Extra pay 111
Ancient traditions rediscovered 114
New traditions revitalised 116
New imperatives 118
Raves in Cyberia 122
Experimenting with ecstasy 124

8. Ecology 126

Meditation and bulldozers 126
Somatic ecology 129
Ecological roots 131
Shades of green 136
Gnostic temptation 138
Hedgehogs, vegans, hunters and prairies 139
Listening neighbourliness 141

9. Earth Mysteries 143

Gaia 144
Micro- and macro-cosmos 146
Ley and Dragon lines 148
Sacred sites 150
Terrestrial zodiacs 152
Sacred geometry 152
Geomancy 153
Earth healing 156
Dragons and rituals 156
The sound of what happens 158

10. Gods and Hedgehogs in the Greenwood   160

    Religion and Theology   161
    The Greenwood   162
    The Otherworld   165
    Pagan deity-talk   165
    Animists and atheists   170
    Ancestors and animals   171
    Faeries, elves and others   172
    Hobgoblins and foul fiends   173
    Pagans in the Greenwood   174
    Theology within Ecology   175

11. History, Sources and Influences   177

    History and folklore   178
    Mythology, archaeology and anthropology   179
    First Nations   181
    Fantasy and Future Fiction   181
    Discworld   185
    Nature   186
    Experience and intuition   188
    Beyond the Enlightenment   189
    Old Religion or New Religion?   191
    Coming home and coming out   192

12. Rites of Passage   194

    From room to room   194
    Life cycles   196
    Paganism and rites of passage   197
    Child blessing   199
    Marriage   200
    Funerals and remembrance of the dead   203
    Initiation   206
    Male mysteries   206
    Passages to health   207
    Paganism as therapy   209
    Rounding off   210

13. Paganism and other Religions   211

    Authority   212
    Inter-Faith Dialogue   214
    Paganism misunderstood   217
    Dealing with defamation   221
    Among the religions   222
    All Our Relations   227

Bibliography   229

Index   243

1

CELEBRATING THE SEASONS

Although every day is sacred and all the Earth is holy, yet there are times and places that seem to be more special. Not all days are alike and not all places are the same. Sacredness collects as if in pools and sometimes splashes over into the ordinary, everyday parts of life. Even in those religions which give primacy to the "supernatural", that which is sacred and that which is profane cannot be kept completely separate.[1] In those religions which refuse to divorce nature from supernature, the mundane is intimate with the sacred. In polytheistic cultures all of life manifests "divine powers and potencies" with which human and other-than-human persons or "all our relatives"—i.e. everything that exists— are encouraged to become increasingly intimate.[2]

Paganism is a polytheistic Nature religion. It is re-creating ways of relating to the Earth and all its inhabitants which express human relationships with all that exists. It is a sense of being "at home" on Earth. The dichotomies of sacred and profane or religious and secular are of little value here because they imply far more than the idea that some things are more significant than others. They set up a barrier between ordinary or "mundane" activities and ceremonial, symbolic or "religious" activities which is not significant in nature-celebrating or life-affirming traditions. Further, they establish a hierarchy in which some things are far above other things. Paganism asserts, however, that our everyday lives are vitally important. Ordinary human activities significantly affect "all our relatives". When we drive to a supermarket to buy plastic-wrapped fruit from the other side of the Earth we casually affect a host of others with whom we share this planet and Life. When we sit in a tree threatened by road builders we affect another range of those to whom we are related by virtue of our shared life on Earth. These two examples illustrate the complexities of contemporary living and the difficulties of creating a life-affirming, nature-celebrating tradition today.

Perhaps "creating" is the wrong word. Pagans spend little time deliberately contemplating the formation of their religion. They rarely indulge in theology or even in sustained thinking about ecology. On the other hand, people who discover the appropriateness of naming themselves Pagan are not thereby compelled to accept a codified set of beliefs or practices. There is no Pagan mission, evangelism or dogma.

---

[1] See Hallowell (1960), Morrison (1992a and 1992b) and Detwiler (1992).
[2] Deirdre Green (1989): 9; and Hallowell (1960).

People decide to call themselves Pagan because they recognise something about Paganism to which they have an affinity, perhaps no more than its respect for the Earth or its celebration of seasonal or human natural cycles. For some it is the discovery that they are not alone in considering traditional Otherworld people (e.g. the faeries, elves, gnomes and dwarves)[3] to be more than childhood dreams or denizens of fantasy-writers' fictions. From these discoveries of affinity, people have to experiment and discover for themselves whether they will follow others further along these paths. There are books and groups which will help the explorer discover the terrain which others have chosen to inhabit. At least they will help the explorer to find a vantage point from which to view the scenery. While it is all too easy to be swayed by force of numbers into accepting the veracity of things that one has not (yet) experienced, most Pagan groups offer their world-view not so much as "Truth" or divine revelation to be assented to, but as "Beauty" to be appreciated. This has permitted Paganism to develop as a fundamentally pluralist tradition. It also means that all Pagans are contributing to the growth of Paganism.

Paganism is evolving, it has no complete, codified or orthodox form. My interest here is not with the seeds or roots of the tradition—comprehensively explored by Ronald Hutton and Howard Eilberg-Schwartz[4]—but with its continuing growth. A reading of this book might conclude that Paganism is not a single tree but an entire wood, not an "-ism" but a broad movement. The roots have produced a tree which has seeded many trees which have evolved in different forms. Whether Paganism is one tree with many branches or several different trees, it is alive and growing. This growth continues to be healthy and vigorous because all Pagans, bringing their own lifestyles, preferences, desires and dislikes, contribute to the evolution. This is not an assertion that there are no problems among Pagans or that Paganism is somehow the perfect way to live. There are considerable differences of opinion among Pagans and there are Pagans whose ego and desire for power or sexual gratification harm others. These harmful facts of life must certainly be dealt with by Pagans and those they relate to, but they do not blight the whole religion.[5]

Biologists identify plants or animals by looking for "taxic indicators": things which distinguish one species from another. All (healthy) spiders have eight legs, but each spider has specific markings which indicate that it is one sort of spider and not another. This chapter explores one taxic indicator of contemporary Paganism: its celebration of seasonal festivals. Most Pagans now celebrate eight annual seasonal

[3] See chapter 10.
[4] See chapter 11.
[5] See Greenwood (1996), Simes (1996) and Bennett (1996).

festivals,[6] but some significant groups celebrate a different cycle. A spider with only four legs would be a sick spider, but categories like "sick" and "heresy" are not useful in the Study of Religions: they are a kind of polemic which should be discouraged even among religious people. So, while asserting that the celebration of natural cycles is a taxic indicator of Paganism, I do not assert that the number or timing of such celebrations indicates belonging to or exclusion from Paganism. At the most, such divergences indicate relationship to a particular type of Paganism. The antiquity or modernity of any celebration is not the central issue, though they are debated among Pagans and will be noted in that context. This chapter aims to provide some insight into the celebration of the eight festivals, followed by a brief introduction to other festive cycles—especially those of the moon, the stars and the twelve calendar months. All these festive calendars encapsulate, express and inculcate similar experiences and themes and have much wider relevance. That is, they are intimately connected with other taxic indicators of Paganism, especially environmentalism, polytheism and colourful, imaginative ritual.

The eight festivals form a "wheel of the year", a cycle which returns the celebrant to the same time each year. The cycle could be said to begin at any point, but one festival is most often identified as the beginning, as a new year feast. Even Pagans who celebrate this cycle sometimes find such a starting point out of harmony with their intuitions, moods and desires and feel free to celebrate the feast without considering it a new year feast.

Samhain

A child is born from the darkness of the womb, day from the darkness of the night. Plants sprout from the darkness of the ground. Many Pagans consider the year to begin with a festival which marks the beginning of winter in the northern hemisphere. (In the southern hemisphere some Pagans continue to celebrate northern hemisphere dates, being perhaps more intimately connected to the traditions of their ancestors than to those of their lands. Others adapt the cycle to the seasons they experience.) With the days growing darker and colder winter is a time for turning inwards towards the centre: the home, the hearth, the individual, the heart. A time to find a secure safe place to care for self. A dark time for the nurturing and nourishment of desire and intentions, waiting for the fertile warmth of spring before full outward expression. A time when old things decay and rot down in preparation for the feeding of new fresh growth.

[6] For the history and origins of these and other calendar customs see Hutton (1996b). Also see Ó hÓgain (1990): 402-5.

This Pagan new year feast is frequently named *Samhain* after an ancient Irish festival. The name is sometimes pronounced as written, *sam-hain* or, increasingly often according to its Irish pronunciation, *sow-ain* ("sow" as in female pig). Some Pagans are happy to call it Halloween after the popular, originally Christian, festival with which it partly coincides. Samhain includes the night of 31 October and 1 November, and sometimes a day or two either side as well. Most of these eight festivals are treated as beginning on the eve of the day, i.e. the feast on 1 February begins at nightfall on 31 January. The night of Samhain (i.e. 31 October/Halloween) is more frequently celebrated than the following day despite the historical precedence of the day over its eve.

Halloween is now widely and popularly celebrated as a time of fun and mischief, a time for ghost stories and witchy goings-on. In Britain it is closely followed by Guy Fawkes Day (5 November), celebrated with bonfires and fireworks and more parties. Soon after that comes Remembrance Day, now held on or as near as possible to the original Armistice Day (11 November) which commemorates the end of World War I and now honours the dead of the two world wars. This day and comparable times for honouring veterans are important to some Pagans (especially veterans or military personnel). Irish mythology and folk tradition in Wales and north-west England associates Halloween with visitations by ghosts and the faery. It is a time when "the veils between this world and the other-world are thin". Pagans combine all these themes into their celebrations.

Some Pagans spend the night out in the woods, in small groups around a fire. They will share food and drink, tell stories (not always ancient, profound or serious ones), remember the past year, perhaps speak of their hopes for the coming year. Some will speak of relatives who have recently died, especially in the past year. Others will name those born that year. Music might be played—drums, bodhrans, penny-whistles and didgeridoos are particularly popular. Lanterns made from hollowed pumpkins and turnips may be hung from the trees or placed on rocks round about the fire. The mood will frequently be light-hearted and not overly "religious", "meaningful" or "precious". To an outsider this may appear to be merely a group of friends chatting around a fire. Even when these friends perform a ritual, it will probably be informal and fairly relaxed. Many groups prefer to meet in a member's house where a room might be set aside and prepared as a "temple" for the evening or permanently. There they might perform a carefully crafted ceremony either prepared by the group or drawn from a respected source. It may be easier to incorporate ritual equipment such as cups, wands, daggers or robes in the context of an indoor ceremony, but these can be used in the woods also. More formal ceremonies will be followed by more relaxed eating, drinking and socialising—perhaps envisaged as "earthing the energy", perhaps for no reason beyond the significant pleasure of good company. Most Pagan rituals begin with greetings to the four cardinal directions: north, east, south, west (not necessarily in that order). Some also greet "the centre" and sometimes "the above" and "the below" also. These greetings may be performed by one experienced or chosen person or by one person per direction. They might also be chosen randomly, "just because they were standing in the north". The directions may be addressed simply as directions, or as the (personified?) four winds who rule them, sometimes by their Greek names: Boreas, Eurias, Notus, Zephyrus. Others address the traditionally associated elements: earth, air, fire and water. Yet others address associated creatures, bear or gnome, hawk or sylph, stag or salamander, salmon or undine.[7]

At Samhain it is deemed particularly appropriate to invite the presence of the ancestors, but this could happen at any festival. The company of other-than-human persons might be requested also. The wood itself, or woodland spirits, or the spirit of place might be thanked for the provision of firewood. The company of trees, rocks, winds and such "natural" other-than-human persons might be acknowledged. Such connections with Nature are made even within a building. The main body of a Samhain ritual will most frequently focus on the honouring of death. Some groups will choose a member to personify death, enabling each participant to "face death". A guided meditation may allow everyone to "die before they die", imaginatively facing their mortality and recognising the role of death in the natural life-cycle.

Note again that the more formal aspects of these occasions are not more important than the "fun and games". Folk tradition and the popular spread of Halloween traditions have provided a range of ways in which the festival can be enjoyed. While Pagans may take some of these traditions "seriously" they are nonetheless entertained by them. They may see blindfold games and apple-bobbing as ways of symbolising the gaining of gifts from the other-world, but their indulgence is marked by as much hilarity as in a purely "secular" context.

Despite the pressures put on Pagan parents by the now slowly dying fears of "Ritual Abuse" accusations,[8] the party aspects of Halloween (in both its popular and its Pagan guises) make it an ideal time for children's participation. Indeed, without children's participation celebrations can lose the spontaneity and "down to earth" character that many Pagans associate with their festivals. Conversely, children's participation does not make the celebration less meaningful. There is

---

[7] For examples compare Vivianne Crowley (1989): 105-8 with Carr-Gomm (1993): 151-5.
[8] Harvey (1995b).

usually a clear demarcation between those parts of a celebration in which children can be present or participants—especially in the context of a prepared ceremony. Samhain, however, can often be celebrated in several stages. Early on, the children can be included in or actually lead games. In a transitional phase a story might give the children an idea of the serious side of the celebration, e.g. honouring our dead relatives. More formal ceremonies might take place later. There are some Pagans who dislike all involvement of children and others who dislike occasions which are not suitable for children.

To summarise this introduction to Samhain: this new year festival in which the dead are honoured highlights the way that Paganism draws on ancient themes and distils contemporary trends—here the growing popularity of a calendar custom. The festival combines concern with human culture and engagement with the changing seasons. The discussion has suggested different styles of celebration from spontaneous drumming in the woods to carefully crafted rituals in "temples". It has introduced some of the other-than-human persons who might be invited to these celebrations, including common ones like trees and usually hidden ones like the faery folk. This has also hinted at the radically animated or living world that Pagans inhabit—even the winds can be addressed meaningfully—and the centrality of Nature. Finally, it has introduced a difficulty and a delight of Pagan celebrations: the presence and involvement of children.

Midwinter

The wheel of the year rolls on into the depths of winter. If most Pagans celebrate Samhain, almost all celebrate the next of the eight festivals, winter solstice. Those who prefer to name themselves Heathens might celebrate the same themes as other Pagans in early November (e.g. the Odinic Rite honour their ancestors on 11 November), but the solstices and equinoxes are marked by all traditions. Winter solstice has the shortest daylight hours and the longest night of the year. The night was known to the pre-Christian Anglo-Saxons as *Modranacht*, Mother Night. Regrettably there are no surviving sources to tell us what this most pregnant name meant. On the other hand, this at least gives people freedom, if it does not actually impel them, to create their own meanings and their own celebrations.

Pagans draw on popular midwinter festivities, many of which have an honourable and ancient ancestry. They go into the woods to collect greenery with which to decorate their homes and, for a while, the home is absorbed into the Greenwood—that part of nature which is less human-dominated, if not actually wildwood, than other places and is thus some steps nearer to the Otherworld.[9] In the dead of winter there is abundant, fruitful life. Holly, ivy, mistletoe, yew and other fruit-bearing greenery are cut—after suitable requests—and brought home. Bringing a Christmas tree indoors has, of course, become a popular custom and is not alien to Pagan homes, though they might call it a Yule-tree.

Pagans name this whole festive season Yule. Its traditional twelve days are frequently counted from solstice rather than from Christmas Day and, as is the popular custom, Pagans focus on a few main days of festivity. The solstice day itself and its eve are especially important, 25 December is significant to some Pagans, as it is to Christians and Mithraists,[10] as the first day following the winter solstice when there is appreciably more light. For Christians, of course, this light is symbolic of Jesus. In Paganism the actual sunlight is important: the sun is returning, the dark diminishing. Pagans are not dualistic: they neither wish to banish darkness nor see darkness as symbolic of badness, "evil" or even "that which is unbalanced". Their celebrations typically honour the fertile darkness, the womb from which the light returns, the earth in which seeds will germinate. Sometimes Pagans refer to "the dark side", meaning those things which they would like to outgrow, move on from or leave behind; perhaps things which they find unhealthy or restrictive. These are typically faced, named and worked on rather than repressed or repented from.

In contrast to Samhain, the celebrations of midwinter take place largely but not solely in daylight. There are a few hardy individuals who spend the long cold night outside and honour it by performing a ceremony at midnight. There are more who say farewell to the setting sun and return home to celebrate in the shelter and comfort of their now forested home. They honour the dark, the cold and the dying but also light candles or lanterns to anticipate the returning light, warmth and growth.

The solstice is a working day for many people, and they will see the sunrise from, or on the way to, work. Others will find a vantage point from which to watch the sun rise, fortified perhaps by flasks of mulled wine or ale. Winter solstice is marked in some Pagan homes, as Christmas is in others, by the exchange of gifts and by feasting. Other Pagans give gifts and feast on both the solstice and on 25 December, as the day on which the sun—sometimes personified as either male or female—begins to return. Yuletide in ancient tradition and popular custom combines quiet family times and more boisterous public occasions. For most people, Pagans included, boisterousness finds its opportunity on New Year's Eve. Those who have celebrated their new

[9] See chapter 10.

[10] The present tense here is not a mistake, there are groups who have revived the mysteries of Mithras.

year at Samhain may not be averse to celebrating again, while others acknowledge 1 January rather than Samhain to be the beginning of the year. Times of quiet reflection and public celebration are separated but held together within a special time—all of life is balanced in the various moods of the festival.

Yule has added to our picture of Paganism a further example of the relationship between the human world and the "natural" world. In cutting greenery to decorate the home Pagans find ways to express their relatedness to other living things. Relationships with other human people are expressed both in gift giving and festivities at home and in partying in more public places. The winter solstice is clearly timed by the relationship between Earth and Sun. In marking this time as special by observing sunset, midnight and sunrise, Pagans harmonise their lives with natural cycles.

Imbolc

Although it is still cold on the hills and snow can be expected in the months to come, Pagans honour the beginning of spring on 1 February. Many use the Irish name, *Imbolc*, sometimes written *Oímelg*. In Irish these are variant spellings and are both pronounced, *iv-olc*; but they are more often pronounced as written. The name means "lactation", referring to the lambing season which traditionally begins at this time. Others name the festival by a variant of the name of a pan-Celtic deity, the Goddess Brigid (Bride, Brighde, Brigantia).

The festival may now be celebrated simply by going to see the first-born lambs of the year, or the first snowdrop flowers, or some other sign that spring is coming. While honouring the beginning of spring, Pagans also honour the wintry dark and cold which can still be dominant in the coming months. If spring can be personified as a youthful Goddess and, in turn, represented by a young girl, the tradition of also honouring the older, wiser aspect of the divine, the Crone, is also popular. London's House of the Goddess has been adapting the Brideog tradition for urban Pagans who are re-establishing a sense of community. A corn-dolly image of the Goddess is welcomed into a chosen home after a week-long journey visiting other homes. It is placed in a prepared bed by the women, who later welcome the men back inside from their own celebrations. Imbolc is also used by some Pagans as a time to express their hopes for individual or communal, personal or political change. Inner intentions become manifest in outer actions just as spring flowers are emerging. Past phases of life are left behind, just as homes are spring-cleaned.

At Imbolc Pagans notice and celebrate the natural expressions of the seasons such as snow and snowdrops. They make connections between such seasonal expressions and their own personal desire for growth and change. Deities are implicated in these cycles, not as almighty, omni-competent, praiseworthy beings, but as those with whom human people share life on Earth. Polytheistic deities send people back to their own "ordinary" living with the sense that everything is infused with sacredness. Pagans can image their deities in material form, and consider that the Goddess can "take up residence" in that image because Paganism is a spirituality which does not denigrate matter and because the physical already manifests divine life.

Spring Equinox

The spring and autumn equinox festivals celebrate the relationship between Earth and Sun. On these two days the sun rises and sets along the equator, due east and due west, making the hours of darkness equal to the hours of light. There is little or nothing to be gained from north-west European tradition about equinox celebrations—they were added to the cycle of festivals in the modern period.

For many Pagans spring equinox is much like Imbolc "only more so". There are more flowers, more young animals, more warmth, more going-out—more spring. The sap is rising in the trees. Spring can be seen as a time when energies rise. Sometimes, however, this can be chaotic, evidenced by the equinoctial gales. It can be seen as a time when all of life is trying to find the harmony already seen in the balance of day and night. Meditation about the individual's desires is balanced with experimentation with more outgoing, self-affirming activities. The myth of St George, the Princess and the Dragon can be re-worked. The dragon symbolises the Earth's rising, wild and potentially chaotic energies which are not destroyed but pinned down, harnessed and channelled in beneficial directions by the Earth-respecting green George and the princess-priestess-Goddess.[11]

Many Pagan celebrations of spring borrow elements from Mediterranean themes such as the return of Kore/Persephone from the underworld, the increase of life (crops and lambs) at Passover, the rising again of a previously cut down God, hero or lover. April was known to the Anglo-Saxons as Eostre, after a Goddess whose festival was celebrated during the month and from which the Christian festival Easter takes its English name. Apart from the name's relationship with the east, nothing is known for certain about this Goddess, but some Pagans theorise that she is the same as Ishtar, Asherah, Astarte and Isis, on whose myths they therefore draw for their celebrations. She is celebrated as spring's powerful personification, sunrise, the gift and giver of life and fruitfulness, the celebrant of her own vitality and sexuality. Popular Easter traditions such as painted eggs, decorated

[11] See chapter 9.

spring-trees and chocolate eggs and rabbits are common too among Pagans in their spring celebrations, though hares might be more earthy, Pagan symbols than the more domestic rabbits. Others enjoy reviving once popular traditions such as rolling eggs down hills.

Equinox is hardly a very distinctive or dynamic time in the Pagan social or festive calendar. Its themes seem to reiterate those of Imbolc or anticipate those of Beltain. However, the discussion has illustrated the way that Pagans draw on a wide range of traditions: ancient Celtic, Teutonic, Mediterranean and west Asian alongside medieval customs. It has shown that Pagans can use old myths to rekindle awareness and celebration of the changing seasons and to create dramatic rituals for these celebrations. The primary importance of the equinoxes, however, is the fact that they provide valuable mid-season celebrations to the new cycle of eight seasonal festivals. These times were once far too busy with either sowing or harvesting (or other work supporting the sowers and harvesters) to allow the luxury of a festive break. Now the additional festivals complete a cycle which provides regular opportunities to revitalise relationships with the Earth, natural cycles and all those with whom human people share life. As they stress the need for balance and harmony, the equinoxes might be seen as the festivals most relevant to the contemporary world.

Beltain

Summer is brought in on 1 May and its eve with fires and flowers, exuberance and larger gatherings. Most Pagans call this festival Beltain (Beltane or Beltaine), an Irish name meaning "bright fire", which originally referred only to the actual fire ceremony in which herds were blessed, but now labelling the whole festival. Pagans have renewed old customs like the Jack in the Green and Hobby Horse, spreading them beyond their original, often limited, geographical locations. They have found new significance in the May Queen who now tends to represent the season or an appropriate deity rather than presiding over village carnivals. Some Pagans also revive the once important Summer King to accompany the May Queen. Many Pagans go into the woods on May Eve and spend the night there around a bonfire. For many it will be a night of love and passion. While few, if any, now decorate the streets with flowers and greenery, or bring back a may-pole or lead village dances, they will almost certainly cut May blossom—after suitable requests—to garland their lover and/or to place in some significant part of their home. In Frome, Somerset, the Secular Order of Druids has participated in the (re-)creation of May Day customs including may-pole dancing (albeit the Victorian ribboned variety), a Hobby Horse and racing round loaves of bread down a steep hill. The bawdy side of the May tradition is also richly evoked by their "Cucumber Dancers".

While the proceedings begin with the Druids naming a cheese at a spring in the town, they make no attempt to add solemnity to the festivities or to advertise themselves. Their participation could be seen by passers-by as merely fooling-around or dressing-up—no-one hands out leaflets explaining the "serious meaning" of the occasion. This is typical of many public Pagan activities which are carried out for their own sake rather than for publicity or to recruit new members. Not infrequently an interested enquirer might be told only that a particular ceremony is in celebration of the Earth, or a protest against the pollution of the Earth.

Beltain is a celebration of the vitality of the Earth. It is a time of love, of carnival, of flowering fertility and abundant provision. Sexuality is a central part of Pagan spirituality, celebrations and relationships, and Beltain is a popular time for weddings, often named handfastings.[12] These "ordinary" or "secular" things are honoured by Pagans. Paganism is not concerned primarily with the unusual or the supernatural, but with the miracle of ordinary life in all its facets.

Summer Solstice

Summer solstice continues the themes of Beltain: vitality and exuberance. Summer solstice is honoured as midsummer's day, usually replacing the traditional date, 24 June, St John's Day. All-night vigils are customary and, given the brevity and mildness of the summer night, not so arduous as a winter night vigil. Watching the summer sunrise is widely perceived to be a habit typical of Druids at Stonehenge, accompanied by the mass of the media, police riot squads and "New Age" travellers. In fact, there are many places where Pagans of all sorts, including the travellers,[13] prefer to watch the sun rise—and many prefer more congenial company than the media and riot squads. Gatherings at midsummer do tend to be larger than those at any other festival, again due largely to the weather but perhaps also to the mood of the occasion: open, celebratory, warm, outgoing. Whatever pressures there may be on Pagans, they do not now live in societies dependent on their crops and flocks. Summer is therefore now far from the dangerous time it once was, with its diseases, storms and raiders. Customs once intended for protection, such as lighting fires and carrying blazing torches around fields, can now be re-visioned as celebrating the life-giving sun. The sun and Earth themselves are far less ambiguous than they might once have been as both givers and takers of life. Solar devastation, which causes melting ice caps, radiation, and desertification in Africa, is now warded off not by supplications to the

[12] See chapter 12.
[13] Many of whom are Pagans who see themselves as making pilgrimage around the land.

sun but by action against human pollutants. Summer solstice is a time for high-profile "Green" protests, many of them growing from Pagan, Earth-respecting motivations.

Midsummer is one of three significant times for making connections with other-than-human persons such as faeries and elves—the other two being Samhain and Beltain. Contemporary Pagan tradition is not always identical with earlier understandings: the faery seem to have returned from their misty Otherworld having become more sociable, more helpful, less tricksy and less belligerent than they once were. There are signs, however, that Pagans are beginning to see the wisdom of the older tradition. Perhaps the faery had cast a glamour which made them appear more friendly than they really are.[14] All this introduces the re-discovery by Pagans that the Nature they honour is not all "fluffy bunnies" but can be sharp-toothed and messy. Such a discovery is part of the process by which many Pagans distinguish themselves from the "New Age".[15]

Lughnasadh or Lammas

This festival of the beginning of autumn is known either as Lughnasad or as Lammas, sometimes by both names. Lughnasadh (Irish, the mourning of the many-talented God Lugh) in Irish tradition included fairs, ball-games and horse-racing but was a pan-Celtic first-fruits festival. Similarly, Lammas (Old English *hlaf-mæsse*, loaf feast) names the Anglo-Saxon first-fruits celebration. After the hard work of the hay harvest and when the barley, rye or wheat was nearly ready for harvest, the first ripe heads of grain were cut and ground for the loaves which formed a central part of the feast. The exact day of the celebration obviously depended on the ripeness of the grain and therefore varied from place to place. There is some evidence, however, of a regular celebration on 1 August in both continental Europe and Ireland.

Although few Pagans now work in agriculture, they do still depend on grains and other harvested crops. Their attempt to renew respectful and intimate human relationships with nature include the awareness that "nature" includes all that we eat and drink. It is not just wild places that are celebrated but all the environment, including human-controlled ones like wheat fields. The traditional song "John Barleycorn"[16] encapsulates the myth popular among Pagans today of the "barbarous" cutting and grinding, baking or brewing of the grain which yet proves to be the "strongest man at last", the one without whom nothing else can happen, and life itself cannot continue. Harvest can be seen as an

---

[14] See chapter 11.
[15] See chapter 13.
[16] Recorded, for example, by Fairport Convention (1978).

acting out of this necessary barbarity,[17] the taking life that life might continue. It can also be celebrated as a willing self-sacrifice by the grain; a giving of life. All this can be effectively enacted in Pagan rituals. An actual sheaf of wheat or barley can be danced around the ceremonial circle, to be symbolically cut down so that a loaf of bread hidden inside can be revealed and shared among all participants. A chalice or horn full of barley wine might also be passed around. The grain, bread and wine are honoured not just as symbols or sacraments but in their own right too. Their ordinary, mundane nature is as sacred as their "spiritual meaning". Conversely, there are forms of life-taking that many Pagans object to, including fox hunting. The original John Barleycorn song ends with a verse bestowing the strength of "Little Sir John" without whom "the hunter he can't hunt the fox". This can be amended into "the hunt-sab[oteur]s they can't fox the hunt".

Autumn Equinox and the Full Circle

There is little to add here to the discussion of spring equinox. Again it is a time to look for balance and harmony. Whereas spring celebrated growing things, autumn celebrates full growth, maturity and harvest. Autumn equinox is a time to pause and honour this part of the cycle and to consider what the year has brought, what has been achieved.

Within this full circle of eight annual festivals Paganism combines celebrations of nature "out there", with that of similar themes or experiences within their own individual and social lives. People take time to observe and immerse themselves in the changing seasons and life-cycles of Earth. Simultaneously, someone who made New Year's resolutions, whether at Samhain or on 1 January, will hope to see their desires or intentions bear fruit. One of the values of the cycle of eight festivals is that roughly once every six weeks people have an opportunity to consider the progress of their lives alongside their celebration of wider natural cycles. They can contemplate themes such as birth, death, marriage, growth, harvest and decay—both "within" and "without". Such contemplation includes consideration of more ecologically responsible living and encourages deeper involvement with "Green" action. Progress through several turns of this wheel further enables the individual to look back at their journey and evaluate their growth. The cycle is not, therefore, a treadmill but it enables considerable personal development in ways chosen by the festival celebrant.

[17] Cp. Tawhai (1988): 859.

Lunar Rhythms

Four of the eight festivals, the solstices and equinoxes, are dated according to the relationship between Earth and the sun. Many Pagans also celebrate times marked by the relationship between Earth and moon. New moons and full moons are particularly, but not uniquely, significant in the Craft of Witches.[18] The moon is full every twenty-eight days, and times the Craft's regular gatherings or "esbats", in distinction from the solar "sabbats". They and many other Pagans are careful observers of the moon, watching its emergence from darkness, growth to fullness and decline back into darkness. In the rebirth of Paganism such affection for the moon has played a central and formative role. Symbolism connected with "the Goddess" frequently includes lunar symbols reflecting back the primacy of the moon among manifestations of the divine. The moon's rhythms are also significant for such things as planting, weeding and harvesting, cutting wands and staffs, and the beginning of new ventures. Few Pagans would marry during the moon's last quarter.

Star signs

Astrological signs and timing are of importance to many Pagans, especially those with more magical leanings. Pagan magazines frequently contain pages comparable to those of newspapers, though of a more thoughtful quality. Many are considerably more elaborate than this and show signs that the writers actually have some expertise in this ancient science and are not just making it up. Astrology can be seen as highlighting the interconnectedness of all things and be used in meditation on situations as well as in finding propitious occasions.

Calendar months

Seasonal or calendar feasts are important to all Pagans, but some prefer to celebrate only or primarily those festivals known from ancient times. Some Heathens stress the three festivals of the beginning of winter (Winter Nights), midwinter (Yule) and the beginning of summer. Others, noting the existence of midsummer celebrations across Europe, add summer solstice to their cycle. The majority of Heathens, however, complete their festive cycle with a celebration on an appropriate date in each calendar month. Some of these days focus on significant dates in history such as the victory of Ragnar Loðbrók at Paris or that of Hengest and Horsa in Kent. Others adapt popular, once Christian, festivals into more Heathen equivalents, e.g. St Valentine's Day (14 February) becomes the feast of Váli, son of Odin, avenger of Balder. If

---

[18] See chapter 3.

Váli is not a romantic figure neither was Valentine, but in fact the adaption depends merely on the rough similarity of the names. Still others adapt the eight festivals to their own tradition but also celebrate other, perhaps monthly, occasions.

This diversity of practice is expressive of a difference between many Heathens and other Pagans. Many Heathens are more concerned that their tradition be historically accurate. Some are scathing of the eclecticism and recent origins of other celebrations and cycles. However, even such diversities do not mask the fact that in their various calendars Pagans and Heathens are celebrating the same themes and seasons, drawing on the same understandings and similarly honouring the Earth.

Listening People, Speaking Earth

All these calendar feasts consciously take the celebrant through the natural cycle of the seasons, Earth in relationship with sun, moon and stars, and the individual in relationship with the environment. They also enable each person to find ways to express themselves and direct the growth of their own identity in self-chosen, self-affirming ways. These themes are based on the understanding that Earth is alive and also a community of related living beings. The human world is not divorced from the natural Earth. This truism applies generally to all human activities: people identify themselves by relationship to rivers (Geordies are people born within a mile of the Tyne) and they wear more clothes in cold weather, fewer in hot weather (even in offices and other air-conditioned buildings). It is, however, programmatic for contemporary Pagans for whom that which is "ordinary" is not divorced from that which is sacred. They recognise no dualism which denigrates matter in favour of spirit. That which is "worldly" is not necessarily indicative of lack of significance, importance or sacredness. What is significant for Pagans is the attempt to discern that which affirms Life and that which negates it.

This chapters has suggested some of the central features of Paganism and introduced some of its diversities. The celebration of a single festival or of a cycle of festivals does not *define* Paganism. Considering the Earth to be worthy of protection from ecological devastation is not the sole preserve of Pagans. Nor are Pagans alone in their interest in self-affirmation and self-development. Theirs is not the only religion which is not interested in evangelism, dogma or hierarchy. The recovery of ancient traditions and their refurbishment as ways of living in today's world are also not unique to Pagans. Pagan reverence for Celtic and Teutonic deities is more distinctive, but theology is not absolutely central to Paganism and there are Pagan atheists.

In short, this introduction has not offered a definition of Paganism and has not suggested that this book will codify what Paganism must be. My intention is to describe the diverse, pluralist, growing and living spirituality that Pagans themselves recognise as contemporary Paganism. Significantly, the name Pagan (and its cognate, Heathen) points to something that *everybody* can do. Whatever the name has meant in its long history, for those who name themselves Pagan it means "those who honour the Earth". Pagans may be the only people who accept the whole package (polytheism, seasonal festivals, nature-centred spirituality and lifestyle, recovery of ancestral, indigenous pre-Christian traditions, ecology, self-affirmation, pluralism etc.) but anyone could adopt any of these things. Even the central theme, honouring nature, can be expressed in various ways, none of them exclusive to Pagans. However, the root, trunk, branch and fruit of the matter is that whatever else Pagans do and however "Green" other people might be, Paganism is a religion centrally concerned with celebrating Nature. Pagans are people who are listening to the living, speaking Earth.

2

DRUIDRY

Like Druids everywhere they believed in the essential unity of all life, the healing power of plants, the natural rhythm of the seasons and the burning alive of anyone who didn't approach all this in the right frame of mind...[1]

Druids have been part of the religious, cultural and charitable life of Western Europe at least since the eighteenth century. There are now Druids in most European countries, and most countries where people of European ancestry live.[2] Not all of them are Pagan, not all of them have Celtic ancestors, not all of them speak Celtic languages and not all of them agree on what "Druid" means. Perhaps the only thing that they all agree on is that human sacrifice is not part of Druidry! Some say it never was and that this was just Roman propaganda to justify the slaughter of a previously respected class of wise and religious people.

This chapter is devoted to the Pagan Druids of the contemporary world. Mention will be made of various groups of Druids, which are referred to as "Orders" or "Groves". The discussion begins, albeit briefly, with some mention of historical Druids of both ancient and modern times. This redresses the balance of scepticism frequently voiced by academics.

Looking back, looking down

Archaeologists often think that they alone have the right to determine the validity of other people's claims to be Druids. They insist that they know what Druids really did and believed, and what they did not do and did not believe. Only Iron Age Druids are authentic. Druids can only be seen as figures of the remote past. An eighteenth, nineteenth or twentieth century "Druid" cannot be considered authentic.

It is claimed that the ancient Druids were a Celtic priestly caste, political leaders entrusted with memorising lengthy genealogies, and had nothing whatever to do with Stonehenge or any other pre-Celtic stone circle. Furthermore, only those to whom this description applies can call themselves Druids. Applying the same approach to Christianity would lead to the rejection of all church-going, hierarchical, creed-believing—and non-Jewish—people who dared claim that name. This is clearly nonsense.

---

[1] Terry Pratchett, *The Light Fantastic*. (1986): 56-7. (*1988): 65.
[2] Carr-Gomm (1996a) contains valuable regional discussions.

17

Druidry may well have ceased to exist as a living tradition during the Roman period, perhaps surviving slightly longer in Ireland. There was no room for their political skills under Roman administration and their religious services may have been replaced by other functionaries. With the rise to power of Christianity any surviving Druids, as in Ireland, rapidly lost their primary functions. There is little doubt that archaeologists and historians have clarified our understanding of ancient Druids and ancient Celtic religions in general but there is no reason for the blanket dismissal of all other users of the name Druid. Being wrong does not negate being religious, just as much as being sincere is no guarantee of correctness. People who named themselves Druids in the eighteenth century had their own reasons for doing so. Some were rejecting the *forms* of Christianity available at the time and developing new social forms which they chose to associate with an ancient, ancestral and archetypal name. In the nineteenth century the name Druid was also associated with close-knit, caring communities of cultured and peaceful people which made it an apt symbol for charitable groups. Druids remained powerfully emotive figures for cultural and linguistic traditions, especially those threatened by dominant and hostile foreign powers. They were recruited into movements aimed at strengthening cultural and national identities, particularly in Brittany and Wales. For some, Druids inspired revolutionary zeal against English or French cultural, administrative and religious control. In England the Ancient Order of Druids was formed and continues as a charitable peaceable fraternity which does not involve itself—as a group—in religion or politics. A considerable number of Druids can legitimately be described as belonging to a distinct type of Freemasonry, one in which antiquarian interests, fraternal clubs and charity combine.

Welsh, Cornish, Breton and other Celtic cultural Druidries could stress the bardic arts without compromising the predominant Christianity of their members. Most Druids until recently have in fact been good Catholics, Anglicans, Methodists or whatever form of Christianity was most culturally vibrant in any particular area. In some areas, especially the Celtic ones, Druidry is still largely cultural and not usually religious, let alone Pagan. The first explicit signal of the rebirth of Pagan Druidry was the publication of a Breton journal, *Kad*, in 1936 which

> announced the formation of a *Breuriez Spered Adnevezi*, a 'Fraternity of Regenerating Belief', inviting the Bretons to renounce the authority of the (French) State and of the Christian Church simultaneously in order to encourage a return to Celtic roots.[3]

---

[3] Raoult (1996): 115.

In the 1960s and 1970s increasing numbers of Pagans began to consider themselves to be Druids and either joined existing Druid Orders or formed new ones. It is these Pagan Druids who are the subject of our discussion here.

Types and Stereotypes

The archetypal Druid is a bearded man in a white robe greeting the rising sun at Stonehenge or talking on equal terms with a venerable oak tree. They are not seen as sinister, unlike witches in folk and fairy tales and in trial records who haunt graveyards at midnight and conjure evil from simmering cauldrons.[4] While the witch stereotype is not applicable to those who name themselves "Witches" today, except in that many are female and they do often meet after sunset,[5] many Druids fit their stereotype more closely. The majority do wear white robes for ceremonies which are often conducted in daylight in public places, though not often at Stonehenge at the moment; many are male, though not all are bearded,[6] and many converse with trees. However, while these things are suggestive they are not of the essence.

Ancient Druidry was divided into three types or classes: Bards, Ovates and Druids.[7] If Bards were essentially poets and Druids were essentially priestly politicians, the Ovates were prophetic seers. In fact these are not entirely adequate descriptions, but they are suggestive of aspects of Druidry which have been significant both in antiquity, in the period of the Romantic revival and in the contemporary world. Druidry is no longer a profession in the sense of a career but is a profession of faith or commitment to a Nature-centred spirituality. It lost political control with Roman and Christian dominance, and lost prophetic authority when the Otherworld became suspect as a source of inspiration. Poets, however, maintained a strong position in many places by reciting lengthy genealogies for the wealthy and entertaining people with traditional stories, epics and songs. Maintenance of the bardic arts, perhaps in a lesser form, permitted the renaissance of Druidry in various ages, beginning with cultural, linguistic and artistic forms. While Druids today may not do or believe the same things as their ancestors, it is possible that the Druidry of the future will be closer to that of antiquity than that of the recent past. The following sections explore contemporary Druidry as the latest incarnation of an abiding obsession with archetypal characters which is reaching towards

[4] For the antiquity and origins of this stereotype see Harvey (1995c).

[5] See chapter 3.

[6] In the past some Druids wore false beards, see Ellis (1994): photograph facing p.129.

[7] Descriptions of Gaul's Druidry speak of *bardos*, *vātis* and *druid*; compare the similar Irish *bard*, *fáith*, and *drui*.

a potential future. Various Druid Orders are mentioned but none is taken as an ideal or a pattern.

Bards

Many Druid activities take place "in the eye of the sun", that is in daylight, out of doors and in public. Of course, Druids do many important things privately, indoors and at night too, and not all of these are merely preparatory for the "open" events. As well as celebrating the midsummer or midwinter solstice sunrises, many Druids spend a night in vigil and some hold a ceremony at midnight. Druidry may no longer require the twenty years' training that ancient writers refer to, but many Druid Orders do encourage study, practice and meditation. Several Orders have guided systems of learning based on correspondence courses and/or recommended reading material. Full participation in ceremonies may require understanding of a considerable body of information, e.g. the associations of the cardinal directions and ceremonial etiquette. All this is dealt with apart from the "in the eye of the sun" celebrations. In local groups or individually, Druids study and prepare. Then they bring their understandings, their crafted poetry, songs, art, experiences and passions to shared events.

According to one contemporary Bard, "to be a bard is to learn to listen".[8] The whole Druidic tradition is said by the Chosen Chief of the Order of Bards, Ovates and Druids to be aural, not oral.[9] Not only do trainee Bards need to listen and memorise stories, songs, poems and other carriers of wisdom, they also need to listen to themselves, to other people and to all the voices of the speaking Earth. They have to hear what is needed and then, drawing on inner resources or tradition, hear the appropriate words or music for the occasion. Bards are distinguishable from entertainers, poets or babblers, by the aptness of their contribution. Bards are not meant to be just poets, but inspired poets, not just musicians but inspired musicians. In practice, anyone who recites a poem, of whatever quality, may be called a Bard by fellow Druids. The title, however, may merely be politely used during the occasion of their recitation. To be spoken of as a Bard between ceremonies, or to be thought of as a real Bard, is a recognition of both talent and inspiration.

In Druidry, inspiration is named Awen and is envisaged as more than motivation or stimulus. It is experienced as descending on people or as rising up through them from the ground. Awen is a "flowing spirit" given by the Goddess. Both the Goddess and Awen can be invoked, invited, called to and called upon to manifest themselves, make themselves known, or express themselves through the Bard. To

[8] Letcher (1996).
[9] Carr-Gomm (1996b): 6.

be possessed by the Muse is perhaps only a weak metaphor for most people today, but it is certainly part of what earlier writers saw in the activities of Awen. Giraldus Cambrensis described people in twelfth-century Wales "called Awenyddion who behave as if they are possessed".[10] They were not only gifted poets but visionaries totally controlled physically, emotionally, intellectually and in every other way by Awen. Today few Bards experience this overwhelming prophetic or shamanic state. According to Andy Letcher, however,

> Stories are precious things and have a life of their own. Open yourself to stories and you open yourself to a depth of understanding that far surpasses the paltry efforts of the intellect. There is an old storytelling tradition that when you tell a story, you imagine the person who told it you is stood behind you. The person who told them is stood behind them and so on. A whole chain of ghosts connecting the tradition and giving it its momentum. You don't need to tell a story, you just need to open your mouth and it will happily tell itself, propelled by the life it has been given by the weight of all those ancestors.[11]

Perhaps these storytelling ancestors include Goddesses—ancestors and deities are frequently indistinguishable from each other in Pagan and polytheistic traditions. Andy Letcher is a talented storyteller and musician—perhaps troubadour is the correct word—who strives to practise and improve his skills, repertoire and delivery. These gifts are, however, reinforced by the clear, palpable sense of inspiration (in-spiriting) when the introductions are over and the story begins or the music emerges from the tuning up.

The invocation of Awen is not only or even primarily an individual activity or experience. Most Druidic ceremonies include some form of chant both invoking and expressing Awen. The assembled group together still themselves, gently take a deep breath and chant "Awen" or "A-I-O" in one long unbroken breath. This is usually repeated three times. Such chanting shifts the consciousness of participants. Before the chant it is possible to feel like an observer of the select few who establish the circular space in which the ceremony takes place and that there is a division between participants and observers or, worse, clergy and laity. The chant makes everyone a participant, which is what they are meant to be from the beginning. Those who greet the four directions and mark the circle are supposed to be giving voice to what the entire company is thinking, feeling, doing, envisaging. Participating in the chant changes this from imagination or intention into experienced reality. The chant enchants; it is not only a symbol or an expression of hope that Awen will descend or rise, but an experience of inspiration. Awen flows not only into the Bard but through the Bard,

[10] Thorpe (1978): 246.
[11] Letcher (1996): 39.

around the circle and outwards, changing the world which witnesses the story or the song.

The following sections return to activities in the circle which might be seen as the preserve of Ovates or Druids. As a central part of many Druid rituals is a specifically bardic event, often named an *Eisteddfod*. These are usually performances by musicians or poets, either prepared beforehand or offered spontaneously, but in both cases intended to complement the theme or mood of the festival or occasion. Performances occur not only during rituals, but also as organised contests or competitions which are central to the Welsh term *Eisteddfod*. The term might also be translated by "session", evocative of events in Irish pubs and clubs the world over in which musicians sit and play together, sharing their tunes and enjoying each other's brief solo performances. Besides the bardic episodes in their ceremonies and the organised contests, Druidic Bards also participate in sessions. These might take place as entertainments during a summer camp, or a pub get-together, while spending a night in the woods, or as an inspiring part of anti-road or quarry protests.

Just as Druids prefer to conduct their public ceremonies in white robes rather than in jeans, many prefer their Bards to play harps—especially the clarsach—rather than electric guitars. However, there are many Druidic Bards who prefer more contemporary means of expression. Equally, some consider the recitation of high medieval epics such as the Branches of the *Mabinogion*[12] to be more bardic than contemporary poetry. Others refuse the traditional insistence that bardic poetry must be in particular metres or languages (Welsh or Breton, for example). They are happy to write and recite poems on contemporary themes in their own style.

Such variations derive from differences between the Druid Orders as well as individual preferences of Bards and their audiences. In ceremonies and Eisteddfodau acoustic stringed instruments are more common than any others. Some Pagans share with New Agers an affection for the clarsach, sometimes accompanied by the human voice. Other popular instruments are drums, especially Irish bodhrans, didgeridoos, guitars, rattles, flutes and whistles. Bagpipes of various sorts (Scottish, Irish, Northumbrian and Cantabrian) are not unknown in rituals but are more common in less formal situations. Part of the appeal of such instruments might be the feeling of other times and other places (Otherworldliness?) they evoke. More specifically, the harps and bodhrans provide a Celtic flavour, evoking the Celtic Iron Age: a popular form of the Golden Age myth.[13] If this can be a symptom of twentieth-century consumerism and, at the same time,

[12] Gantz (1976).
[13] Bowman (1994) and (1996).

dissatisfaction with such "market-led" lifestyles, it is also true that such instruments affect an alteration of consciousness. The complex harmonies of the harp and the powerful rhythms of the drum demand a re-focusing of attention on things other than the noise of traffic, the bustle and hassle of everyday life and the call to the pursuit of wealth. The poet and the singer provide additional enchantments, seducing or provoking the listener to seek access to and expression of increased intimacy with the Earth.

Some Druid Orders are involved in the revival of folk traditions like the Abbot of Misrule, May and other seasonal festivities. The Secular Order of Druids refuses the trivialisation of these traditions in their polite Victorian forms, in which they are subverted for the education of children or improvement of adults. They include a boisterous, humorous and blatantly sexual Cucumber Dance in the Morris tradition in their very public May Day celebrations. They also encourage adults to dance round the maypole, have created a new Hobby Horse like Cornwall's Padstow Horse, and include a Fool or Jester among the chief officers in their ceremonies. All these have a serious intention: to cause a much wider response than a preciously "spiritual" event might attract. Even in their serious involvement in protests against quarrying and restricted access to sacred sites, the Order attempts to use colourful drama and humour to gain a sympathetic hearing. Sometimes this has been misunderstood by more "serious minded" Pagans, but is frequently effective in enticing people to celebrate the seasons and participate in festivities and protests.

Druid Bards are not strangers to technology, though they might object to some of its uses and indeed to *some* technologies. Their involvement in music is not just for the entertainment and enlightenment of fellow Druids, but is often well known outside Druidry. Although they do not advertise their Druidry there are Druidic Bards in all corners of the music industry: from traditional Irish to Rave. As with many other Pagan paths, Druidry does not seek converts or attempt to persuade everyone to join their group, agree with their beliefs or participate in their activities. Much of the "message" of Druidry is concerned with the affirmation of life—that of the individual and that of the Earth. The bardic arts of music, storytelling, poetry, literature, painting, photography and so on, are excellent vehicles for encouraging people to live more ecologically responsible or more just lives, for example. To this end Druid Bards participate with like-minded and similarly concerned people in all manner of artistic activities.

Awen is therefore evoked not only by harpists wearing "Celtic" jewellery but also by the DJs and other musicians in (Acid) House clubs. In such events everyone is encouraged and enabled to participate and not merely to observe. According to Terence McKenna, Rave music, lights and dance replicate rhythms intended to

> actually change neurological states, and large groups of people getting together in the presence of this kind of music are creating a telepathic community, a bonding...

In such communal experiences people experiment with Shamanic techniques and re-contextualise Shamanic worldviews.[14] These technological Shamans

> act as exemplars by making this cosmic journey to the domain of the Gaian ideas, and then bringing them back in the form of art, to the struggle to save the world.[15]

One British club, Megatripolis, opened with a Druid ritual. At another the organiser was initiated as "the first Bard of the dance of the modern age"—the latest expression of a tradition of Druid involvement in the arts. This is motivated partly by a desire to encourage and celebrate popular participation in the arts, partly by an affirmation of recreation or re-creation and creativity and partly by a recognition that the arts manifest the spirit of the age. The dialogue between the spirit of the age and the flowing spirit of Awen might be difficult in some circumstances, but not, for some Druids at least, in the case of Raves which articulate Gaian awareness. Rave techno-shamans and Druid Bards celebrate their dwelling within the interconnected ecosystem of a living Earth, their relationships with "all our relations". They are also involved in "the struggle to save the world" and participate responsibly in the "ecology of souls".[16]

Returning from the Rave to the Grove, it is worth noting that much of the ceremony of Druidry is bardic. Druids process into the circle, carrying signs and symbols of the natural or ancestral worlds, chanting or playing instruments. They greet the cardinal directions or invite Celtic deities to participate. Within the circle, apart from the Eisteddfodau, there is movement and drama, for example the enactment of the John Barleycorn folksong at harvest. Much of this certainly depends on a depth of understanding that must be acquired by study and experience, but it is typically expressed in poetic or dramatic form. Druids do not interrupt their ceremonies to preach evangelistic or educative sermons. They celebrate. Observers may witness drama and hear poetry and music, but they will not be offered creeds to assent to or "meanings" to understand. This may be baffling to those who desire information, but celebration is not the way Druidry imparts information; it prefers to celebrate the seasons and Nature, honour life

---

[14] See chapter 7.
[15] The Shamen with McKenna (1993).
[16] McKenna with Zuvuya (1993).

and affirm the various relationships of participants and others. The private learning sessions and the public celebrations balance one another, but the most typically Druid events are the celebrations which re-enchant life. Lengthy explanations prevent such enchantment taking place, much as they destroy the impact of a joke. There are, however, books and correspondence courses which impart information. Production of these teaching materials is part of the function of the Druids, who are discussed after the following section on Ovates.

Ovates

If the task of the Bard is to bring the wisdom of the past to bear on the present, then the task of the Ovate is to discover the wisdom of the future. If Bards are those who listen to ancestral voices, Ovates are those who listen to the voices of the Otherworld or other-than-human people. Both listen to Nature and respond to Awen, but their typical methods of expression vary. Bardic poetry and music aim to encourage the flow of Awen, so that listeners can respond and themselves be inspired. Ovates are facilitators, healers, changers of situations. They interpret signs, blend remedies and ask questions. Few Druid Orders have specific groups labelled "Bards" or "Ovates" distinguishable from their "Druids" but most recognise the usefulness of such terms if applied broadly or loosely. Orders might also differ on exactly where the province of the Bard ends and that of the Ovate begins.

One of the most common techniques of gaining understanding in Druidry is through a complex system of tree lore. Each tree is associated with a particular mood, action, phase of life, deity or ancestor. Stories gather round the trees, along with other, more "natural" inhabitants like birds, insects, fungi and animals. All these, singly or together, can tell the observant Ovate much. Certainly much of this system is of recent origin, an inspired response to the needs of the contemporary world. It draws, however, on aspects of folk tradition, story and legend, combined with a knowledge of natural history and traditional human use of particular trees. For example, the alder tree naturally grows by water, and its wood was used for bridge piles, and its bark for tanning leather; a decoction of its bark, buds or twigs can be used to relieve sore throats, and it is linked to the character Brân the Blessed in *Branwen Daughter of Llyr*.[17] Contemplation of these and other properties of the alder will reveal it to be an apt symbol for companionship and support.

A series of symbols for each tree can be carved on sticks or drawn on cards, perhaps with a picture of the tree, to form portable divinatory systems akin to the better known runes.[18] Iolo Morganwg and Robert

[17] Gantz (1976): 66-82.
[18] See chapter 4.

Graves—themselves inspired Bards—are the two people most responsible for these complex but elegant and evocative systems.[19] The most commonly used symbols are those of the Irish ogham (pronounced *oam*) alphabet, of which the earliest examples seem to have been carved on stones in the 4th century CE. By an "imaginative play with the initials of the letters of the alphabet"[20] a medieval scholar associated the ogham characters with tree names and placed them in what is now regarded as a traditional order, beginning "Beithe Luis Nin".[21] Robert Graves made this the centre of his "historical grammar of poetic myth", *The White Goddess*.[22] He is said to have written to a stranger in 1955:

> Some day scholars will sort out the White Goddess grain from the chaff. It's a crazy book and I didn't mean to write it.[23]

In fact scholars (especially classicists, historians and folklorists) have not received the book well. Poets, playwrights and Pagans, however, have mined it for materials to use both as foundations and adornments in their own works.

Another set of symbols, carved on wood and bearing similar associations, is called coelbren. This system was possibly invented by Iolo Morganwg, collector and creator of Druidic traditions, about 160 years before Graves was inspired to write his book. Its greatest exposition so far is in the works of Kaledon Naddair who, like Graves with whom he often disagrees, associates the symbols with characters, creatures and episodes in an array of "Keltic Folk and Faerie Tales".[24]

Just as others might cast a series of runes, so Ovates cast ogham or coelbren sticks or lay out cards. These might guide a meditation, develop a story, give insight into a problem or foretell future possibilities. The authors of the many books, pamphlets and sets of cards related to ogham or coelbren also intend their users to increase their understanding of trees and not merely to parrot the books they read. It is surprising but not uncommon, however, to find considerable ignorance about trees: some Druids seem unable to tell an oak from an ash, or may from blackthorn.

Apart from divination, Ovates also engage in healing therapies. These too might be related to tree and plant lore: herbalism and homeopathy are both popular. The entire range of conventional and alternative therapies is used by and practised by contemporary Ovates.

---

[19] There are more uncharitable designations for their work in this context.

[20] Personal correspondence from Dáithí Ó hÓgáin, University College, Dublin.

[21] See Calder (1917): an edition of *Auraicept na n-Éces: the Scholar's Primer*, a seventeenth century transcription of medieval texts.

[22] Graves (1948).

[23] Seymour-Smith (1982): 405.

[24] See especially Naddair (1986 and 1987).

If many of these therapies deal with the body, some also focus on more "spiritual" adjustments, treating disease and dis-ease.

Sweat lodges have become increasingly popular in European and American Druidry in the last decade—perhaps an expression of the popularity of shamanism.[25] These are temporary domed structures from which all light is excluded and in which rocks heated in a fire outside the lodge are sprinkled with water which becomes steam. Their role among contemporary Druids, as learnt directly from Lakota, other native Americans or through ethnographic descriptions, is communal personal rededication to honouring the Earth. The intense experience undergone both in preparation for the sweat lodge—including fasting, building the lodge, collecting fire wood, rocks and water—and within its dark, steamy confines is a purification. The body sweats out impurities, but the sweat lodge is far more than a sauna taken for hygiene or pleasure. Jordan Paper describes the traditional ceremony as

a potent, communal ritual of confession, catharsis, decision-making, and direct communication with sacred beings.[26]

If "those Oglalas who still keep the traditions" are the "Earth People",[27] this too is an apt description of Druids who participate in such ceremonies. Unlike New Agers, who seem to do it for the "spiritual fix" or individual self-affirmation which it seems to provide,[28] Druids treat sweat lodge as an initiation. They are refined through affirming neighbourliness and facing weaknesses. Everything about the sweat lodge—its structure, materials, experience, atmosphere and effects— reinforces a message about relating respectfully to the Earth and to "all our relations", including those with whom one shares this creative womb. The Ovate facilitating the ceremony, for example, introduces participants to the etiquette involved in relating to stones. Participants—initiates—take time to consider their motivations, aims, desires, abilities, weaknesses and relationships. They emerge as new people, taking their first steps towards different or more dedicated ways of walking the Earth. As such, perhaps Ovates are initiators of personal ecological responsibility and of justice in all human dealings with wider Nature.

Ovates function as therapists healing individual illnesses and rifts between humanity and those we share Earth with. They introduce people to other-than-human people such as trees and rocks and guide them in considering ways of expressing their inclinations towards ecological living. Whether using ogham or sweat lodges they teach that

---

[25] See chapter 7 and Adler (1986): 430-4.

[26] Paper (1988): 302.

[27] Wallace Black Elk, quoted in Detwiler (1992): 243.

[28] Perhaps valid motivations in their own right, but hardly a respectful learning from a rich and robbed tradition.

the world is not all that it seems, and that there is more than is seen. Bards listen to the voice of the ancestors and repeat what they have heard in stories, poems and songs. Ovates look at the world and show it to others in signs, symbols and models.

To traditional Christians the world is a temporary dwelling, a departure lounge where people determine their eternal destination: heaven or hell. In Druidry and other Nature religions Earth is home and there is no other destination to which to aspire. However, the world recognised by secular science is only a part of the whole according to Druid tradition, there are other places and other dimensions. In Celtic mythology the Otherworld, its regions, seasons and inhabitants frequently erupt into this "ordinary" world. In birth, death and lesser crises people can be affected by the Otherworld, not always in ways that they welcome. At seasonal festivals the Otherworld and this world stand open to one another. Much of this mythology is accepted by contemporary Druids, but it does not eclipse participation in the everyday world of "mundane" reality. Another way of looking at the world (the clarification of which might also be the work of Iolo Morganwg) is as a series of concentric circles. Our current lives take place within the Circles of Abred which are formed both by the multiple relationships of living beings—the "web of life"—and by the process of rebirth.

Classical sources say that the Celtic Druids believed in the "transmigration of souls", or metempsychosis. Some today see this as the equivalent of reincarnation, though not as a vicious circle from which to seek liberation. Others understand it to mean that some essential part of each individual can join with others within new physical forms when their present body dies. Whether people have "progressed" from being animals or plants, or whether all physical forms are equal but different within these circles, the idea expresses the kinship and mutuality of living beings. The Circles of Abred emerge from the Circle of Annwn (pronounced *anoon*): a chaotic simmering cauldron containing all potential forms and manifestations. Annwn and Abred are more complex than merely "past" and "present". They exist simultaneously, and there is a temporal progression within the Circles of Abred as the manifest forms, which have emerged from Annwn, are born, grow, die and are reborn. Contemporary Druids disagree on whether there is a purpose or goal to life in the Circles of Abred. Are people intended to improve and progress to "higher" forms, or is it enough to experience the rich diversities of life? Beyond Abred is the Circle of Gwynvid, a state of perfection for each and every form. Beyond that but pervading everything is Ceugant, the causative and perhaps divine realm. Not all Druids are convinced by this model of the universe, some seeing it as too heavily influenced by Christianity, especially in its eighteenth century Deist form, but it is evocative for others.

Whether drawing on classical sources, medieval poetry, the creative writings of the "Druid Renaissance" or more recent facts and fictions, contemporary Ovates offer guidance in relating to the world. By leading people to various "points of view", which reveal the possibilities open to them Ovates, help them to find their place in the world.

Druids

Ancient Druids were powerful political and spiritual leaders. Today's Druids are leaders of groups whose central spiritual concerns have political ramifications. Whatever Druidry was in the past, it is now a variety of Paganism, an honouring of Nature and of ancestral sacred sites. Although not all Druid Orders divide their members into the three groups, Bards, Ovates and Druids, it is still useful to consider the activities of some members of such groups as Druidic. That is, just as there are Druidic Bards and Druidic Ovates, there are Druidic Druids. Conversely, while it is possible to speak of Druids as people who perform particular functions, roles or activities, *most* members of Druid groups call themselves Druids, whatever they do. There is no suggestion here that only leaders can legitimately name themselves Druids any more than only bishops can call themselves Christians. That said, this section discusses the role of Druids within contemporary Druidry.

The primary activity of a Druid is organisation. Local groups (groves) and national organisations (Orders) are centred on Druids. Their leadership is based on natural or learnt abilities, on their understanding of the tradition, their inspired vision of potentially fruitful activities. Most contemporary Orders expect their leadership to be capable as Bards and Ovates but also to be able to act decisively and facilitate group activities. They are expected to respond to the inspiration of Awen and to be in touch with the ancestors and the spirit of the age. Druidry, in common with other varieties of Paganism, is not a rejection of the world, a retreat into utopian dreaming or a revolutionary overturning of the existing order. It might sometimes express similar aspirations or engage in similar activities to utopian or revolutionary groups, e.g. in its celebration of nature or its opposition to motorway building, but Druids are engaged with the world. Druids are expected to provide opportunities for Bards and Ovates to fulfil their roles and improve their skills. They arrange gatherings in which celebration combines with recreation and planning. The Order of Bards, Ovates and Druids arranges summer camps at which people who might know each other only through a newsletter or correspondence can meet to work and celebrate. There are workshops, sharing sessions, Eisteddfodau, ceremonies, sweat lodges, walks in the woods, socialising and the opportunity for initiations. People make contacts which are fruitful of continuing contacts—e.g. they might discover a common interest in working with environmental groups or in regular visits to a particular ancient sacred site.

In addition to arranging such gatherings, Druids act as ritual leaders during ceremonies. They might lead processions into and around circular ritual areas, initiate the conversion of these spaces into sacred places, call upon others to participate, guide ceremonies through their stages and finally declare their endings. Druids do not usually act alone in such ceremonies; they are communal affairs with a number of actors or speakers, in which all are encouraged to participate. Druids introduce the chanting of the Awen and the declaration of "the Druid's Prayer". In its original eighteenth-century form this addressed God, but in its more contemporary Pagan form it is addressed most often to Goddess, but sometimes to God and Goddess, God alone, God/dess or to Spirit.

> Grant O Goddess, thy protection
> and in protection, strength
> and in strength, understanding
> and in understanding, knowledge
> and in knowledge, the knowledge of justice
> and in the knowledge of justice, the love of it
> and in the love of it, the love of all existences
> and in the love of all existences, the love of Goddess and all Goodness.

For most people who recite this "prayer", three things seem to be central: first, acceptance of a place within a tradition; secondly, the desire for greater understanding with its concomitant responsibility; and thirdly, the affirmation of justice and love. To say these words with others "in the eye of the sun" *is* to be a Druid, to be linked to all other speakers of the words, and all Druids, including those from before the prayer was written (again by Iolo Morganwg). People who join Druid groups want to understand the way the world works, how it came to be as it is, how it might be possible to prevent ecological disaster, how to relate more intimately or more justly with trees and other living beings. The Druids of the Orders facilitate their initiatory path and exploration of these areas and encourage the expression of knowledge, not only in intellectual form but in responsible living. This necessarily involves teaching. Druids provide instruction to other members of their group, they write books or correspondence course material, and they give lectures or participate in discussions. Druidic teaching is not dogmatic or doctrinal but exploratory of different ways of responding to ancestral, visionary and contemporary inspiration and to the spirits of place and the age. While the different Druid Orders draw on the same traditional material (including mythology, history, poetry, imagination and places), they express their understandings in different ways. They might be more bardic, more public, more politically involved, more esoteric, more interested in Stonehenge, Glastonbury or another sacred site, more ceremonial and so on.

Druids also act as the public representatives of their groups. Contact between one Order and another, or between the Orders and other religious groups, the media, police and other interested parties, is largely the responsibility of Druids. For example, the Council of British Druid Orders is an umbrella organisation for many, though not all, of the British Orders. Observers from other organisations (e.g. the Pagan Federation and Breton Druids) also attend. The Council is not a controlling organisation but a forum for debate and for arranging potential mutual activities, such as seasonal celebrations or representations to organisations affecting Druid interests. It also produces a journal, *The Druids' Voice*, which contains features, debate, news, reviews and matters of interest to all sorts of Druid groups.

Druids have also initiated the Gorsedd of the Bards of Caer Abiri, a celebratory network of people who celebrate at Avebury stone circle. This is open to anyone who has an affection for Avebury, not only Druids and not only Pagans. It is not in competition with other groups and focuses on bardic celebrations rather than teaching or activism. On the other hand, the existence of many different Druid Orders, who may co-operate in some ventures, indicates a diversity which on occasions is far from harmonious. The Orders remain distinct and offer their members different styles, activities and attitudes.

Druids lead the more public presentation of Druidry, engaging in Inter-Faith Dialogue with other religionists or in media events. Isaac Bonewits' vision for the future of Druidry includes far more public events, some mediated by TV stations and others led by a professionally trained clergy. His "A Druid Fellowship" (ADF) is one of the many American Pagan organisations establishing a clergy training programme and wishing to offer its services in ways similar to those of other religious communities.[29] Aside from any problems with Christian fundamentalist opposition, he is aware that this would radically change the current inclusive and non-hierarchical social structures of Paganism.[30]

Given that Paganism is rooted in a deep concern with ecology and is in part a response to intimations of disaster threatening Earth's life, Druidry is necessarily involved in eco-drama. In many Pagan traditions knowledge brings with it responsibility to act. Ovates cannot treat trees

[29] Also see Kelly (1992): 142-3.
[30] Bonewits (1996).

merely as symbols in arcane divinatory systems. Their discovery of the natural history of trees will, sooner or later, reveal the extent of the destruction of trees, woodlands, forests and the rich habitats they provided. In Druidry this cannot remain simply an idea or awareness, it must be translated into some sort of action. Just as the Welsh and Breton Druid renaissance was conceived as a response to cultural and political oppression, so the Pagan Druid renaissance frequently involves itself in contemporary demonstrations of affection for Nature. The Roman accusation that the Druids were bloodthirsty slaughterers has rarely been evoked and the Druid as peace-loving, wise and just nature venerator has insinuated itself deep into the modern consciousness. The sight of Druids non-violently opposing the destruction of an oak wood by motorway builders might provoke re-consideration of the values of a society willing to cover the land with tarmac.

Druids function within Druidic Orders as leaders, facilitators, organisers, initiators. They are not priests controlling congregations, nor are they administrators continuously demanding increasing commitment of workers. Their role is closely allied to the ideal set by representative democracy: a few are chosen to speak for the majority, but they are expected to be completely accountable to those they represent. Druids are expected to continue to use the bardic and ovate senses: hearing and seeing. They are not expected to be exclusively vocal.

Grades, Hierarchies and Druid Time

The three functions discussed above—Bards, Ovates and Druids—once labelled jobs done by Druids. Now they can be treated as initiatory grades: newcomers, even ones who may be neither musical nor poetic, are Bards. They progress, if they can, to being Ovates and thence become Druids. They might tell their friends that they are Druids, which functions both as a goal and as the name of their spirituality. Many Druid Orders are trying to alter the perception that a Bard is merely a trainee Druid. Since the Druid tradition is primarily bardic and survived only because of Bards, this is a positive move. Progression within Druid groups can easily be marked in other ways, just as improvement as a Bard can be marked best by greater recognition as a Bard, rather than applying the label Ovate.

Most Druid Orders are led by a Chosen Chief, who outsiders, especially the media, frequently call the "Arch Druid". Arch Druid is traditionally an honorific, suggesting significant contributions to the Order. Chosen Chief better expresses the degree to which leaders of groups maintain their positions by the continuing choice of the group and their own acceptance of that position. Most Druid Orders are currently led by male Chosen Chiefs, but this is not obligatory. Some Chosen Chiefs have an equal female partner who shares the role and title of Chief.

There are other roles within the different Orders: e.g. scribe, sword-bearer, secretary, jester. These have significant functions to play in the running of the Order and in ceremonies. One Chosen Chief regularly refers to the "Conscience" of his Order whose unofficial burden is to remind the Chief that noon has long since past, the ceremony should be in full swing and it is time to leave the pub. Despite the offices and efforts of the "Conscience", Druid ceremonies run according to Druid Time which rarely coincides with any mechanical or electrical method of time keeping. Though this title may be unique, the relaxed attitude to time and the humour with which it is treated are widespread in Paganism and other Nature-respecting religions.

Stonehenge

We have already seen that Druids are popularly associated with Stonehenge and oak trees. Their relationship with oaks is made problematic only because of the devastation of woodlands. Druid activities at Stonehenge continue in a variety of ways. Some Orders are vociferous in asserting the right of free access to all sacred sites. This has brought them into conflict with this century's administrators of Stonehenge, who see Druids as just one more form of tourist, and the place as either an ancient gem to be guarded or a valuable popular entertainment to be exploited. The conflict of interests also involved a Free Festival held within the sacred landscape surrounding Stonehenge. Some Druids see this as growing from the spiritual roots planted by Wally Hope (founder of the free festival), and consecrated by the scattering of his ashes within the circle.[31] Others argue that since English Heritage now permits small groups of any sort to have access to the centre of the circle, out of regular opening hours, by arrangement and on payment of £15 per head, the only question is whether anyone should pay and in what numbers access will be allowed.[32] The issue further depends on the future development of roads and other features of Stonehenge's site.

Looking Forward

Druids are not the only Pagans who speak with Celtic deities or are concerned with Celtic and pre-Celtic sacred sites. Many other Pagans draw inspiration from their understanding of Celtic religion. Developments in Druidry run parallel to the growth of such Pagan

[31] Harvey (1994b).
[32] Shallcrass (1995).

understandings. At the end of the nineteenth-century Druidry was thought of as a monotheistic philosophical tradition. Now it has more in common with the rich and varied polytheism archaeologists have reconstructed from Celtic Iron Age finds. Druids and other Pagans now refer to a host of deities and traditions which earlier, more Christian Druids would have considered irrelevant and ungodly. This is not to argue that contemporary Druids are necessarily practising exactly the same religion as the Iron Age ancestors, but only that they are trying to do so. Druidry is not a thing of the past, it is a present reality which shows every sign of growing significantly, both in the number of its adherents and in coherence, in the future. It is one of the most vibrant ways in which people in the West are seeking to find ways to relate more justly, more harmoniously and more pleasurably with the Earth and all her inhabitants. Druidry encourages the use of all the senses in responding to the speaking, living Earth.

3

THE CRAFT OF WITCHES

Artists and writers have always had a rather exaggerated idea about what goes on at a witches' sabbat. This comes from spending too much time in small rooms with the curtains drawn, instead of getting out in the healthy fresh air.[1]

Of all the varieties of Paganism it is Witchcraft—the Witches' Craft—which receives most media attention. More words are written or spoken about Witches than about any other group. Not a few of these words are written or spoken by Witches themselves. Despite all these words the popular image—or is it the media image?—is mostly inaccurate. Terry Pratchett summarises this image as "dancing around naked", "all that business with goat-headed gods", "the bits of reptile and so on", "mystic ointments" and "sabbats".[2] He does not say that the prevalent idea of a Witch is of an elderly and wicked woman practising "black magic" against neighbours and their property. This sinister image is, of course, a more exciting one than that presented by those who, in the present, call themselves Witches. It is also an ancient image,[3] one that is easily evoked and not easily dismissed.

This chapter introduces the Craft of Witches and Witches themselves. Some of the key words here are polarity, initiation, circlework, energy, power, magic and secrecy. Although there are varieties or subdivisions within the Craft, these distinctions will not be our exhaustive concern. That is, there are no separate sections devoted to "Gardnerian", "Alexandrian", "Traditional", "Hereditary", "Hedge", "Progressive", "Dianic" and other branches. However, the chapter includes both those forms of the Craft in which initiation is central and those in which it is not. These *could* be seen as expressing two types of religion: a Mystery Religion in which the individual initiate is central and a Nature Religion in which the honouring of the Earth is central. In fact, however, there is no clear demarcation separating personal growth from celebrating Nature. Initiating and non-initiating traditions are interested to some degree in both. Their difference is one of secrecy or openness. While much of the following discussion focuses on communal expressions of the Craft, there are increasing numbers of solitary or non-affiliated Witches whose experiences are more individually nuanced.

---

[1] Terry Pratchett, *Witches Abroad*. (1991b): 17. (*1993): 20.
[2] Pratchett (1991b): 19.
[3] Harvey (1995c).

The name "Wicca" is preferred to the words "Witch" or "Witchcraft" by some Pagans, especially those initiated in British Gardnerian and Alexandrian covens. Perhaps because of the association with these more closed traditions, others dislike the label "Wicca". In North America "Wicca" is used more widely as a synonym of "Witch" or "adherent of the Craft" without distinguishing between traditions. Because my interest is in all forms of the Craft, I use the wider term "Witch" or "the Craft" but if necessary distinguish what Wiccans (in the British sense) do from what others do. Note too that male Witches are also "Witches"—terms like "warlock" and "wizard" have been rejected by contemporary Pagans.

The Charge of the Goddess

In the Craft there are two main ways in which people relate to or envisage deity. The first is in the way they hear the words of various "Charges", especially the "Charge of the Goddess", a form of self-revelation by the deity manifest in a Priestess or female leader. This is related to an experience called "Drawing Down the Moon". Secondly, deity is manifest (expressed, revealed, experienced, touched, tasted, incarnate, sensed, represented, immanent) in Nature.

Various forms of the Charge of the Goddess are used, adapted according to the preferences of those who use it. The following version appears to follow Doreen Valiente's original prose version.[4] Many people prefer to update the archaic "thee", "thou", "ye" and "men". Others drop the lines about "sorcery" or nudity. Others think the language is "more poetic", "more spiritual" or "more traditional" than contemporary idiom. It is spoken by the leader of the group or coven, frequently called the "High Priestess". Sometimes this is a position or rank held by one person. In other groups members take turns leading the ceremonies. The Charge is introduced by a man in the role of High Priest or ritual leader,

> Listen to the words of the Great Mother, who was of old also called among men Artemis, Astarte, Dione, Melusine, Aphrodite, Ceridwen, Diana, Arianrhod, Bride, and by many other names.

Then the priestess, manifesting, channelling or being the Goddess, says,

> Whenever ye have need of anything, once in the month, and better it be when the Moon is full, then shall ye assemble in some secret place and adore the spirit of me, who am Queen of all Witcheries. There shall ye assemble, ye who are fain to learn all sorcery, yet have not won its deepest secrets; to these will I teach things that are yet unknown. And ye shall be

---

[4] See Farrar and Farrar (1981): 42. Cf. Crowley (1989): 160-1; Jayran (1994): v; Starhawk (1989a): 90-1; Luhrmann (1989): 50-1.

free from slavery, and as a sign that ye be really free ye shall be naked in your rites and ye shall dance, sing, feast, make music and love, all in my praise. For mine is the ecstasy of the spirit, and mine also is joy on Earth, for my law is love unto all beings. Keep pure your highest ideal, strive ever towards it; let nought stop you or turn you aside. For mine is the secret door which opens upon the land of youth and mine is the cup of the wine of life and the Cauldron of Ceridwen, which is the Holy Grail of Immortality. I am the gracious Goddess who gives the gift of joy unto the heart of man; upon Earth I give knowledge of the Spirit eternal, and beyond death I give peace and freedom and reunion with those who have gone before. Nor do I demand sacrifice, for behold I am the Mother of all living, and my love is poured out upon the Earth.

After the priest exhorts the group to "hear ye the words of the Star Goddess", the priestess continues,

I who am the beauty of the green Earth and the white Moon among the stars, and the mystery of the waters and the desire of the heart of man, call unto thy soul, arise and come unto me; for I am the Soul of Nature who giveth life to the universe. From me all things proceed and unto me all things must return, and before my face, beloved of Gods and men, thine innermost divine self shall be enfolded in the rapture of the infinite. Let my worship be within the heart that rejoiceth; for behold, all acts of love and pleasure are my rituals. And therefore let there be beauty and strength, power and compassion, honour and humility, mirth and reverence within you. And thou who thinkest to seek for me, know thy seeking and yearning shall not avail thee not, unless thou knowest the mystery that if that which thou seekest thou findest not within thee, thou wilt never find it without thee, for behold I have been with thee from the beginning and I am that which is attained at the end of desire.

In essence the Goddess reveals herself: she is gracious, giver of life and death, infinite and immanent, and has a sense of humour. She suggests full moon as an appropriate time to meet her and indicates attitudes in which to approach her: naked, with music, love, beauty, strength, compassion, honour, humility, mirth and pleasure. She affirms her manifestations in Nature: Earth, moon, waters, desires of the heart, the Soul of Nature, death. The climax of the Charge, however, is the affirmation that "if that which you seek you find not within yourself, you will never find it without".

Two primary things are taught by the speaking, hearing and experiencing of the Charge. The first is that deity is experienced in the ordinary things of life—a woman speaking, the Earth and moon, food, drink, dancing, the human body, humour and music. While there is wisdom to be gained (this is how "sorcery" in the Charge appears to be understood) and learning to be done, the Goddess does not require "faith", "belief" or assent to doctrinal "truth". As Starhawk explains, "we do not *believe* in rocks... [and] in the Craft we do not believe in the Goddess."[5] Both are tangible and experienced in the ordinary realities of life.

The Charge also teaches that whatever you want or need to learn must be looked for "within" and not "without". The Goddess has already provided everything—the Goddess *is* already everything—she need not add lessons in morality, spirituality, ecology, theology or whatever else people might seek. The Goddess sends enquirers back to themselves, to self-exploration, self-development and discovery of the world. What is needed is already available without the need for divine revelation. The "Wiccan Rede"—"An it harm none, do as you will"[6]— encourages Witches to discover what they really want ("will" refers to "your true self") and then to follow their best ideals as long as this does not conflict with the good of others. This is often quoted as the essence of Wiccan ethics.

Deirdre Green, writing about Vedic polytheism, could be describing the message of the Charge of the Goddess when she writes that it

> shows an expression of joy and delight in the beauty of life, which is seen as a wondrous gift from the gods, and an organic vision of living as part of a cosmic whole. There is the suggestion that this entails an appreciation of life in all its diversity as a manifestation of divine powers and potencies.[7]

The Craft's use of the singular "Goddess" and the singular "God", combined in "the Goddess and the God", is different from explicit polytheism which speaks of "Goddesses and Gods". However, at the heart of the Craft's understanding of deity and of its dramatic rituals is the manifestation of both the Goddess and the God in triple forms, e.g. the Goddess is "virgin, mother and crone". Furthermore, the question of numbers is not the most significant difference between monotheism and polytheism, but only the most obvious one. The Craft is polytheistic in that its "Goddess" and its "God" send us back to ourselves and our mundane human lives. Unlike monotheistic Gods they refuse to let us become obsessed by the divine, the un-human, the otherworldly. If people seek an escape from the world into "spirituality" or "heaven" or "enlightenment" they are clearly told that the divine and the human exist in this world of food, drink, sex, humour, sadness, desire, constriction and ecstasy.

I have noted that the Charge of the Goddess is spoken by a priestess or female leader manifesting the Goddess. That manifestation occurs because, to work backwards, the speaker has experienced the Drawing Down of the Moon.

---

[5] Starhawk (1989a): 91.

[6] Although it is clearly Anglo-Saxon for "if", some Witches say that "An" here means "and". "Rede" is an archaism for "wise advice" or even "binding injunction" or "rule".

[7] Green (1989): 9.

Drawing Down the Moon

The Craft most often speaks of the divine as the Goddess and the God, usually linked in much the same way as the Yin and Yang of Taoism.[8] Almost everything that is commonly thought of as living is gendered as male or female, and deity is not so alien or transcendent as to be "beyond gender".[9] In ritual the Goddess is "drawn down" into the High Priestess or female leader. Sometimes the God is "drawn down" into the High Priest or male leader. The Moon has been popularly associated with the Goddess at least since the Romantic poets were inspired by classical Roman and Greek sources to speak of and to the Moon as Goddess. The lunar cycle resonates with women's menstrual cycles, with wider cycles of growth, maturity, decline and those of birth, death and rebirth. It is richly evocative for those seeking significant roles for Nature and women in religion—frequently a male preserve, permitting women to observe and support but not to lead. It is possible to limit the Moon to typically "feminine" receptive roles, in the patriarchal sense: "The moon only reflects the sun's light". However, in the Craft's view the Moon's control over ocean tides and such "watery" things as human emotions makes it as fully creative and destructive as the Sun.

Besides expressing herself as the moon and all her other manifestations mentioned in the Charge, the Goddess "comes down" on or into the priestess when invoked or called upon in ceremony. "Drawing Down the Moon" is an enchanting title for this rite involving Goddess and priestess which primarily takes place at full moon. The Moon itself is hardly mentioned,[10] but is the Goddess's brightest manifestation. The Goddess is experienced, manifest, revealed in the priestess. What the priestess is as woman, teacher, leader, mother, healer, sister, maker, wife and so on, expresses or reveals the Goddess. Women and men reveal deity in their ordinary lives, they can address each other with the words, "You are the Goddess", "You are the God". Everyday human living expresses and resonates with the greater cycles of Life; it does not merely symbolise or point to them. In ceremony, after being invoked (called or invited), the priestess becomes an icon and a channel. The invocation allows that which is already immanent, innate and incarnate to be seen, revealed and experienced. It makes those involved—both invoker and invokee[11]—aware, and permits a shift of consciousness. The Goddess becomes manifestly obvious.

Vivianne Crowley describes the experience from the perspective of an initiating High Priestess.

---

[8] See chapter 10. Also see Jones (1996).
[9] Claims that "God is beyond gender" are usually an excuse for calling God "he".
[10] Jayran (1994): 190.
[11] Crowley (1989): 144.

Andy, as High Priest, knelt before me and began the invocation to the Goddess. There was a stillness and silence within me. Then the flow of the power came, down through my crown chakra, down to my feet and out into the circle. She had come.

She continues to describe her awareness during her recitation of the Great Mother Charge:

I was far away, deep into samadhi; that state of consciousness whereby there is no longer any 'I and other', 'this and that', 'far and near', only a sense of oneness with the universe. As though from a long way off, I heard Andy's voice stop. The power of the Goddess flowed through me once more and I made ready to respond...[12]

This experience is initiated by the priest as the invoker. First, he ceremonially kisses her from the feet up to the crown of her head by way of the knees, womb, breasts and lips. Next, he visualises links between the chakras (energy centres) of his own body with those of the priestess—beginning at the base of her spine and working up. When the two are connected, linked like electrical circuits, and the energy is flowing between them, he envisages the form of the Goddess behind the priestess. Then the Goddess is asked to "descend into the body" of the priestess.[13] It is not unknown for other participants in the ceremony to see changes in the priestess as she becomes inspired, filled with the Goddess. The language used here is similar to that used by charismatic Christians, New Age channellers, traditional Shamans, mediums, oracles and others describing forms of possession. The invocation is an enchantment for all concerned, altering their state of consciousness and preparing them to hear the Charge of the Goddess and to participate effectively in the rest of the "work" of the circle. We return to this "work" after noting that the there are dissenters from the traditional Wiccan accounts followed above.

Polarity and sexuality

As Rae Beth says,

Sexual imagery is the strongest recurrent theme in witchcraft. It is the witches' main symbol of integration. In this image, the witch seeks to harmonize with the natural flow of life, as well as to reconcile the intuitive and the rational, the inner and the outer, the passive and the active, within his or her own nature.[14]

Summarising the sexual polarity which is central to many Wiccans, Vivianne Crowley says,

---

[12] Crowley (1990): 77-9.
[13] Crowley (1989): 144.
[14] Beth (1990): 31.

The divine forces are always invoked into someone of the same sex as the deity by someone of the opposite sex.[15]

However, Wren Sidhe introduces her much earthier way of Drawing Down the Moon[16] by saying,

It only took 2 days and didn't include anyone using their male polarity to bring out the divine essence in my female polarity... I did it myself inspired by the creative divinity in another woman. The Gardner/Valiente Book of Shadows states that "woman and woman should never attempt these practices together, and may all the curses of the Mighty Ones be on any who make such attempt". Reading this I firmly returned these curses whence they came and gave thanks to She-Who-Mightily-Loves-Her-Twin for the many blessings she has brought. Didn't She say "All acts of love and pleasure are My rituals"?

Then she digs a pond, fills it with fish and plants and draws down "not just the moon, but the whole sky". She also notes,

For those without gardens: a saucer of water placed on a windowsill will also Draw Down the Moon.

Her ceremony transforms the world, and celebrates life and herself.

In Starhawk's version the Goddess is "invoked into each member of the circle", including the men, and not only into one chosen Priestess or the High Priestess. As for men's participation, including the degree to which they manifest the Goddess, she asks, "Why should our imagination be limited by the shape of our genitalia?"[17]

Although Shan's version of "Drawing Down the Moon", the centrepiece of a "Lovers' Blessing",[18] is written as if performed by a heterosexual couple, she is careful to note that it can be adapted for "lovers of the same sex". The occasion begins with the priest or the one doing the honouring, whichever gender they are, ceremonially kissing the priestess or the one being honoured from the crown of the head to the feet by way of the forehead, mouth, breasts or nipples, navel and genitals. The one giving honour ends up kneeling, looking up at the one being honoured. The action and the energy moves from above downwards and ends in a traditional honouring posture. (In the more typically Wiccan form the priestess' head is bowed at this point so that the priest can kiss her head. He will, however, soon bow to her.) Two glasses of water, which had been placed where they could "soak with moonlight", are then blended together and drunk by the lovers. The action, the energy and the moonlight are brought down into the circle and the celebrants—either or both of whom manifests the Goddess.

[15] Crowley (1989): 144.
[16] Sidhe (1991).
[17] Starhawk (1989a): 99, 229-30.
[18] Jayran (1994): 190-5.

In contrast to these dissenting voices, it is arguable, that (some) Wiccans are merely following widespread prejudices in the area of gender and sexuality.[19] This is perhaps, as Michael Kelly suggests, because Wiccans have presented their "philosophy as a type of fertility religion".[20] Perhaps they are still strongly attached to the shaky foundation of Margaret Murray's stress on fertility, the God, male leadership and phallic symbolism.[21] However, Ken Rees argues that

> the gender stress has little to do with any "fertility" roots of modern wicca and more to do with the tantric influence included by Gardner in his composition.[22]

Many Witches celebrate with considerably more diversity than Vivianne Crowley's "always" suggests.[23]

The vehemence with which this debate is conducted might suggest that some Wiccans have enshrined two essentialist dogmas at the heart of their Craft.[24] First, a deity's gender and sexuality are more important than anything else that could be said about them. Secondly, gender and sexuality are the most important similarities between beings of different types (in this case deities and humans) and overrides any dissimilarities. On the other hand, as the dissenters show by not entirely abandoning similar practices, many different qualities, energies and skills are inculcated by these experiences of divine indwelling, independent of gender.

Acknowledging the importance of gender and sexuality is immensely valuable when compared with the denigration of bodies and sex, especially women's bodies and sexuality, typical in some religions.[25] It allows people to act as whole people not as "souls". Women and Goddesses are able to take central and significant roles. All aspects of embodied life can be celebrated. Sometimes the Craft brings sex into the circle, into the context of its honouring of deity and life.[26] Whether this must only be in the context of the polarity between heterosexual Goddess and God is debated. Whether the relationship between Goddess and God, or that between deities and humans, must be seen in the Jungian terms stressed by some Craft writers is also debatable. Many Pagans reject the idea that there are "masculine" and

[19] See Martin (1994); Cal (1995).

[20] Kelly (1995).

[21] Hutton (1991): 334. Murray (1921) and (1933). Also see Simpson (1994): 92; and Rees (1996).

[22] Personal communication.

[23] See, for example, the debate occasioned by Vayne (1995) in subsequent issues of *Pagan Voice*.

[24] Rufus (1992): 2.

[25] See Crowley (1993) and (1994): 109-10; and Jayran (1996).

[26] See Voigt (1992). Almost all Craft books discuss sex in ritual at some point—usually pointing out that it is exceptional rather than common.

"feminine" characteristics, e.g. rationality as masculine, intuition as feminine. Such differences are part of the diversity and pluralism of the Craft and of Paganism generally. It will be interesting to watch future developments.

Nature

In order to complete the discussion of the main ways in which the Craft experiences deity it is necessary to interrupt this backwards exploration of the typical Craft ceremony or circle. What attracts most people to Paganism now is the stress on honouring Nature. This is true too of the Craft. Alongside inspiration, motivation and techniques for honouring Nature, initiatory traditions offer inspiration, motivation and techniques for self-development. Nature "out there" and Nature "within", i.e. human nature, are inseparable. Personal development without honouring Nature is not only egotistic (not in itself a vice in Paganism) but a delusion. To pollute what gives you life demonstrates a severe misunderstanding of the place of the individual and of humanity within the Earth's ecology.

The Charge of the Goddess proclaims that the Goddess is manifest in such aspects of Nature as Earth, moon, waters, desires of the heart, the Soul of Nature and death. Food and drink, pleasure, dance and meditation are also revelatory, expressive of the divine. In other Craft writings (poetry, prose, ceremonies, invocations) every conceivable aspect of Nature manifests the divine. Bodily functions, psychological moods, weather, geology, flora, fauna, astronomical and terrestrial phenomena, earth, air, fire and water—the divine is immanent in all things. Not only place but also time reveals deity. Within the Craft the lunar cycle and especially the eight festivals are not only rites of the four seasons but also the rites of passage of the Goddess and God. The celebrant enacts and experiences this cycle from birth, through growth, sexuality, decline and death and into rebirth.

Having seen something of the ways in which the Craft envisages deity in the Charge, Drawing Down the Moon and in Nature, it is important to note the primary form and context of Craft celebrations: the circle.

Into the Circle

Pagans do not sit in neat rows facing an altar or pulpit in their ceremonies or gatherings. They form circles which speak eloquently about the way Pagans understand themselves, their religion and its various traditions. The actual mechanism of casting a circle can be briefly noted as a preliminary to discussing the character of the Craft in further detail.

Whether a particular group of Witches conducts its ritual naked (or skyclad as some say)[27] or dressed in special costumes, they disrobe or robe before forming the circle. The Charge of the Goddess declares nudity to be expressive of freedom from slavery. This is glossed as stripping away the various disguises people present to the world, expressing their love and trust, aiding or expressing their shift of consciousness to a more trusting openness.[28] Robes similarly effect a shift of consciousness—what you are about to do is different to what you do in ordinary clothes.

The real beginning of a ritual is the formation of the circle. It is "cast" or marked by someone walking its perimeter and imagining the drawing of an actual circle, sometimes using a wand or a knife kept specially for such occasions. Then the four cardinal directions (east, south, west, north—usually but not always in that order) are greeted or invoked. Exactly how this is done varies according to the tradition and/or the preferences of participants. Some are content to address "the powers of the north"; others refer to the elements traditionally associated with the directions.[29] In Alexandrian Wicca (following the tradition established by Alex Sanders) the four winds of Classical mythology are welcomed too. Craft teaching provides detailed correspondences between the directions, the elements, ritual tools, colours, aspects of the personality and so on. All of this is drawn into the pot or cauldron which is the circle.

Within the circle the group or individual is acted upon by all that they associate with the casting of the circle and the invocation of the quarters. Within the circle consciousness is altered—more poetically, Witches say that the circle is "between the worlds". This is true too of the opening of any religious ceremony, the difference is that Witches are both conscious of and deliberate about making the alteration. In other religions the clergy (perhaps assisted by a choir, maybe using incense or processions) are psychopomps taking their congregation into the other world of religious devotion. The Craft teaches each initiate how to make the changes, effect the shift, by and for themselves whether working alone or in a group.

Within the circle all are priests and priestesses—or aspiring to be such. Even in those groups which are not hierarchical, there is no laity, everyone seeks experience in priest/ess craft. The Craft usually presents itself as a mystery religion.[30] It provides a structure in which people can follow the ancient advice or instruction "Know Yourself". Alongside its particular ideas about the nature of Nature (alive, interconnected, sacred, divine) and about time (cyclical, marked by

---

[27] A phrase probably derived from Jain ascetic tradition. Gardner (1954): 49.
[28] E.g. Starhawk (1989a): 60-1; Crowley (1989): 59-60.
[29] As noted in chapter 1.
[30] Crowley (1996).

solar and lunar festivals), the Craft teaches people that they manifest divinity and are also not alien to animals and other inhabitants of Earth. Some Witches are happy to perform their own initiations, guided by books, other people's ideas and their own intuition. Others insist that initiation must take place in prescribed ways. Only properly initiated priestesses and priests can properly initiate others. This can simply mean that to be a priestess or priest means to be recognised by someone; it is not a question of your opinion of yourself. More often it is understood that individuals can dedicate themselves to a path but initiation is a greater step, one which involves others shaping the experience. Among Wiccans initiation involves relationships with the lineage of the group and the tradition. It is not just a matter of relationship with deity—that is direct, unmediated and personal—although, precisely because it is personal, an individual is encouraged to be guided by those who already enjoy the experience. It is possible to be misled: intuition and imagination are insufficient guides given that they are unlikely to have been moulded by Pagan understandings. "Self indulgence is a Pagan virtue"[31] and self-blessing is encouraged, but initiation can be thought to go beyond this. Others again are willing to teach the skills of the Craft in much the same way as Shamanic "techniques of ecstasy" can be taught outside a traditional environment.[32]

Exactly what takes place in Craft initiations is recorded in a number of recent works.[33] Given the detail provided in these and many other books written for Witches by Witches, it is unlikely that much now remains secret. Some claim that the personal names of the Goddess(es) and God(s) are only revealed to initiates. Such names are said to be particularly effective—it is only to be expected that using someone's name, even if that someone is a deity, is more likely to lead to a positive response. It is also worth commenting that self-initiation is unlikely to be as memorable as that surrounded by mystery, uncertainty, surprise, anticipation and so on. On the other hand, much of this may be hype. In the end, the validity of self-initiation can only be determined by asking whom it involves. Self-initiates are unlikely to gain full access to a mystery religion or to a group concerned about descent from "properly connected" initiates. Perhaps openness also depends on whether the Craft is *primarily* a Mystery, and on how much more open it will become to all who wish to learn its ways of listening to the speaking Earth. The increasing availability of open meetings and of information in books will probably lead to less hierarchical structures in the Craft, but initiatory rites will certainly continue to mediate powerful experiences of transformation.

[31] Jayran (1994): 231.

[32] See chapter 7.

[33] E.g. Crowley (1989, 1990); Starhawk (1989a); Farrar (1984); Crowther (1992).

What Witches do is recorded in their *Book of Shadows*, a sort of recipe book initially copied by initiates from their initiators and then added to as they gain experience. What is written is not received or treated as scripture that is infallible or revealed. The *Book of Shadows* is necessarily diverse and increasingly individual in its expansion around a traditional core.[34] It is a collection of ceremonies and techniques which have worked in the past, since what has once been effective might be expected to continue being so. However, it can always be improved and made more personally applicable. Just as there are various forms of the Charge of the Goddess, so each Witch's *Book of Shadows* will contain variations, e.g. on the words and actions for celebrations of the festivals.

Within the circle the work of the group can take place. Time and space have been set aside for something to happen. Consciousness has been altered. In the circle cyclical time is celebrated above linear time. These two ways of marking time are common to the world, though perhaps rarely labelled or considered. Our calendars and watches teach us to see time as moving in a straight line from the present to the future and to look back at the past. Things began, things exist now, and they will continue until they reach their climax or goal. On the other hand, our calendars also teach us that we return to the same season, the same hour, the same day of the week. Calendar customs have the same double function. Birthdays and New Year's Day remind us that time moves on and that we get older. January sales, summer fashions, colder winters than we used to have and hotter summers than last year remind us that we have returned to the same season. The cycle is, of course, not a monotonous, endless circle—the weather is different, fashions change, we do not eat the same food as we ate last week. It is a spiral combining both linearity and circularity: repetition and change, growth and stability. Pagans are not alone in noting that we experience time in two different ways. Other religions also make this kind of shift between linear and cyclical time in their festivals. Perhaps it is something Pagans do more consciously than other people or other religionists, though not all Pagans would express the idea in this way.

I have already noted that within the carefully marked circle deities become manifest in humans and people honour one another. People are initiated and become increasingly adept at altering their consciousness to be the kind of people who do things in this special time and place. They will eventually close the circle, saying farewell to those they invited, including the directions, elementals, deities and each other. They will return to the regular patterns, rhythms and places of their lives. If the experience has been effective, if it has been initiatory, it

---

[34] This has been published (with some expansions) in the books already quoted. Especially see Farrar (1984) and Kelly (1991). Also see Rees (1996).

will continue to affect them outside the circle. Men will continue to honour women and vice versa. People will continue to perceive deity in everything. They will continue to celebrate the physical as sacred, the location in which deity is manifest and life is lived. It remains to note too that Witches "work" within the circle. They engage in magic: an activity that is intended to make changes.

Using Energy

The circle acts as a container, a cauldron, in which something new can be formed. It might be new ways of perceiving the world or experiencing deity, or new roles and relationships within the group. One of the circle's primary functions is to contain the "energy" built up by Witches until it is ready to direct it to bring about desired changes.[35]

All group activities, from football crowds to prayer meetings, establish a mood, an almost tangible atmosphere which takes on a life of its own. People come away from powerful shared events glowing, enthused, excited, "high", but anticipating—perhaps unconsciously—a "coming down to earth" away from the group and the event. Some try to keep the mood "up" by further shared experiences: e.g. drinking, fighting, socialising, nightclubbing. Witches see the "electricity" of such events as something that can be used and deliberately, consciously "raise energy".

Within the circle, after the foregoing preparations, casting and invocations, Witches frequently share energetic activities. They "raise energy", understanding that it cannot be destroyed but only changed. Some chant, others dance or run around the circle, some beat drums. Usually these activities begin slowly and build up to a crescendo. All this time the participants are picturing the energy forming into a spinning spiral, a "cone of power", or another agreed shape, perhaps a sphere, fountain, wave or spear. The circle keeps the energy together until, as the running, dancing, chanting or drumming reaches a climax, it is "sent" to affect an agreed situation. It might be directed to healing a member of the group, or one of their relations. It might be used for the good of the rainforest, to stop road-building, quarrying, nuclear tests or animal experiments, and a whole array of goals desired by the group. Such (imaginative?) uses of energy do not prevent Witches from participating in other methods of affecting the same situations. Their experience is a powerful one, but is rarely an opiate preventing engagement with the world. Many Witches may prefer "alternative" health care (herbalism, homeopathy, etc.) to allopathic medicine, but the use of some sort of therapy is not seen as a "lack of faith" in the power of the circle or group. The two are complementary. Witches may

---

[35] Cp. the magician's circle in chapter 6.

meditate for the benefit of the rainforests, but are also likely to support organisations like Greenpeace and are not strangers at protests and demonstrations against whatever endangers life.

All of this—meditation, running around in circles and active protest—can be seen as "magic". Many Witches describe it as "changing reality according to the Will" or "changing consciousness according to the Will". Some see it as both at the same time.[36]

Having directed the energy, the group or solo practitioner is likely to touch the ground or drop to the floor. They deliberately "ground" themselves and "earth" the energy. This coming down to earth carefully alters consciousness again, not leaving people too "high" to leave the circle without experiencing dislocation and stress. It also subtly allows the ecstasy to be integrated into ordinary life.

Cakes and Wine

Before the circle is closed and the celebration ended, the group is likely to share "cakes and wine". This is often a prelude to a less ceremonial socialising, sharing food, drink and conversation. The transition allows participants to link what happens in the separated space and time of the circle with "ordinary" life, empowering the Witches' daily honouring of themselves, their surroundings and their "neighbours" (all that lives). The sacredness of the cakes and wine spills over, affecting regular meals. Or maybe the bringing of cakes and wine into the circle reminds people that all that they eat and drink comes from the Goddess(es) and the God(s).

The actual communion of cakes and wine may be ritualised or it may be very simple. In Wicca a priest holds the cup of wine, symbol of the Goddess, into which a priestess dips a ceremonial knife called an athame, a symbol of the God. For some this symbolises intimacy between Goddess and God, men and women, masculine and feminine. For others it shows that "the two divine forces are ultimately reconciled in One".[37] All drink from the cup and then share blessed cakes, sometimes in the shape of the crescent moon. Alternatively and more simply, the food and drink allow a more complete "earthing" and a brief time to express gratitude for the results of previous "work".

The sharing of food and drink, formally and informally, re-emphasises the words of the Charge, "Ye shall dance, sing, feast, make music and love". Fun, laughter, spontaneity and even saying the wrong words or making the wrong gesture are all part of Craft celebrations—humanity is not left outside the circle.

Socialising also points to the potentially significant relationships built up within groups. Craft events are either "closed" or "open". The

[36] See chapter 6.
[37] Crowley (1989): 160.

former are restricted to initiated coven members; the latter welcome people from outside the particular group or coven. Some events are even more "open", e.g. the House of the Goddess arranges an annual Halloween Gathering in London and Starhawk's Wind Hags coven organises public rituals and political actions.[38] However, the Craft is often said to be secretive. As with the Freemasons, the big secret is that there is no secret. For the purposes of initiation it is useful to build up the mystery. However, what is "revealed" in initiation is already available in books, conferences and conversation.[39] The word "secret" misleadingly implies arcane knowledge. In fact, the Craft is not secretive but private. It consists of small groups of people who work closely together. For the "work" to be effective they must trust one another, and this depends on fairly close friendships. Pagan groups are continually changing as people join and leave. New groups are formed, existing ones close.[40] People cannot just turn up on the doorstep and expect to be allowed to participate. They have to be invited and will be welcomed once the group is happy with their degree of interest, commitment or initiation. Like Jews, Mormons, Communists and Christians, Pagans too have been wrongly accused of performing human sacrifice, cannibalism and child abuse. In this climate it can be no surprise that Witches tend to keep themselves to themselves. Not advertising every celebration is no more secretive than not advertising a house-warming or wedding beyond friends and family. Nobody welcomes gatecrashers—especially those from the media looking for a "good story" or, more commonly, looking for photographs to attach to a pre-written salacious story.

On the other hand, there is considerably more openness among Pagans, of all sorts, now than there was as recently as the early 1980s. Margot Adler credits this to large festive gatherings across North America.[41] In Britain the first point of contact with Paganism for many people was in the Free Festivals of the 1970s and '80s (which included spirituality and land-rights claims); the many open festivals and conferences since the mid-1980s and the spread of informal gatherings in pubs in almost every British town and city in the 1990s. Some of these are purely social, some also educational, e.g. Talking Stick's regular London meetings. They have clearly affected the degree of privacy or openness in the Craft. Finding alternatives to domineering leaders, stuffy groups or boring rituals is now fairly simple. There are plenty of ways to learn other ways of doing things, or other things to do.

[38] Starhawk (1989a): 222. Also see Starhawk (1990).
[39] Though many Witches are disappointed by this and some see it as a betrayal of vows not to reveal the inner workings of the Craft.
[40] See Simes (1996) and Greenwood (1996).
[41] Adler (1986): 421-30.

Types of Wicca

This broad introduction to the Craft has occasionally noted differences between traditions within the Craft. By now most of these are represented by, or discussed in, books by Witches. In many countries there are umbrella organisations and world-wide-web sites providing information on the Craft, obviating the need to list or note the different traditions in any great detail.

Gerald Gardner's ideas can be followed in his own books.[42] They are also fundamental to other writers,[43] including some who add their own modifications or those initiated by Alex and Maxine Sanders which became Alexandrian Wicca.[44] There is now a growing movement of solo practitioners of the Craft.[45] Many Witches are developing less ceremonial and more nature-based ways of working.[46] Some are developing what they call "Progressive Wicca" with less hierarchy, more commitment and more frequent practice of magical.[47] Most Pagans have been influenced in one way or another by feminism, but there are explicitly feminist groups or movements within the Craft.[48] A version of Wicca which invokes primarily Saxon deities has gained some adherents in America.[49]

Most of these movements (and others) are admirably introduced by insiders in *Voices from the Circle* and in *People of the Earth*.[50] For the Craft in North America in particular, Margot Adler's *Drawing Down the Moon* is essential reading.[51] Australian Witchcraft is the subject of a couple of articles and a forthcoming book by Lynne Hume of the University of Queensland.[52] There are Witches in throughout Europe, South Africa and most other countries settled by people of European origin. However, the Craft is not restricted to Europeans but there are, for example, a growing number of Japanese Wiccans.

Granny Weatherwax, Nanny Ogg and Magrat Garlick

It is impossible to discuss Witchcraft without reference to Terry Pratchett.[53] His Discworld novels are widely acknowledged to include the most acute observations of Witches and Witchcraft. His (New

[42] Gardner (1949, 1954, 1959).
[43] Especially see Valiente (1975, 1978).
[44] See Farrar (1981, 1984); Crowley (1989, 1994); Clifton (1992); Kelly (1991).
[45] Beth (1990); Green (1991); Cunningham (1993).
[46] Valiente (1975); Green (1989); Jayran (1994).
[47] Morgan (1991); Rainbird (1994).
[48] Starhawk (1989).
[49] Buckland (1971, 1974).
[50] Jones and Matthews (1990); Hopman and Bond (1996).
[51] Adler (1986).
[52] Hume (1994, 1995).
[53] See in particular Pratchett (1988, 1991b, 1993).

Age?) Wiccan, Magrat Garlick, is instantly recognisable at Pagan events. There are also not a few cloak-draped Witches decorated with occult jewellery, some of whom really do call themselves names like Diamanda, Perdita or Amanita. Witches like Granny Weatherwax—with no time for "paddlin' with the occult"[54] but clearly Pagan in her protection of the land and her "headology"—can be found. The more earthy Nanny Ogg, vociferous singer of raunchy songs, is less obvious, regrettably. Pratchett also has much to contribute to the understanding of magic, nature, rites of passage, death, deities, humour and bigotry in religion. Not all Pagans enjoy his sense of humour but many recognise his characters—sometimes in themselves.

New Old Religion

Witches are polytheists even if some of them refer to "the Goddess" or "the God and the Goddess". The exact number in which the divine is experienced is not the central issue: polytheism can embrace devotion to one or two deities as easily as it celebrates many. More important, it refers to the way in which deity interacts with, relates to and is manifest in the world. The all-inclusive Goddess of feminist Witches or the Goddess and God of Wicca are polytheistic deities.

The Craft is a Nature religion, even if some Witches hold most of their celebrations in the comfort of their own homes. They honour seasons and the cycles of Earth, Moon, Sun and Zodiac. They celebrate the human and other natural life-cycles, including sexuality. They envisage deity as experiencing a quite "ordinary", natural life cycle. Embodiment is celebrated and not considered a restriction of spirituality.

Although Witches regularly incarnate their Goddess(es) and God(s) they do not become or follow gurus or messianic figures. Representing, expressing, manifesting deity is treated as a perfectly normal activity for a human being. There are respected teachers and valued books in the Craft, but none has or claims the authority that might expected in New Age circles or in many other religions. Even greatly respected teachers will not expect what they say to be treated as "the whole truth and nothing but the truth", nor will they expect great financial rewards.

The Craft is a fundamentally pluralist tradition, despite regularly hearing (their) Goddess revealing her nature and her desires. This self-revelation discourages "followers", "faithful devotees", "true believers" or evangelists. It does not expect faith and obedience. On the other hand, it encourages personal growth and maturity. The Craft has therefore developed as a series of systems for exploring identity,

[54] Pratchett (1993): 86.

relationships with the Earth, and growth towards personal responsibility.

Despite having fairly easily identifiable characteristics derived from a "received tradition", the Craft has no scriptures. Leaders and traditions are respected for their effectiveness rather than, ultimately, merely for their lineage. Gerald Gardner is important less because he represents the "Traditional Craft" and more because he taught people effective techniques for raising energy and affirming themselves.

The Craft attracts people because it combines the honouring of Nature with techniques for self-exploration. It tends to form close knit groups, separate from wider society but working for the good of others (in its own self-understanding). It provides a context in which something can be done about threats to the planet.

Many Witches call the Craft "the Old Religion". It is clearly a new religion in the sense that it has evolved since the 1930s. It is new in the sense that it is not even the same now as it was when the first proto-Pagan groups began to blend ceremonial magic with folk tradition and the ideas of Margaret Murray. It is new in that it arises out of modernity in some ways and anticipates postmodernity in others. It is new in the sense that it eloquently expresses the problems and delights of the modern world. There are, nonetheless, old traditions within the Craft. Celtic, Saxon, Egyptian, Greek and other deities are venerated. Some ancient agricultural festivals have been blended with more modern urban lifestyles. Its most archaic aspect is the sense of "return" to a Golden Age when humanity spoke easily with animals, trees, deities and "all our relatives". The celebration of Nature within the Craft excavates an ancient theme of vital importance to the contemporary world. The Craft is not the Old Religion of pre-Christian Europe, nor is it an old religion. It is a new religious movement with a message of timeless (ancient, contemporary and future) importance: the Earth is our home, we are Earth's people.

4

HEATHENS

> In fact the Gods were as puzzled by all this as the wizards were, but they were powerless to do anything and in any case were engaged in an eons-old battle with the Ice Giants, who had refused to return the lawnmower.[1]

While contemporary Pagans often claim Celtic origins for their traditions, the ancestors of many British people were Germanic or Scandinavian in origin. This is true even in the so-called Celtic areas and a growing number of groups and individuals are drawn to the traditions and history of these peoples for inspiration. Many, though not all, such people and groups prefer to name themselves Heathen rather than Pagan; both names are now commonly associated with the countryside, natural and wild places, the difference being that one originates in Germanic languages and the other in Latin. There are other ways of referring to such people and traditions, some preferring the Icelandic name Ásatrú, "allegiance to the deities", others preferring to be named Odinist.

Along with other Pagan traditions Heathenism is growing numerically and in coherence. It has adherents throughout northern and western Europe (including France, Belgium, the Netherlands, Britain, Germany, Scandinavia and Iceland), North America and Australasia. Heathenism shares many of the same characteristics, interests and problems as other Pagan traditions. It also has distinguishing features.

The significant groups in Britain are two named the Odinic Rite, Odinshof, Hammarens Ordens Sällskap and the Rune Gild.[2] These groups are represented in other countries too, especially but not only in northern and western Europe and in the Anglo-Saxon diaspora. The Odinic Rite has French and German groups. Nordlandia in Belgium combines interests in spirituality, culture and economics. In America the Ásatrú Alliance, the Ásatrú Folk Assembly, the Odinist Fellowship, the Ring of Troth and the Rune Gild are important.[3] Since 1973 Ásatrú has been one of the officially recognised religions of Iceland which has legalised its marriages, child naming and other ceremonies and provided benefits for tax purposes. (There were 172 registered Ásatrúarmen in Iceland on 1 December 1994.)[4] Each Heathen group has its own emphasis and not all of them are mutually exclusive, i.e. some people belong to more than one organisation. There is also a

---

[1] Terry Pratchett, *The Light Fantastic*. (1986): 16. (*1988): 18.
[2] These are discussed in further detail in Harvey (1996).
[3] Apart from their own publications see Kaplan (1996).
[4] Letter from Jón A. Baldvinsson, Embassy of Iceland, London, 24 November 1995.

wider audience for those things which are of central significance to
Heathens. Books on runes and Norse mythology abound and appear to
be gaining extra space in the relevant sections of many bookshops, i.e.
especially under 'Religion' or 'Mind, Body, Spirit'.

Rather than focusing on the deeds and thoughts of any particular
group or individual, this chapter is interested in the Heathen movement
as a whole. It begins with a sketch of the cosmology that *many*
Heathens consider to be their inheritance,[5] introduces festivals,
hierarchies, the use of runes and other means of communicating with
the other-than-human world, and explores distinctive issues of ecology,
race and deity-talk.

Northern Cosmology

The world in which we live is one of nine, all of which are linked to a
vast tree called Yggdrasil. Our world, Midgard (popularised by Tolkien
as Middle Earth), can be presumed to be central to the other worlds:
some are above it, others below. The exact manner of this linking
varies in both the ancient sources and in contemporary re-tellings.
Sometimes other worlds are said to revolve around Midgard while
elsewhere they are said to be in either the roots or the branches of the
tree.

Each world is predominantly populated by one race or type of
being: human in the case of our world, giants in one world, divinities in
two others, elves in one, dwarves in another, and so on. There is
continual movement between these worlds by those who are able to
travel, particularly the divinities and the giants. Not all is peace and
harmony; indeed there is usually conflict between these. There is also
movement up and down the World Tree, Yggdrasil, which is itself
continually being gnawed and nibbled away by the various creatures
inhabiting its roots, trunk and branches. However, the tree is not only
continually renewing itself but it also nourishes those who devour it.
The World Tree (and indeed much of this cosmology) is a 'memorable
image of perpetual movement, destruction and renewal'.[6]

There are two groups of divinities in these worlds: the Æsir and the
Vanir. The Vanir are "fertility deities of the earth, with Freyr and Njord
and the goddesses Freyja and Frigg as the main powers", while the
Æsir are "gods of sovereignty, magic and warfare".[7] Both groups have
their own world or home. A primeval conflict between the two was
resolved after an exchange of hostages who became significant allies,

---

[5] See the works of Hilda Davidson for greater detail and discussion of the historical
and archaeological sources and of this cosmology. Especially see Davidson (1993); but
also (1964) and (1988).

[6] Davidson (1993): 98.

[7] Davidson (1989): 105.

friends and marriage partners. The number of divinities of either or both groups is hard to calculate. Some are given more than one name, and Odin has many more than one. It is possible that some names apparently applied to separate divinities may in fact refer to a hypostasis of a more well known deity.

The difference between the Æsir and the Vanir is not one of gender, both groups including Goddesses and Gods. Nor are Goddesses second class citizens in this cosmology. While Northern Mythology is interested (obsessed at times) with fighting and breeding, the Goddesses are not all fertility symbols nor are all the Gods macho warriors. There is much multi-functionality which makes Georges Dumézil's 'three functions' only broadly applicable.[8] This multi-functionality and the conscious and expansive polytheism illustrate the wider diversities of north European history, cultures and cosmologies. Even the broad unities of place and language are offset by many diversities, especially those of clan and kin loyalties.

Polytheism makes possible the celebration of our everyday 'mundane' lives, whereas monotheism tends to diminish them in favour of the exaltation of an after life of divine worship.[9] Heathenism and other polytheistic traditions find meaning and value in the varied ordinary lives of human beings. Deities not only demand allegiance and worship but introduce us to ourselves. As with everything else in Nature, Gods and Goddesses have beginnings, albeit long before human memory, and their deaths can be remembered in some cases, e.g. Balder, and anticipated in others. Deities are not eternal.

At the foot of the World-Tree are three sisters, the Norns. They are now popularly thought of as 'Past, Present and Future' and as the only three spinners of Wyrd (something like karma or fate)[10] in all the worlds. The *Edda*, however, presents a more complex situation in which Wyrd is a web spun out by the combined actions of many, perhaps all, beings. The *hamingja* (more than 'luck' but not quite 'destiny', and something more poetic and mythic than 'genetic inheritance') of the group and sometimes of the individual is also significant. The three Norns are certainly central to this web. Their names might be better translated by 'Initiating, Becoming, Unfolding'. Northern mythology and history suggest a great ambivalence between fatalism and complete free-will. Fate could be striven against rather than meekly accepted.[11] If "resignation to [God's] will constitutes the classic monotheistic solution to the problem of coming to terms with

[8] Dumézil (1973) and (1988).

[9] Miller (1974); Bowes (1977); Green (1989).

[10] Also called Orlög, though some writers distinguish this from wyrd, seeing it as implacable, unalterable and more cosmic than individual.

[11] See Stone (1989).

the contingencies of life",[12] heroic effort is encouraged in Heathen myths. Within the great web of all things there is room for all individuals, in relationship with others, to manoeuvre within their wyrd.

There are many other significant other-than-human inhabitants of the nine worlds. A group which was particularly important to the many migrating and settling folk of post-Roman Europe was that of the 'hooded men' or 'land-spirits'.[13] These have survived into northern English folklore as 'boggarts' and 'Brownies'. Hilda Davidson suggests that they now survive cunningly disguised or ignominiously belittled as garden gnomes.[14] 'Land-spirits' are those who help but sometimes hinder those humans who give them respect and share the same territory. They are inhabitants of this world and in some way mediate between the land and human inhabitants. Such other-than-human people illustrate an important feature of this cosmology: human relationships with other-than-human beings were a matter of contract and co-habitation, relationship and proximity, or perhaps 'neighbourliness'. While they were clearly polytheistic ancient Heathens might choose to show especial honour to, or 'trust' in, one or several of the deities and their local land-spirits. Freyr, Thor and Odin were particularly popular in various places at various times.

In the past, hearth and home were central locations for religious ceremony. There were temples and sacred sites, including significant trees or rocks, which were foci for large public gatherings. Generally, though, priestly functions could be enacted by anyone. In a tradition where there was no great barrier between the sacred and the profane and in which everyday events like birth, death, sex and cooking were of interest to other-than-human people, the honouring of deities was not an unusual or specialised activity. The spiritual world and the physical world were one and the same.

These are some of the features of the cosmology of pre-Christian northern Europe. Many of them remain significant in contemporary Heathenism.

The Nine Worlds Now

Some Heathens are convinced that the northern cosmology in all its grandeur and evocative power is an accurate, if poetic, description of the cosmos. There are deities of culture and nature, there are other realms to which it is possible to journey, everything began in the interaction between fire and ice and everything will end with a cosmic conflict or a grinding down of all matter. They assert that the virtues of

---

[12] Lerner (1995): 306.
[13] Davidson (1989).
[14] Davidson (1989): 114.

an earlier age are still valuable, especially honour, kinship, trust and strength. The tree which links all of life, and is itself threatened by those who live in it, is a powerful icon for contemporary ecological engagement.

Mythology also provides maps of people's inner worlds. Those convinced by Jung might apply his ideas to the idea of the nine worlds. One realm might represent the deep unconscious which could be explored therapeutically or imaginatively for greater understanding of the self and its condition. Another might be inhabited by pure archetypal forms that could be approached for another level of understanding. Some see the deities as humanity's intellect or "higher self" and the giants as instinctual urges. Or perhaps the giants represent inertia, the tendency towards entropy, while the deities represent the varied manifestations of the evolutionary urge against entropy.

Some approach the deities to honour them, some even to worship. Others hope to gain wisdom, understanding, power or visionary insights. It is the intention of the more magically orientated to emulate particular deities and, by doing so, to become truer to themselves. There are even those who speak of "becoming deities", being drawn onwards by the current deities who are themselves also evolving into higher forms.

The therapeutic and psychological riches of the Anglo-Saxon tradition, which Brian Bates introduced to many people through his book *The Way of Wyrd*, are now fully and richly revealed in his *The Wisdom of the Wyrd*.[15]

All these interpretations and uses of the northern cosmology are expressed in similar forms. People tell the stories, elaborate upon them, study their symbolism, especially as encapsulated in the runes, and explore their relevance in everyday life. They also chant runes, make similar gestures or symbols, drink mead and form groups with those who share such interests. Some tend to be dismissive of other Pagan paths. The following sections provide greater detail on the activities, beliefs and organisations of contemporary Heathens.

Festivals (time and place)

Some Heathens celebrate the same eight seasonal festivals as other Pagans—the solstices, equinoxes and the four quarter days. They also celebrate the lunar cycle with gatherings or ceremonies at new and/or full moon. Others dismiss these festive cycles as of recent origin and assert that the original celebrations of the Anglo-Saxon, Teutonic and other northern European peoples are more significant occasions.

---

[15] Bates (1983) and (1996).

Three ancient festivals are Winternights, Yule and Sigrblot. The first and last mark the beginning of winter and summer respectively, while Yule still marks midwinter. While these remain the most significant Heathen festivals, additional celebrations also occur.

Winternights combines the celebration of the onset of winter with a harvest festival and the honouring of the dead. Yule combines the celebration of the darkest, longest nights of winter with that of New Year and a time of oaths and fateful encounters. Traditionally, the dead and otherwordly or divine visitors were either entertained or kept away by gifts, sacrifices, parties and carefully spoken promises or other expressions of honour. Sigrblot (victory celebration) marks the beginning of summer and celebrates the return of greenery and abundance. The "victory" of the title might refer to that of summer vitality over winter gloom, a popular theme of folk customs associated with this time of year. Alternatively, the feast may have anticipated victories in the coming trading or raiding season. Given the popularity of midsummer celebrations in Scandinavia and Germanic countries, it is almost certain that midsummer (perhaps the solstice itself) was celebrated widely and vigorously in pre-Christian times. It is certainly popular now among Heathens.

Apart from such undoubtedly ancient festivals, Heathens frequently celebrate additional festivals throughout each year. They typically devote days to heroes of the Heathen past, such as those who resisted the violent efforts of the Christian missions or who led armies and settlers to new lands. Some groups devote regular celebrations to particular deities, e.g. Thor, or groups of deities, e.g. the Goddesses. In common with wider Pagan practice, such celebrations might take place on the same date every year, perhaps in the evening to be convenient for those who are employed during the day, or at the nearest weekend.

Heathen festivals tend to include poetic invocations and expressions of honour and commitment (oaths) to deities and other significant peoples, e.g. the elves. Many of the liturgies of these occasions draw on or imitate the diction of ancient Norse or Anglo-Saxon poetry, frequently including archaic or traditional words. Typically, mead or ale is drunk, following its offering to leading deities (especially Odin and Thor), and fires, torches or candles are lit. Many Heathens dress in the style of their ancestors, especially of the tenth century, with woollen tunics over linen shirts and woollen trousers. If "Celtic" patterns and jewellery are popular among other Pagans, New Agers and others, Heathens recognise much of this (e.g. knotwork), more accurately, as of Norse origin.

A hammer sign is perhaps the most frequently used symbol among Heathens, occurring as pendants, in art and as gestures in rituals. It can indicate a particular though not exclusive affinity for Thor, while three interlocked triangles, a *walknot*, indicate an affinity for Odin. However, the hammer can also be worn as a symbol of the entire religion, much as many Christians wear a cross. These symbols express something essential about their respective religions and their interfaces with other religions. The hammer symbolises the energy or vitality of Heathenism as a religion celebrating Nature, itself energetic and vital. It is the hammer of Thor, *mjölnir*, the spinning, never-ceasing energy of the universe. It is the wheel of life, turning through growth and decline, ever returning to its apparent starting point, only to move on again. It is wielded against the inertia of opposition, pulverising immovable and intractable objects into primal matter which then supports the evolution of life. Barriers become bridges. The hammer does not encourage self-sacrifice, though this has its place and might be symbolised by the tradition about Odin hanging in Yggdrasil for nine days and nights.[16] Nor does it suggest humility or self-negation. Rather it inspires strength of character and indicates refusal to work quietly behind the scenes for change. The hammer sign as a personal ornament or pendant appears to have arisen in direct opposition to, and as a distorted reflection of, the cross sign worn by Christian armies, missionaries and converts. Based on traditions about Thor's hammer, it was a clear statement of a refusal to "take the cross" and also an expression of the vigour of Heathenism. The old religion was not dying out when Christianity arrived. The hammer continues to symbolise the strength of the revived tradition and its honouring of life, creativity and strength.

In common with Wicca and (Pagan) Druidry, Heathenism has roots among early twentieth-century "back to Nature" groups, such as Kibbo Kift and Woodcraft Chivalry. The outdoor emphasis of such roots remains significant, reiterating ancient nature veneration. Such roots also balance the indoor trend based on traditions of feast halls and temples. These are not really alternatives, and many celebrations easily combine both indoor and outdoor aspects. An indoor feast might precede or follow an outdoor ceremony. For example, the Yule tree traditionally remained outside and was decorated and received offerings as one part of the celebrations many of which, especially given the cold winters, took place indoors. Like its ancient form, contemporary Heathenism combines the honouring of trees, rocks, rivers and other "natural" places with the celebration of good company and the harvested fruit of human interaction with nature's fields and flocks.

Priests and people

Heathenism—like most contemporary religions—is made of groups of people who have chosen to associate with one another. The groups

---

[16] Davidson (1964): 143-4.

have leaders, some of whom are teachers, some initiators, others administrators.

Many Heathen groups name their leaders by Icelandic or Germanic titles. For example, the Odinic Rite has a ruling Council, the Court of Gothar, *Gothar* being the plural of priest, *Gothi* (male) and *Gythja* (female). Odinshof's Council is called the Witan Assembly, after the Anglo-Saxon royal courts. It describes Gothar as being "parish priests or priestesses" who oversee local groups called Hearths, each of which is overseen by a Hearth Guardian. Some Heathens use the Icelandic forms *Goðar*, *Goði* and *Gyðja*. The Ring of Troth renders *Goðar* and *Gyðja* as Godmen and Godwomen, using an inclusive form, Godwo/men in its publications.[17]

These priestly labels should not obscure a diversity of leadership patterns among Heathen groups. Group leaders might be administrators or secretaries in charge of mailing, facilitating the group's networking and handling enquiries from interested outsiders, e.g. the media. Others are recognised as more capable, adept, learned or wise in areas that group members wish to gain competence. Someone knowledgeable about the runes and adept in their use might be surrounded by those wishing to learn. As long as the adept keeps ahead of the student their relationship will continue. The larger organisations have more formalised structures, with central offices and officers, including both administrators and teachers. During rituals some of these leaders fulfil a priestly role: they direct ceremonies, bless mead, co-ordinate and draw others into the occasion. Few Heathen ceremonies are led by one person alone, and all provide opportunities for group participation. Heathen priests are not intermediaries between people and deities. They facilitate ceremonies in which the group participates. Teachers within these groups tend to direct individual study, not always through books but also in practical skills and crafts, e.g. story-telling or brewing. Some groups encourage the development of counselling skills and an awareness of more professional sources of help in various areas: medical, therapeutic, psychological, legal and so on. Of particular importance to many groups is the knowledge of and ability to retell traditional lore derived from sagas, myths, legends, histories and other sources. Such people might be called skalds, equivalent to bards, or lore-speakers.

In order to explore the more priestly functions in greater detail the following section discusses three ways of using symbols in communicating with the other-than-human world.

[17] E.g. Gundarsson (1993).

Runes: Galdr, Seidr and Taufr

One of the best known aspects of northern tradition is runes. These are popularly considered to be a series of symbols used in fortune-telling, perhaps equivalent to the tarot cards but carved on sticks or stones. Such understandings are partly correct but might prevent a full appreciation of what Heathens do and believe. There is a wide gulf between books on "runes for fortune-telling" and those which integrate the runes into a complete cosmology and religion.

The runes may have been created simply as an adaptation of the alphabet for the writing of Teutonic languages. It is now traditional, however, to use them as an elaborate system of symbols which encapsulate and evoke the richness of Heathen cosmology.[18] Each character can be associated with a deity, one of the nine worlds, a mood, an action, a season or some other aspect of northern life, belief and thought. They can be used as a divinatory system: a rune stick can be drawn out of a bag or bundle and taken to be an answer to a question, albeit one that needs interpretation. A rune associated with Thor might suggest that success in a given venture will require vigorous effort. Heathens use the runes in such attempts to discover what Fate or the Norns are spinning, or to discern the shape of the Web of Wyrd, or all things. They also use the runes in their communications with other-than-human people.

Heathen ceremonies commonly include the chanting of runes. Written versions of Heathen liturgies might just note "Galdor" at the point when one or more participants chant one or more runes. Some Heathens chant the entire runic alphabet at the beginning of their ceremonies, each rune having a particular note and pitch. Sometimes the chanters assume a posture replicating the rune or they might make a gesture with their hands in that shape. During a ceremony a competent chanter might be called on to chant a single significant rune, suitable to the occasion. Other participants might echo the chanted rune. The purpose of Galdor is literally an attunement, or an attempt to resonate with what is of significance for the particular ceremony or occasion. Chanting enables a shift of consciousness, from the simple focusing of attention on the matter in hand, leaving behind affairs of work and play, to the experience of ecstasy and communion with other-than-human people. These are not, of course, alternatives but desired stages in religious ceremony. The initial chants and other preambles enable participants to withdraw from their many individual concerns and to unite in developing a communal feeling, mood or understanding. Once the many disparate interests have been focused into one community, sometimes thought of as a group-soul, then further Galdr within the

---

[18] Especially see Aswynn (1990) and Thorsson (1991).

ceremony express the desire and the fact of human communication with the divine.

Seidr is a more contentious aspect of some Heathens' practice and experience. It can refer to the making of potions and remedies, including both herbalism and brewing. However, something less acceptable and less controlled is suggested by some references to Seidr. Although Odin was taught Seidr by Freya, this does not legitimate the tradition; Odin can be somewhat tricksy at the best of times, and anyway his quest for wisdom embraces all experiences. Seidr was considered less than respectable for men and not entirely acceptable for women.

Today Seidr is taken to be some form of Shamanic practice. Freya Aswynn says,

> Seidr is the name of a variety of magical and shamanic practice involving sorcery, divination and "soul journeys".

She translates it literally as "seething".[19] Similarly, Thorsson says it "involves attaining of trance states and often involves sexuality".[20] The most sustained discussion and practical advice is given by Jan Fries who calls Seidr a "seething trance".[21] Fries begins by extending the herbalism association into a metaphor: the body of the practitioner is the pot or cauldron which can be brought to the boil. The first effect of the alteration of consciousness is trembling, shaking or seething. In fact, Fries indicates that such states can be induced by deliberate gentle shivering and progressing to more uncontrolled shaking. This can "increase the pyrotechnics in the brain which then gives way to the full phenomenon". Along with chanting runes and other shamanic exercises, shaking is preliminary to the alteration of consciousness which enables communication with other-than-human people, whether they are thought of as spirits or as deities, elves, totem animals or personal guardians. For example, a trance, which might be light or deep, opens up the possibility of becoming a channel, medium or "horse" for deities. Freya Aswynn acts in this way for Odin, allowing the deity to speak to those who honour him. Though she does not necessarily follow Jan Fries' techniques for entering trance, her descriptions of Seidr are similar and certainly lead to similar results. In truly shamanic style she surrounds herself with the signs, symbols, costumes and accoutrements of the deity with whom she is most intimate. His choice of her as a means of communication is expressed in a shape-shifting in which she seems to disappear and he is seated in his prepared high-seat.

---

[19] Aswynn (1990): 258.
[20] Thorsson (1991): 277.
[21] Fries (1993): especially 176-9.

If Galdr and Seidr are two contrasting ways of communicating with deities and other other-than-human people, Taufr is a third. Taufr is the making and use of talismans or symbols, e.g. carving runes on wood or stone, making pendants or rings and marking symbols on other objects. The maker or carver is not just decorating objects, but is engaged in a sacred activity. An otherwise mundane object like a beer mug can be hallowed by its marking with runes. These might dedicate the mug to use only in religious ceremonies, or might attempt to ensure that the contents will always be health-giving. A hammer bought from a hardware shop might make a perfectly acceptable sign or ritual tool evocative of Thor's mjölnir and useful in invoking Thor, but most Heathens would consider it necessary to mark the hammer with suitable dedicatory runes.

In the contemporary practice of magic some Pagans use symbols called sigils, made up of various discrete letters or signs combined into one pattern.[22] The runes lend themselves to a form of sigil called a bindrune. A series of runes expressive of the carver's interests and intentions, beliefs and practices, can be combined into a more complex pattern. The Pagan environmental action group, Dragon, uses a complex cosmological bindrune both as a group logo and as a part of its eco-dramatic rituals against roads, quarries and other devastations. Six different runes are combined into a single tree-like symbol, representative of Yggdrasil, rooted in the rotten decay of the underworld and reaching to the divine realms of Asgard by way of Swartalfheim, Midgard and Ljossalfheim. These realms are understood both physically as the mineral, vegetative and other natural cycles of Earth and psychologically as references to conscious, subconscious and "super-conscious" realms of intuition, action, thought, imagination, intention and inspiration. Dragon explain each rune separately, giving its elemental, divine and human associations, as well as explaining the entire symbol. They encourage the use of the sigil in meditation, ritual and action. It can be painted on threatened trees or used as a banner in demonstrations. It can be empowered and power can be drawn from it. So many and various are the uses to which the Dragon bindrune can be put that it has been referred to as a "magical Swiss Army knife", with multiple functions and applications.

Much of the Heathen use of signs and symbols, whether verbal or physical, chanted or carved, illustrates the validity of Jonathan Z. Smith's explanation of ritual as,

> first and foremost, a mode of paying attention. It is a process for marking interest.[23]

---

[22] See chapter 6.
[23] Smith (1987): 103.

Ordinary objects are taken and used in ceremonies and thereby become sacred. Ordinary hammers, written symbols, rings, drinking vessels, sounds and stories are made sacred by being used in the service of divine or other-than-human powers and influences. In using and so making these things sacred, Heathens pay attention to their tradition, their deities, their wyrd and the world around them. The archaic nature of some of these ritual objects, e.g. drinking horns and runes, does not negate their "ordinary" origins. Rather, the juxtaposition of such archaic forms with contemporary situations enables people to pay attention more closely. The following sections discuss three areas of interest to which Heathens are paying attention: ecology, race and deities.

Ecology

Heathenism is as involved in ecology as any other Pagan path. Michael York quotes a comment in *The Odinist* (the newsletter of the Odinist Fellowship) that it "came as a surprise that few Odinists are interested in ecology".[24] Perhaps there was a fault in the questionnaire on which this finding was based. Although ecology might not be the primary religiously inspired activity of Heathens, it is certainly of great interest to most of them.

Besides the seasonal celebrations which engage people in conversation with Nature, the ideology of Heathenism stresses the honouring of the land and its deities and other significant beings that are intimate with specific places and landscapes. The fact that northern cosmology speaks of nine worlds does not lead Heathens to a quest for life in any other world but Midgard, Middle Earth, the place of our ordinary mundane existence. Midgard is home to humans but its destruction or devastation would also involve the other worlds. There are stories about life after death which suggest that at least some of the dead dwell elsewhere, in Valhalla, or with the lowerworld's ruler Hel, or with a deity to whom one had been devoted. Other stories suggest that the dead remain in their burial mounds, from which some were able to communicate with their relatives. None of these stories, however strongly affirmed by contemporary Heathens, predisposes people to belittle life here and now in favour of some more "spiritual" option.

The deities of Heathenism are intimately related to the land. Although they can be said to inhabit their own realms, Asgard and Vanaheim, they are not strangers to Midgard. In fact, it is probable that both ancient sources and contemporary Heathens envisage the nine worlds as overlapping and integral to this world. Certainly, some

---

[24] York (1995): 126, quoting *The Odinist* 117 (1988): 1.

traditions and groups associate the Vanir deities with agriculture. The large number of other significant beings—landvættir (land-spirits), elves, dwarves and others can also be encountered in this world and not only as visitors but as inhabitants. Respect for them entails respect for the ordinary places of the world.

Heathen ecological activity has involved, for example, tree planting, raising money to buy a wood which will be protected from human exploitation, and protests against the widening of the rail-link between London and the Channel Tunnel. *Hammarens Ordens Sällskap* have established a "land-army" which is working towards self-sufficiency by small-scale farming (smallholdings and allotments) in combination with a barter system. They have been working with the local council to make their skills available to unemployed people, not only to Heathens. They also work with countryside wardens to protect an area of natural beauty and scientific significance. That this area also includes a site of historic importance to Viking settlement in north-west England is not incidental to their involvement, but it is not their sole motivation either. They are deeply concerned with both the history and the natural history of the area and encourage others to root themselves in their own landscapes.

Race

Many Heathen groups lay considerable stress on race. They assert that Heathenism is the aboriginal or indigenous tradition of the Anglo-Saxon or Teutonic peoples. Some make it clear that they consider other indigenous traditions equally valid for other peoples, and that they are not claiming a racial or religious superiority. They object strongly to multi-culturalism and to the blend of cultures and traditions caused by the mix of peoples in the contemporary world. Some suggest that there is something in the collective unconscious of people of northern European descent which gives them a greater affinity with runes, Heathen deities and Heathenism itself.

Other Heathen groups distance themselves from such views, refusing to distinguish a stress on race from racism. It is undoubtedly true that Heathens are likely to be politically right-wing and generally conservative in their views, e.g. on sex, politics and history. This alone makes their tradition difficult for many other Pagans, who tend to be politically left-wing and generally liberal or radical in their views.

There is a continuing debate among Heathens about the degree to which the Nazis were inspired by Heathen traditions. The undeniable use of runes by some Nazis does not necessarily mean that their entire ideology was Heathen. On the other hand, the fact that some rune-users were persecuted does not mean that the Nazis had no interest in the runes. It seems clear that the Nazis drew on whatever sources might appear to justify their power and their actions, but that their ideology was formed from a blend of traditional Christian anti-semitism, Germanic nationalism and racial pride. Such pride gained power from the Social Darwinism popular throughout the West at the time and from a reaction to the suppression of German freedoms after the First World War. The closest this comes to Heathenism is in Wagner's patriotic and Nietzschean versions of the sagas and mythology of the Teutonic peoples, and in Guido von List's eccentric version and interpretation of the runes.[25]

People who are drawn to the deities and traditions of the Anglo-Saxon, Norse and Germanic peoples have to take a clear stand concerning the racial ideas now commonly associated with the tradition. Many avow such views, but there are a number of such groups for whom the tradition is open to anyone attracted by its wealth of powerful and evocative stories and symbols. They have no trouble repudiating racism, sexism, homophobia or any other ideology that they perceive as negative but prevalent among other Heathens. These things are simply not part of the tradition which attracts them or the groups which they join. Further discussion of Heathen deities may clarify what attracts some people (of various shades of politics) to this tradition.

Gods and Goddesses

Sustained thought about deities is not typical or central to Paganism. Even in small tight-knit groups of Pagans of a single tradition there is likely to be a diversity of views on the nature of deity. Some are happy to talk of a single Goddess, others of "the Goddesses and the God", others of many. There are also Pagan atheists, agnostics, animists and others who are not particularly interested in deities, considering human life to be a human concern. Heathens tend, however, to be much more definite about theology. If the deity-talk of feminist-influenced Pagans uses a female form, the*a*logy, then perhaps it would be appropriate for Heathen deities-talk to use a plural form, the*oi*logy, that is if Heathens did not have a strong preference for north European words and strong antipathy towards southern European ones. If there is no equivalent word in common usage among Heathens, this is because their approach to deities does not inspire the kind of abstract, philosophical or systematic God-talk that theology has become within Christianity. Traditionally Heathens spoke of their Gods and Goddesses in the context of poetry and stories. There are complex riddling poems like *Vafþruðismal*, The Words of the Mighty Riddler; poems that combine wisdom and prophesy, like *Hávamál*, and *Voluspá*, Prophecy of the

[25] See Fries (1993): 68-73.

Seeress; and poems about journeys between the worlds, like *Hymiskviða*, Hymir's Ballad, and *Thrymskviða*, Thrym's Ballad.[26] Some contemporary Heathens also draw on more recent mythological works, such as those of Tolkien. From such sources they produce liturgies in which deities are spoken of and spoken to, not in creeds but in further poems and invocations.

Heathenism today is as strongly polytheistic as its traditional sources. Heathens acknowledge and experience the presence and activity of an indeterminate number of Goddesses and Gods, including Odin, Thor, Frey, Freya, Balder, Tyr, Nerthus, Idun, Sif, Vidar, Vali and many more. Festivals may be devoted to them, individually or in groups. Their deeds and relationships are the subject of poetry and stories the purpose of which is not instruction or improvement, but enchantment. That the deities indulge in eating, drinking, sex, fighting, farming, travelling and other mundane pursuits is an important aspect of the polytheistic assessment of the natural, material world. Every aspect of life—not only its "spiritual" aspects—is celebrated, often with humour and delight.

Most Heathen groups have been largely focused on honouring the Æsir and those Vanir deities who are closely related to them. Perhaps this is because the Heathen revival so far has been concerned with providing meeting places for deities and humanity (or the Anglo-Saxon "race"). The deities that have had most connection with culture have renewed their acquaintance first. Currently, however, there are signs that the Vanir deities are being approached and encountered by various Heathens. Perhaps this coincides with a renewed emphasis among some groups on the land. Similarly, Heathenism has until recently been a thoroughly patriarchal movement both in its stress on Gods—either Æsir or Vanir—above Goddesses, and in its male control. This too is changing under the impact of significant strong women and perhaps in line with wider changes in society which make explicit patriarchy less easy to justify. In addition to those groups which call themselves Ásatrú, "those who honour or trust the Æsir", there are now Heathens who prefer the title Vanatrú, "those who honour the Vanir", and a few who prefer Dísitrú, "those who honour the Goddesses". A British journal, *Folkvang Horg*, is dedicated to "Harmony through Beauty Restored: Æsir and Asynjur in Balance"—i.e. it aims to encourage Heathens to rediscover and restore the honour given to the Goddesses. It has received a positive response from larger Heathen organisations.[27]

If many Pagans are ambivalent about the nature of deity or deities— are they poetic metaphors, psychological archetypes or a species within cosmic ecology?—the majority of Heathens are certain of the

---

[26] For a brief introduction to these and other poems see Davidson (1993).
[27] Also see Metzner (1994).

personality and ontological existence of deities. In short, "the basic relationship between god/esses and humans is one of gifts given by each to the other".[28] Heathens are engaged in reciprocal relationships with their chosen ancestral Gods and Goddesses as part of their web of relationships with the world around them.

Pride and Prejudice

Heathenism is in some ways distinguishable from the broader Pagan movement, but it is similar in that it is growing numerically and also gaining increasing confidence as a religious tradition.

Wiccans and other followers of the Craft often suffer from the deeply instilled cultural negative stereotype of the 'witch'. It is rarely possible to utter that word without evoking deep fears and prejudice. Druids perform open outdoor celebrations in public places such as Avebury and London's Primrose Hill (if not at Stonehenge) and, at the worst, face humour rather than hostility. Heathens stand somewhere between the two. They can be public about some of their activities and views without the barrier erected by the word 'witch', but some of their traditional symbols (e.g. the swastika) and interests can cause alarm.

Undoubtedly many Heathens hold views on race and sexuality which are considerably to the right of the political centre. Some certainly hold neo-Nazi views. These matters make their relationship with other Earth-respecting groups difficult. On the other hand, some groups nuance these views carefully and others reject them altogether.

More positively, Heathenism has much to teach Pagans about the value and power of a self-consciously polytheistic tradition. Many Pagans moderate their polytheism with the confusing claim that 'all Goddesses are one Goddess'. Heathens are aware that polytheism encourages the celebration of the ordinary facts of life—eating, drinking, working, relating, surviving, growing, dying etc. Some Heathens have become increasingly involved in ecology and in celebrating their tradition in more "Shamanic" ways. They are spending more time around fires, on hills, heaths and in woods—both celebrating their tradition and protecting the land. Some are rediscovering ancient ecstatic and trance traditions and techniques. The contentious aspects of Heathenism can be seen as a human-centred conversation about race and a male-centred conversation about power. The deities of importance to Heathens and their celebration of Nature engage them in conversations with Nature. In such ways Heathens are listening to the diverse voices of the living Earth.

[28] Gundarsson (1993): 59.

5

GODDESS SPIRITUALITY

Something else was happening, in a place as far away as the thickness of a shadow.[1]

Feminism has found a spiritual or religious expression in the re-valuing, re-discovery and re-creation of Goddess-talk. For this Naomi Goldenberg has coined the term "thealogy".[2] Not all of this is Pagan. Within many or perhaps all other religions women have at least begun to look again at the maps to see if they chart women's spaces and activities or indicate the horizons women notice.

In its Pagan manifestation this Goddess-talk has primarily been concerned with the embodied living of life by women. "The Goddess" is not equivalent to "Woman" as archetypal being but more like "the innermost being of women" or "that which exists between women encountering each other". The diversities and particularities of women's lives are significant, not merely some overarching archetypes to which people might be expected to conform. Asphodel Long sums up her view by affirming that, "In raising Her we raise ourselves; in raising ourselves, we raise Her".[3]

The particular realities of women's lives are affected by their discovery of the Goddess. Similarly, their imaging and descriptions of the Goddess are affected by their lives. For example, the Goddess can be portrayed, especially following Robert Graves,[4] as young, maternal or elderly, or as virgin, mother or crone. Goddess Spirituality refuses to limit such portrayals to fertility but links "the Goddess" with the everyday processes of women's growth from infancy through maturity towards death. Aspects of their lives ignored, marginalised or shunned by patriarchal religions are released and women are enabled to realise the sacredness of, for example, menstruation, sexuality and maternity. Women's desires, intuitions, moods, thoughts and opinions are significant. They do not have to wait until they are widowed or elderly to be able to celebrate their own religious intimations.[5] In short, they do not need men's authority or approval.

[1] Terry Pratchett, *Equal Rites*. (1987): 170.
[2] Goldenberg (1979): 96. My use of hyphenated "re-" is dependent on Mary Daly's re-forming of the English language to refuse the giving of authority only to that which males value(d), discover(ed) or create(d). See, for example, Daly (1987).
[3] Long (1994).
[4] Graves (1948).
[5] Cp. Sered (1993).

Goddess Spirituality takes people's embodied experience, their spatiality, their ordinary lived reality into consideration. It does not require a valuable "religious experience" to be "numinous" or revelatory of the supernatural, non-human world.[6] What is significant to women is significant to Goddess(es) and to this influential aspect of Paganism.

This chapter explores the diversities of Goddess Spirituality. It notes the books most often referred to and the groups in which spirituality is encouraged, taught or experienced. To make what is happening clear, some New Age thoughts about "the feminine" are also discussed. Much of what is said here is not only descriptive of activities of explicitly feminist groups, but also applies to many other Pagans. That is, Goddess Spirituality crosses the boundaries of traditions, influences other ways of being Pagan and participates in cross-fertilisation within Paganism. Even those Pagans who say they are not feminist are influenced by feminism, just as they are affected by ecology.

Avalon from the Mists

My first exploration of Goddess Spirituality was occasioned by Joan Leonard's article discussing the teaching of Feminist Spirituality in a Catholic liberal arts college in the United States.[7] My interests at that point were in the role of Goddess(es) and women in a variety of Pagan groups—not necessarily explicitly feminist ones. I distributed a questionnaire among two Druid Orders, a Wiccan coven, a Heathen group, and a Thelemite Order, and sent it also to many individuals, e.g. members of Goddess-centred or New Age groups. In addition to asking about roles and understandings I also asked how Goddess Spirituality is taught and/or learnt. The resulting article summarised the responses, which suggest that discussing women and Goddesses makes possible an approach to some central aspects of Paganism.[8]

"Equality" was the most common answer to the question, "What is the role of women in your group, especially in meetings?". In practice, some groups do not distinguish between people by gender but only by their abilities—and encourage them all to extend their areas of competence. Some say that women are "more intuitive" and that their "natural gift is [their] attunement with the innerworlds", whereas men are said to be "more outgoing than the females" and "tend to stick to the letter of the law". Men "tend to enjoy sacerdotal dignity and formality" more than women. Wicca, in which "women represent the Goddess and control the circle", was thought by some to be more

---

[6] See Raphael (1994) and (1996).

[7] Leonard (1990).

[8] Harvey (1993). The questionnaire had a limited circulation so its results must be seen as suggestive rather than definitive.

attractive to women than Druidry. A Druid, meanwhile, stressed the balancing of the "dominant god energy" by women—not, interestingly, by Goddesses. The gender balance in both the Craft and Druidry is, in fact, fluid; there are both completely male covens and completely male Orders, there are also completely female covens, though as yet no completely female Orders. Most Pagan groups are fairly evenly balanced, with active and leadership roles taken by women and men. The Heathens who responded also stressed the equality of women with men in all positions and activities of their group. However, most other Heathen groups are more male-dominated than this group, though there are significant women among them. There are also Heathen groups who give pride of place to the Goddesses.[9] Only one response, from a New Ager, said, "Feminism [is] unconstructive, negative, belligerent". Certainly a wider sample would show that more Pagans dislike feminism, but men-only groups are rare, and only Mithraists[10] have no place for Goddesses or women in their tradition or ceremonies.

These respondents describe the Goddess(es) in various ways. She is the Earth, Mother Earth, an archetype, a symbol, Creator or co-Creator with a God. Some only speak of plural divinities, some never refer to Goddess(es) without also referring to God(s). Several speak of "the three faces of the Goddess: virgin, mother and crone". Others note that several have triple aspects, like the Morrigan of Irish tradition[11]. The celebration of sexuality without reference to fertility or reproduction is honoured by the Secular Order of Druids in the "fourth face of the Goddess: the scarlet woman".

When asked how they honour the Goddess(es) two related themes were referred to: honouring the Earth and honouring people, particularly women. Contexts in which honour can be expressed are the seasonal festivals, the countryside, and sacred places like Stonehenge or Glastonbury. Recycling everything possible and other such mundane and ecological activities are mentioned. Knowing the desire of the heart is also significant. No-one in these responses uses the word "worship". Only occasionally do Pagans ever talk about worship and when they do they tend to note carefully that they mean something different to what Christians mean.[12]

In Leonard's article Goddess Spirituality is taught using Marion Bradley's *The Mists of Avalon*[13]—an imaginative retelling of the Arthurian legends from the perspective of some of the women. My article shows that within Pagan groups people are encouraged to explore Nature and to trust that their experiences are revelatory of that

---

[9] See chapter 4.
[10] Of whom there are a few—though not all of them call themselves Pagan.
[11] See Ó hÓgáin (1990): 307-10.
[12] Further discussed in chapter ten.
[13] Bradley (1984).

which matters. No one referred to a sacred text but many significant books were mentioned. Introductions to a tradition's Goddesses and Gods, and much else of significance to Pagan groups and individuals, take the form of getting to know Nature, both the individual's own self, human-nature and the environment.

Despite certain weaknesses in *The Mists of Avalon*, it is

> instructive in helping women uncover the dimensions of their own experience of life from beneath layers of male formulation, interpretation and domination... In the novel we see how much of value the world has lost when Avalon slipped from us.[14]

The conclusion to my article notes that Avalon did not just "slip away"; it went because patriarchal Christianity[15] would not tolerate any truth or beauty but its own. The pluralistic, creative "many-coloured land" might be seen to be returning now with postmodernism, feminism, Paganism and especially Goddess Spirituality acting as its forerunners.

This discussion is not an attempt to claim that Paganism is equivalent to feminism, that all Pagans are feminists or that all Pagans are positive about feminism. It notes that Goddesses and women are significant in all branches of contemporary Paganism, except perhaps Mithraism. Paganism provides a wider audience in which feminism, like ecology, finds echoes, resonances and a ready hearing. The remainder of this chapter explores the ideas and activities of women with explicitly feminist spiritual interests and commitments.

History and Herstory

A major concern of the Goddess spirituality movement is research about and reclamation of history. Traditional history writing has ignored or marginalised women and also presented male dominance as the norm from the origins of humanity until today. Such patriarchal narratives present history as "his story" and also justify the continuation of that story. Feminists are now uncovering, exploring and recording "her story". Some present "her-story" history as objective fact, a more accurate presentation of "what really happened" than conventional or dominant views. Others are happy to see it as an empowering mythology: one that is true to life if not necessarily historically factual. Yet others are ambivalent: impressed by seemingly authoritative research but not entirely convinced by the need for a glorious past. Golden Ages and Utopias are, they say, best worked

---

[14] Leonard (1990): 134.
[15] Until recently there has been no other sort.

towards rather than sought in the past. Briefly told, her-story history is as follows.[16]

The earliest human communities gathered around women. Women were honoured as life-givers and therefore central to all that was important. They grew and gathered food, crafted pots and clothes, and celebrated creativity. Some say that women ruled these communities, but they did so for the benefit of all and did not discriminate. Matriarchy is not a mere inversion of male power in favour of women, it is a different sort of system altogether. Others prefer to call it "gylany" which implies egalitarian, women-respecting organisation rather than dominance models.[17] There was no war. Deity was imaged as and perceived to be female and not (or only secondarily) male. The divine, Goddess or Goddesses, was experienced in the natural processes of the Earth—people did not look to the sky to find powerful manifestations of deity—and in women's life cycles. Some say that there was one Goddess, others that there were many.

At some point patriarchal hordes overthrew these peaceful, egalitarian, nature-venerating agricultural communities and imposed the rule of sky-Gods and men. (I can find no sustained discussion about how these hordes themselves became patriarchal; it seems to be accepted that this does not need explanation.) They brought weapons and war, class or caste differentiation, hierarchies, dualism and the denigration of women. They valued the crafting of weapons more highly than the production of pots. They invented "Nature" as something other than "here" or "home",[18] something alien to be feared, something wild to be tamed or something virginal to be penetrated and dominated. In short, they brought Patriarchy.

Neither Goddesses nor women disappeared, of course. They survived in subservient, oppressed, second-class positions. The sky-Gods had mothers, sisters and daughters. They took wives and seduced or raped Goddesses, women or other female beings—and meanwhile fought each other for supreme power. Goddesses were allocated jobs that were beneath the dignity of the Gods, e.g. listening to the prayers of women in the labour of childbirth, agriculture or home-making. In polytheistic but patriarchal societies Ultimate Reality could even be imaged as female—after all, like women, it sometimes seems nurturing and sometimes seems unconcerned for human (i.e. male) interests.

[16] See, for example, Harding (1971), Stone (1976), Spretnak (1978), Gimbutas (1982) and (1989), Olson (1983), Lerner (1986), Sjöö and Mor (1981) and (1987), Eisler (1987), Göttner-Abendroth (1987), Orenstein (1990), Gadon (1990), Long (1992) and Morgan (1996). These works do not all present a single view and my presentation of "her-story" does not follow any one of them—or completely represent the richness of the tapestry. Also see Sered (1994): 205-6 and Rees (1996).

[17] Especially see Eisler (1987).

[18] See Le Guin (1986) and (1992): 161-3.

In historical times, Christian patriarchy demoted Goddesses into saints. Not all the richness of the divine could be portrayed in female form: patriarchy would not tolerate too much independence. Women, especially female saints, could not be uppity but had to be mainly virginal and meek. Many of them were victims of male aggression, but Goddesses were not so easily cowed—I deliberately use this term, which in patriarchy denigrates females and animals, but which equally contains the seeds of liberation. Disguised as saints, the Goddesses maintained their watch over women and men too, though with some sadness. They permitted an approach to deity when the impassive, imperial and stern God of the theologians distanced himself from the mundane. When the time was ripe, they began to manifest themselves again. Some words which had once abused and belittled women and nature, now revealed their power to transform and heal. Some words that patriarchy valued were, of course, irredeemably oppressive or revealed as tawdry and pathetic illusions. "The thing about words is that meanings can twist just like a snake."[19] The patriarchal snake/word charmer cannot be certain that he will not be bitten. Goddesses and "Womanwords"[20] have asserted their independence and their ability to empower women who hear them.

Herstory is sought for in theological, anthropological, archaeological, historical, folkloric and hagiographical writings. Ancient and contemporary Goddesses from every continent meet with saints, heroines, historical, mythical and poetic female characters and together receive attention and provide inspiration and encouragement to women seeking liberation. This quest results not only in books but also in art, music, ceremony and drama. Herstory is studied not only by lone individuals but also by groups of women. It is enacted in groups who challenge the way things are with a vision of greater justice and community.[21]

It is neither my role nor my intention to criticise, question or support the accuracy of this history *as history*. Religious Studies takes seriously people's affirmations of self-understanding, it listens respectfully to the stories they tell, the myths and metaphors by which they live. Its purpose is to note people's beliefs, experiences, approaches and methods. It evaluates the role of myths and rituals within religions and in relation to the outside world. It can legitimately ask whether a belief or practice is experienced—both by adherents and by those affected by them—as liberating or abusing.

It is clear in this case that Herstory is a conscious exercise in empowering women. It repels the many prongs of the patriarchal

---

[19] Pratchett (1993): 170-1. For inspired insights into the workings of language in the war of the sexes see Grahn (1984), Daly (1987) and Mills (1991).

[20] Mills (1991).

[21] Long (1996), including her development of Grigg (1995).

assault on their self-esteem, their ability to act freely and creatively within society. It provides a new context for sisterly power-in-relation.[22] More needs to be said about this, and about other effects of—or allegations about—Goddess Spirituality. Before that, the following section says something more about the Goddess, not as ancient deity of a matriarchal or matrifocal society nor as Christian saint, but in her various contemporary guises.

Goddess and Goddesses

Talk of "the Goddess" is easily mistaken for a revision of monotheism in which a single all-powerful, dominating, female deity (Goddess) replaces a single all-powerful, dominating male deity (God). Instead of God with a beard we get God with a dress.

In fact, "the Goddess" of Goddess Spirituality, and perhaps the deities of other feminist spiritualities, is better understood within polytheistic deity-talk. Divinity encapsulates the single inter-connected reality in which everything exists and everything is embodied. At the same time it is also experienced in a plurality of beings, forms or manifestations. Goddess*es* are as real as *the* Goddess—and are more frequently experienced, which is more important.

But this is not the whole picture. "The Goddess" also refers to the inner motivations and most significant foundations of a person's life, however it might be changing. The initial attraction of Goddess-talk to many women is a new vision of self-worth. More systematic thinking about thealogy sometimes follows later. Asphodel Long summarises this thinking in her invaluable article "The Goddess Movement in Britain Today"[23] which also comments on comparable activities in North America. She describes some foundational thinking of the Matriarchal Study Group:

> In some ways the term 'the Goddess' was a synonym for a woman with newly regained self-worth. "I am in the image of the divine; I am acknowledged. I have, all this time, been told a lie. I am not—and never was—inferior, subordinate."[24]

She describes the various ways that the Goddess is described or, more significantly, related to and spoken to in ceremony and in life. Carol Christ summarises three major views of who the Goddess is.[25] The view that there is a "real Goddess out there" who can be "invoked in prayer and ritual", much like the deities of other pantheons, does not negate other understandings and experiences. The Goddess as personification

---

[22] Grey (1991).
[23] Long (1994).
[24] Long (1994): 15.
[25] Christ (1979): 278.

of the natural processes of life, death and rebirth is equally important, and the "affirmation and beauty of female power" remains central. Asphodel Long adds:

> The Goddess is to be recognized in many aspects of female life, which have been denigrated—menstruation, childbirth, etc.[26]

Such ordinary experiences manifest the Goddess and can thus be revalued by women. They can be included within women's spiritualities.

In her writings and her evocative art Monica Sjöö stresses motherhood as prime symbol and embodiment of the Goddess.[27] The Matriarchy was a time of rule by mothers. The Earth is Mother—Mother Earth or Earth Mother—and she is the Goddess, the Great Mother, our Mother. Asphodel Long questions the linking of Goddess and motherhood. She suggests that women's creativity, e.g. in arts, technologies, agriculture, science and so on, is not a function of their being (potential) mothers.[28] Much of Monica Sjöö's work does stress the Goddess as Mother and portrays her birthing, or pregnant with, life. However, while this is a significant choice of image, it is not a limitation of Goddess to maternity, fecundity or fertility.[29] Nor does it imply that only mothers can image, represent, manifest or understand the Goddess. It is a powerful claim on readers and viewers (respondents?) to act upon their intimate relationship with the ultimate source of life.

In Paganism and particularly in Goddess Spirituality, models of divinity, "the meaning of life" and religion are worked out in everyday life. Birth, menstruation, eating, drinking, making love, getting angry, being hurt, growing older and growing old, learning, making, breaking, working, forgetting, remembering and inventing—these and all other aspects of people's ordinary lives are not divorced from the lives of other-than-human people, however exalted they might be. Embodied living provides significant manifestations of the divine and is authoritative because it is the location in which people explore "reality"—the Goddess "*is*" reality".[30] The Goddess, whether "out-there" or "within", shares similar experiences and similar cycles with women, men and other-than-human people. Starhawk writes:

---

[26] Long (1994): 16.

[27] See Sjöö and Mor (1981) and (1987), and Sjöö (1992).

[28] Long (1981): 18; and (1994): 17. Also see discussion in King (1989): 146-53.

[29] Sjöö (1992): 126. For a critique of the linking of *female* deities and fertility see Hackett (1989): 75.

[30] Starhawk (1989a): 22. Also see Spretnak (1982) and Luhrmann (1993): 223-6.

The Mysteries are the most ordinary events—and ultimately, we don't decide who or what the Goddess is, we only choose to what depth we will experience our lives.[31]

As with any discussion of deity or religion, it has to be said that all these words are stories which attempt to carry rich and varied experiences. The experiences are always bigger than the containers; life is too messy and wild to be controlled by a single story. If this is true in most religions it is an acknowledged and welcomed facet in Goddess Spirituality.

This feminist Goddess does not always manifest herself as caring, nurturing or "nice". She is also the Dark Goddess: death-giver and life-taker. If life is a web, the Goddess is the spider, a predator as well as a mother. "If God is God She is not nice", according to the title of Catherine Madsen's paper introducing a roundtable discussion.[32] Starhawk responds:

No, the comforting, nurturing Goddess is not all there is, but She can be comfort and nurture. And maybe women who have been struggling within the patriarchy deserve a few years of comfort and nurture. The Hag will show Her face in time.[33]

Here, finally, the word "Goddess" frequently refers to many Goddesses rather than to a singular deity. It might be easier if people consistently said "Goddesses", and an increasing number do.[34] There are good reasons for doing so, as we shall note in discussing some feminist objections to Goddess Spirituality. I hope, however, to have suggested that this is not a monotheistic tradition, even when practitioners do, in fact, talk of one deity.[35] The Goddess and the Goddesses are experienced in many and varied ways, and are related to in the style of polytheistic traditions. The following two sections introduce a few of the contemporary manifestations of Matriarchy—the groups which are the tradition—and then ask, where does this tradition take people, what does it do for them, and what is its attraction?

Manifestations of Matriarchy

The books referred to above are the tip of an iceberg of expressions of the Goddess Spirituality movement. The many readers of the books and their many responses form the bulk of the iceberg, hidden but not so far away. The movement is not all about books or about reading, writing, studying, thinking, discussing. It is also concerned with living life. If

[31] Starhawk (1989b): 106.
[32] Madsen (1989).
[33] Starhawk (1989b): 106.
[34] See, for example, Culpepper (1989) and Eller (1993).
[35] See chapter 10.

feminists affirm the slogan "The personal is political", so feminist spirituality honours the personal as spiritual. The following section asks what effect the tradition has on its members, its practitioners or celebrants. Before that, some examples of the groups and activities of the movement are noted.

Many women's first contact with Goddess Spirituality is in a discussion group, an affinity group or perhaps an evening class. Some of these are formed by friends who have discovered that they share an interest in exploring ancient Goddess traditions. Others are run by knowledgeable women who arrange and advertise classes for women. Such classes will almost certainly be structured learning programmes, much like those of any other subject. They will, however, encourage more than factual knowledge by their concern with personal growth, self-affirmation and the affirmation of all women.

In Britain there are a number of venues available for the exploration of themes of importance to this movement. The Worker's Educational Association (WEA) and the Continuing Education (or Adult Education) departments of many universities support evening and weekend classes on any and every imaginable subject. Typical examples are series of classes concerned with ancient Goddess, matriarchal history and archaeology, the recovery of female saints as potential feminist role models, seasonal festivals, lunar phases and sacred sites. Women who attend one such class frequently go on to participate in others. Many also keep in touch with others, having formed close friendships. They may decide, for example, to celebrate the summer solstice with a beach party, watching the sunset and waiting through the night for the following sunrise. Intellectual education is creatively combined with personal experience and group celebrations.

Having established a grounding in Matriarchal Studies, a frequent title for such courses, many women join networks such as the Matriarchy Research and Reclaim Network (MRRN). Their own continuing research and experience are shared with others in such forums, or through the various journals or magazines. Some of these are for women only; others are open to women and men. In Britain the journal *From the Flames* is primarily devoted to women while *Wood and Water* is produced by women and feminist-influenced men. Similarly, MRRN is a women's network, whereas the Fellowship of Isis is open to all for whom Goddesses are central in their spirituality. This does not necessarily mean that all such people are feminists.

Going beyond study groups are more activist groups such as the combined Ama Mawu political spirituality group and the End of Patriarchy Movement, who are proclaiming the end of patriarchy in controversial ways. Their first public action was the interruption of a service in Bristol Cathedral with a procession, the singing of "The Burning Times" (a song linking the medieval "witches" with ancient and contemporary Goddess worshippers), and the display of Monica Sjöö's painting "God giving Birth". This coincided with a dance protest through a Tesco superstore. The "official beginning of the end of Patriarchy" was declared to have been 1 August 1993. Apart from the creation of affinity groups, the movement has also included the use of "graffiti, letters and article writing, discussion, music, painting and making new links to support the cause". They also note:

> Bringing about the End of Patriarchy incorporates women's involvement on many levels: political-outward-action, spiritual-inward-personal, transformation, healing, daring, confrontation, and much more.[36]

The movement is also committed to creating a multi-racial movement and has held day conferences to this end. In doing so they counter one of the strongest criticisms of feminist spirituality: that it is a white middle-class phenomenon. More is said about this below.

A final example of the Goddess Spirituality movement, which again illustrates its activist wing and its interaction with other Pagan paths, is some of the Greenham women. Greenham Common in southern England was a U.S. airforce base with nuclear capability. For some years in the 1980s it was surrounded by a number of peace camps, mostly of women. Many of the women were attracted to various forms of feminist spirituality, not necessarily Pagan or Goddess centred forms, though these were not rare.[37] Most of the camps closed with the withdrawal of cruise missiles from the base, and the women found other places to continue their explorations and express their commitments. Many have formed new affinity groups or strengthened existing networks. Their form of Goddess Spirituality again combines the personal, the political, the spiritual, the artistic and the activist.

Circles empower

Feminism provides women with a voice, a hearing and a space.[38] It also allows women to see for themselves. As Lorraine Gamman and Margaret Marshment argue,

> In most popular representations it seems that men look and women are looked at. In film, on television, in the press and in most popular narratives men are shown to be in control of the gaze, women are controlled by it. Men act; women are acted upon.[39]

Lynne Morgan comments on this:

---

[36] "Report on the Ama Mawu/End of Patriarchy Movement", privately circulated, undated, 1993.
[37] Also see Long (1994): 27-8 who notes the influence of the works of Starhawk especially (1982) and Budapest (1976).
[38] Daly (1987); Morton (1985); and Wolff (1929).
[39] Gamman and Marshment (1988): 1.

As we have been looking at ourselves through male eyes for something like two thousand years we are bound to have a distorted view of how we are. So it is time for a re-assessment and women's spirituality allows us to do that.[40]

The first effect of Goddess Spirituality is that women look at themselves and at female images, female role models, female activities in history and myth. Women's estimation of themselves changes: the more they notice women and Goddesses, the more they "remember a time when [they] were not slaves".[41] Instead of inferiority, subjection, humility and docile domesticity, women can reaffirm their strength and creativity, their industry and their imagination. They can, in short, choose to see and to do in their own way.

Mary Jo Weaver asks, "Who is the Goddess and Where does She get us?"[42] Since ancient traditions about Goddesses are not normative for Goddess Spirituality "in the way that Scripture is normative for Christians", they can be adapted and re-told to affirm women's lives now. Goddess Spirituality follows the principle that "women's experience as named and confirmed in community" is the foundation and standard against which other claims to authority are judged, or winnowed.[43] The Goddess, like the many deities of polytheistic societies, sends people back to their own "ordinary" lives. In the case of women, whose ordinary lives have been marginalised if not threatened within Patriarchy, the Goddess does more than liberate from "psychological dependency on men and male authority"[44]—she also affirms women's power, bodies, sexuality, religious insights, experiences, desires and heritage.[45]

What is significant about Goddess Spirituality, within feminism, is

not the rejection of God, but the determination to live a life rich with religious experience, ritual and community.[46]

The movement becomes a context for celebration, not merely a forum for accusation or rebellion against Patriarchal theft of history, value, significance or life. The Goddess does not save by intervening but by being. Her existence, discovered in her-story, archaeology, history, mythology, ritual, celebration, communal bonding and sharing, allows women to give birth to themselves again. They can, slowly and experimentally, create themselves and their lives in new, strong, free and affirming ways. Beyond this, as the first editorial of the Matriarchy Study Group's *Goddess Shrew* said,

[40] Morgan (1996): 95.
[41] Wittig (1985): 89.
[42] Weaver (1989).
[43] Weaver (1989): 59; especially discussing Carol Christ (1985) and (1987).
[44] Christ (1979): 275.
[45] Christ (1979): 276 and (1987): 111. Also see Woodhead (1993) and Foley (1994).
[46] Weaver (1989): 61.

We do not wish merely to contemplate the past. Our aim of understanding the past is to influence the present. We see the part that male-based religion has played in demeaning and exploiting women. In exposing this, we want to share our regained confidence in ourselves with other women...

Further, we see that such control of the spirit as well as of our bodies will extend the possibility of change in society... We move from the importance of feminist social demands to total reappraisal of patriarchy in politics generally.[47]

To highlight the significance of these wide-ranging aims, the following brief section notes some contrary voices.

Contrary Voices

Not all women are feminists, of course, and some still exhort other women to display "feminine" virtues. According to New Age neo-Shaman, Brooke Medicine Eagle, "the feminine, receptive, allowing, surrendering energy" has been "very much overbalanced" by "the thrusting, aggressive, analytic, intellectual, building, making-it-happen energy". Her message, addressed to "women specifically", including native American women, is that "we need to put more emphasis on surrendering, being receptive, allowing, nurturing".[48] This startlingly reactionary call to women to "surrender" and "allow" *more* can only come from a New Age detachment from the realities of life.[49]

Peter Roberts regrets the "restriction of [Goddess-spirituality's] form and content to provide a platform for feminist politics" and its

inability or unwillingness to create stabilising structures that will assure its continual development and ability to take advantage of opportunities to feed into established structures that could extend its own potentiality.[50]

Many women who have found a meaningful context for their religious experiences in Goddess Spirituality, might well hope that the movement will not fulfil Roberts' hopes that it will become "a major New Age expression of religion". Perhaps in place of this kind of backlash, women and men might learn to hope that

it is just possible that the unheard testimony of half of the human species which has for so long been rendered inarticulate may have something to tell us about the holy which we have not known.[51]

---

[47] Quoted in Long (1994): 14.
[48] Medicine Eagle (1991): 89.
[49] Contrast Sjöö (1992).
[50] Roberts (1991): 12.
[51] Saiving (1976): 197; quoted in Raphael (1994): 526. A stress on the authority of experience(s), particularly women's experience(s), rather than on that of belief, hierarchies, and a universal message might indicate why Roberts' hope is unlikely to be fulfilled. See Woodhead (1993): 179, n.41.

In addition to such contrary voices there are a number of questions addressed to Goddess Spirituality by feminists and others which deserve a hearing. The fact that many feminists continue to be either uninterested in or hostile to Goddess Spirituality, seeing little difference between it and any other form of spirituality, should not be ignored. Janet McCrickard concludes that women cannot afford what she sees as a limiting fundamentalism.[52] Feminist archaeologists have criticised Gimbutas' work, both in method and conclusions, and explored the patriarchal nineteenth century underpinning of many Matriarchal narratives. However, they tend to acknowledges the value of this myth for modelling the future and spurring allegedly more academic archaeologists to reflect on their own presuppositions.[53] Other feminists assert that existing religious traditions can be changed from the inside and that there are resources for women's empowerment within Christianity, Judaism, Buddhism and other religions.

Cynthia Eller claims that the Goddess of the movement "stands completely apart from history":

> It is not that she is distant from her worshippers—quite the contrary, she is a radically immanent deity. But spiritual feminists' contact with the Goddess is limited to sacred time, and history is profane time.[54]

She implies that the Feminist Spirituality Movement dislocates women from ordinary time and traps them in an obsession with a comforting Golden Age. Her reliance on Mircea Eliade here prevents her from seeing that the her-story told by Goddess Spirituality is not necessarily an escapism but an affirmation and an inspiration of change *now*. If the Golden Age in the past is an untrue myth and cannot therefore come back, the idea that the Golden Age is coming in the future is no more (or less) liberating if it remains an apocalyptic or redemptive myth like "heaven" or "the revolution".[55] It is as a goal to work towards now that it is empowering. In other words, Goddess feminists are in contact with the Goddess at all times and in all places. In their homes, in their spiritual-political protest camps and marches and in their coming together they represent, experience and express the Goddess: they are Goddess. To quote Asphodel Long again, "In raising Her we raise ourselves, in raising ourselves we raise Her."[56]

Emily Erwin Culpepper discusses her discomfort with

[52] McCrickard (1991): 66.
[53] See Conkey and Tringham (1995) and Meskell (1995).
[54] Eller (1991): 293.
[55] Rees, personal communication.
[56] Long (1994): 17.

any monotheism of "the Goddess". She tends to become "the Great Mother" and sweep diverse realities into one cosmically large stereotype.[57]

The diversities of particular concern to her are those of

the inexplicable miracle of be-ing and the inexplicable horror of suffering and cruelty.

She mentions the beauty of magnolias and the horror of racist lynchings. She cites various ways of "finding divine imagery adequate to the problem of evil" but is also clearly interested in finding imagery for positive or welcome experiences too. Instead of the singular Goddess she prefers polytheistic symbols which can more powerfully evoke the entire array of experiences, "but they are not all nice", they do not always nurture and protect people but can sometimes be angry or distant.[58] Many women within Goddess Spirituality groups certainly share this preference for multiple images. A single Goddess, especially one drawn from a particular polytheistic tradition, cannot be given all the work of all the Goddesses. Perhaps it is time for the writers of books and the course tutors to stop saying "Goddess" and to start saying "Goddesses". Instead of an all-embracing but essentially shapeless and nameless "Goddess" they could name, and thereby evoke the presence of, specific Goddesses. They could find that particular Goddesses from different traditions are already accustomed to doing the various jobs required by the diversities of women's experiences.

The fact that many of the Goddesses drawn upon for the composite "the Goddess" come from European tradition is inescapable.[59] This is changing under the influence of womanist (i.e. "black feminist or feminist of color")[60] and Native American writings, e.g. those of Alice Walker, Anne Cameron and Paula Gunn Allen,[61] which are insistent that feminists must deal with racism as well as sexism and classism. Similarly, Margot Adler discusses the age-ism of many Pagan portrayals of the Goddess.[62] It is undeniable that many Pagan paintings of Goddesses are unable to deal with age. Even when portraying the divine as "Crone" or "Hag", many Pagan artists seem obsessed by nubile breasts. Is self-affirmation a youthful or middle-aged white middle class luxury? If Mary Lefkowitz's question "What educational values will Goddess religion preserve?"[63] unnecessarily denigrates the learning of many women in the movement, it does suggest that

---

[57] Culpepper (1989): 107. See too Culpepper (1987) and Lefkowitz (1993). This is parallel to the generally accepted rejection of the "generic erasure" (Culpepper, 1987) of women's diversities by the term "Woman", see discussion in Hackett (1989): 66.
[58] See pp.80, 173 and 181.
[59] E.g. Morgan (1996).
[60] Walker (1984): xi.
[61] Walker (1983) and (1984), Cameron (1984) and (1989), Allen (1990).
[62] Adler (1986): 209-10.
[63] Lefkowitz (1993): 268.

something should be learnt. People should be expected to reach beyond
their stereotypes and beyond the narrow margins of Patriarchal
conditioning. For example, Asphodel Long shows that the Matriarchy
Research and Reclaim Network has "helped to discredit" the idea that
"the Jews" are responsible "for the death of the Goddess".[64]

Finally, it has been suggested that it is precisely by noting that the
classical Goddess cults were celebrated within Patriarchy that they can
speak powerfully to today's still patriarchal world. For example, the
Eleusinian rites and myths of Demeter and Persephone had

> a public aspect, whereas the spiritual feminist versions turn the story inward
> towards a strictly female world; it is still a myth of female individuation,
> but is no longer a complex part of the social and religious life of a whole
> society.[65]

Goddess Spirituality is not just a therapeutic help to women, but a
movement aiming at widespread changes in society—e.g. in politics,
economics, religion, communal life and family life.[66] The Golden Age
is not just a myth about the past, it is a goal to aim for in the future. In
the present "pregnant darkness"[67] women are birthing and being birthed
by a new way of living.

Impact on other Pagans

Although many women's first contact with Goddess Spirituality has
been through reading a book or attending an evening class, many
others have identified themselves with the movement as a further step
in their Pagan path. For some this means that they became dissatisfied
with their existing group or tradition, finding it too male-centred, or
insufficiently feminist. For others, Goddess Spirituality is a natural
confirmation and expression of their understanding of Paganism. Just
as they had discovered that what they had previously thought of as
their own eccentric ideas now turned out to be called "Paganism", they
then discovered Goddess Spirituality as a more complete affirmation of
their intimations.

Meanwhile, feminism has affected all Pagan traditions in one way
or another. These influences are noted in other chapters, or are clear
from the discussion so far, but will also be summarised here. The Craft
has always held "the Goddess" and "priestesses" to be central. In more
recent forms it is strongly feminist, especially in the Dianic Covens and
as taught by Starhawk.[68] Druidry had a distinctly male bias until it

---

[64] Long (1991): 130-1. She also discusses all these issues in greater detail in Long
(1994).
[65] Foley (1994): 210.
[66] E.g. see Spretnak (1989).
[67] Cp. Eller (1991): 288.
[68] See Adler (1986): 176-229; Starhawk (1982) and (1989a).

became increasingly Pagan during the 1970s and 1980s. Now the
Pagan Druid groups are not only open to female and male membership
equally, but most Orders have significant female leaders. One of the
most frequently used Druid invocations once began "Grant O God thy
protection". It is now more popular to say "Grant O Goddess thy
protection", although some Druids still write "God/ess" and may say
"God and Goddess". One of the largest global networks of Pagans is
the Fellowship of Isis which is dedicated to any and all manifestations
of deity in female form. Although most people see Heathenism as a
thoroughly male-centred tradition there are individuals and groups
dedicated to making significant changes here too. Freya Aswynn
devotes much of her book to the "feminine mysteries" despite, or
perhaps because of, her devotion to Odin.[69] There are also groups that
stress their primary devotion to the Goddesses of the Anglo-Saxon or
Teutonic tradition by their use of the self-designation Dísitrú, trust in
the Goddesses. Folkvang Horg is using the undeniably less central,
though never forgotten traditions honouring Goddesses to rebalance a
dominant interest in the male deities of the Heathen tradition.[70]

Liberation Thealogy

Goddess Spirituality is perhaps the most explicit "liberation
theology"—more properly thealogy—of contemporary Paganism. By
various approaches it explores the past, the present and future hopes for
intimations of other ways of living. It proposes that the honouring of
the Earth must go hand in hand with the honouring of women. Assaults
against one echo, reinforce and authorise assaults against the other.
Within this vibrant movement, women are recreating themselves and
finding that they have authority to write their own stories: they are their
own authors, writing in both factual and creative modes.

   One of the most frequently quoted exhortations of this movement is
that of Monique Wittig:

> there was a time when you were not a slave, remember that. You walked
> alone, full of laughter, you bathed bare-bellied. You say you have lost all
> recollection of it, remember. You know how to avoid meeting a bear on the
> track. You know the winter fear when you hear the wolves gathering. But
> you can remain seated for hours in the tree-tops to await morning. You say
> there are no words to describe this time, you say it does not exist. But
> remember. Make an effort to remember. Or, failing that, invent.[71]

By both remembering and inventing, Goddesses and women are raising
themselves, liberating themselves, creating themselves and expressing

---

[69] Aswynn (1990).
[70] See chapter 4. Also see Metzner (1994).
[71] Wittig (1985): 89.

themselves. They are also going out into the world to "do justly and love mercy".[72] This is a major part of the "something else" that is happening in "a place as far away as the thickness of a shadow".[73]

[72] Long (1996): 8.
[73] Pratchett (1987): 170.

6

MAGIC

Magic wasn't difficult. That was the big secret that the whole baroque edifice of wizardry had been set up to conceal. Anyone with a bit of intelligence and enough perseverance could do magic, which was why the wizards cloaked it with rituals and the whole pointy-hat business. The trick was to do magic and get away with it.[1]

Not all Magicians are Pagans, but a significant number are. Not all Pagans engage in magic,[2] but a significant number do. What Magicians and Pagans mean by magic varies greatly. This chapter discusses the varieties of magic in which Pagans engage, the techniques they use, and the results they expect. It is chiefly interested in individual practice even when this occur in communal contexts like lodges. It begins by exploring what Pagans mean by magic.

What is Magic?

When asked what the word "magic" means, Pagans are likely to refer to a wide variety of experiences from the unusual to the mundane. It might simply be "what people enjoy". The exclamation, "It's magic!", meaning that something is special or worthy of celebration or sharing, is not alien to Pagans (however trite it may be). These mundane and prosaic uses of the word "magic" should not be ignored as they form an important background against which more considered and more elaborate uses occur. Pagans can affirm that life (ordinary daily experience) is "magical": significant, imbued with value, sacred or paradoxically suffused with transcendence. However, this is to reiterate the matter of other chapters. This chapter focuses on particular techniques or particular philosophies or theories, particular ways of relating to or manipulating the world.

Pagans do not tend to think of "magic" as "conjuring tricks" such as rabbits from a top hat. This might, however, function as a weak metaphor for the transformation and personal growth for which most magicians aim. In this vein Starhawk writes, "Magic is the art of turning negatives into positives, of spinning straw into gold."[3] More broadly, the elaborate philosophical, imaginative, ethical, emotional

---

[1] Terry Pratchett, *Moving Pictures*. (1990): 150. (*1992): 189.
[2] I will at times follow the preference of *some* Pagans and *some* other practitioners for the spelling, Magick.
[3] Starhawk (1982): 99.

and intellectual preparation required by some magical traditions might transform an insecure adolescent into a mature adult.

When asked what "magic" means Pagans often quote definitions which seem to them to make sense of their experience and intentions. Aleister Crowley encapsulated his ideas and experience into the phrase, "Magick is the Science and Art of causing change to occur in conformity with Will".[4] A complementary and not contradictory definition is attributed to Dion Fortune, "Magic is the art and science of changing consciousness according to the Will". These definitions, but not necessarily their creators, remain popular among Pagan and other magicians. They suggest two facets of magic: attempts to change things or situations and attempts to change the practitioner. Some magicians stress one of these approaches over the other but rarely deny the value of either.

Another valuable definition of magic is provided by Georg Luck according to whom it is

> a technique grounded in a belief in powers located in the human soul and in the universe outside ourselves, a technique that aims at imposing the human will on nature or on human beings by using supersensual powers.[5]

Richard Sutcliffe[6] points out that this definition not only locates contemporary ritual magic in the Western Gnostic-Hermetic tradition rather than in medieval Christian demonology, it also reveals the centrality of human will and shows that magic is rooted in a system of beliefs. In other words, magic is not devil worship but a coherent way of understanding the world in which something within each person— the will—can be used to effect change or affect others beyond the self.

What do magicians mean by "the will"? In Luck's definition it appears to be related to something in "the soul". If "soul" refers to a central, characteristic and essential but not physical aspect of each individual which can commune with significant (perhaps "spiritual") others, "will" might be a synonym. However, "will" strongly suggests an intellectual, emotive and imaginative focus. It is, perhaps, a secular counterpart to the religious "soul". If the soul is linked to divine beings and can imply human dependence, the will allows an assertion of human maturity, independence and self-reliance. It expresses the intentions, desires, hopes and creativity of the ensouled person. Over-eaters and smokers are encouraged to apply their will-power to changing their habits. Magicians apply their will to changing their situation or their perception of reality. Will is not just a part of the person which can be used to make changes, it is the "true self".

---

[4] Crowley (1973): 131 and (1976): xii.
[5] Luck (1987): 3.
[6] Sutcliffe (1996): 111.

Whatever the person is or, deep down, would like to be, is "the will". Will is also something beyond the individual, it connects each discrete being in the universe, permeates all things, and is the essence of the true nature of reality. By discovering their own will and living according to it magicians aim to align themselves with ultimate reality. Magic is an alchemical and/or therapeutic process in which practitioners seek their true selves and then express them in relation to the cosmos as it is and as it will be when humanity re-aligns itself harmoniously.

Tanya Luhrmann's study of ritual magic reiterates her view that magic is a strange thing for modern Westerners to engage in. She is interested in how "people accept outlandish, apparently irrational beliefs... [and] learn to find it eminently sensible".[7] This makes for an interesting but flawed study which keeps the reader on the outside looking in through opaque glass.[8] The practised eccentricity of some magicians should not blind the observer to the intimate relationship between the contemporary practice of magic and the rationality of modernity. Nor should it obscure the secularity and rationality of their engagement in magic. Berel Dov Lerner's analysis makes considerably more sense of magic.[9] Humans and human societies are faced by things which affect "life, health, prosperity, security and so on" and are "beyond the control of available technology". "People must find ways to recognize their own limitations without being paralysed into inaction." Prayer is one response, but it requires "recognition of one's dependency on God and resignation to His will". Sometimes the Gods are silent but magic might be efficacious. Magic is a largely secular and human-centred technique which is arguably more rational than prayer. In the modern world there are other technologies for coping with the contingencies of life and, like magic, they are human-centred—they affirm human agency, independence, abilities and growth. Despite the prevalent view that such "primitive" peoples are deeply spiritual, they and the magic some of them practise are often as secular as modern Westerners.[10] Western magic—Pagan, Gnostic, Christian, Kabbalist or whatever—is primarily a means of personal growth and self-expression. As such it is far from being a degeneration into "superstition", but it bears considerable similarities to other contemporary quests for self-understanding and growth.

---

[7] Luhrmann (1989): 7.
[8] For contrasting anthropological views of anthropology see Flaherty (1991) and Düerr (1985).
[9] Lerner (1995). The following account summarises her argument.
[10] Also see Douglas (1990): 73-82; and Lewis (1989): 35-8.

Esotericism

From a phenomenological perspective, contemporary magic is deeply embedded in a modern, western, esoteric spirituality which is itself rooted in the Enlightenment. This esotericism has a particular form, observable by "outsiders" *and* identifiable by "insiders". It is most clearly described by Antoine Faivre who identifies four intrinsic (i.e. necessary or essential) elements:

> (1) correspondences, (2) living nature, (3) imagination and mediation, and (4) the experience of transmutation.[11]

A brief summary of each of these elements follows.

Correspondences. Magicians believe (or act as if they believed) that everything in the universe is like everything else. Working with one thing can affect those other things with which it corresponds. Moving a symbol in a ceremony is like moving something affecting a person or situation. Drawing another symbol is like paying attention to whatever it symbolises and thereby giving it energy or influence. The universality of correspondences also means that apparently unconnected things affect each other continuously. Rising planets can correspond to a growth of personal energies.

> These correspondences are considered to be more of less veiled at first glance, and they are therefore meant to be read, to be decoded. The entire universe is a great theater of mirrors, a set of hieroglyphics to decipher; everything is a sign, everything harbors and manifests mystery.[12]

Living nature. The universe is not only a set of symbols that correspond to one another by open or hidden means. It is also a radically interconnected living system. Beyond the individual relationships between individual living things (and everything can be treated as if alive), the whole of Nature (the totality of that which is) is alive, ensouled. The Gaia hypothesis has considerable popularity among contemporary magicians. It seems to reiterate this older approach to Nature, treating all things as alive and in some way kin to humanity. It is possible for humanity to relate to the world because it shares both soul and matter, will and form, with humanity. Both Gaian science and esoteric magic encourage the understanding that affecting one part of Nature will have implications for other parts. The fact that these parts are living, perhaps ensouled, requires ethical consideration before actions are taken.

Imagination and mediation. It is not only the physical, material living things of the universe which are connected and/or correspond to each other. Internal moods, desires, attitudes, beliefs, feelings and

---

[11] Faivre and Needleman (1992): xv. Also see pp. xi-xxii.
[12] Ibid: xv.

imagination are integral parts of the universe too. They not only affect other internal states, but also change outward, material things. The belief or imagined idea that a place is full of spiders will prevent an arachnophobe entering. A delight in wild places might inspire a Nature-lover to protect a threatened woodland. Magicians manipulate their inner Imaginal[13] world in order to affect both their growing understanding of the universe and their actions in the world. A change within someone is already a change in the radically interconnected universe and will have at least as much influence in the outer world as the spreading of the metaphorical butterfly's wings in Chaos mathematics. Far from being "unreal" or "mere fantasy" the Imagination is a powerful intermediary between desire and action, and therefore between individuals and the world they wish to see changed. It is central to alchemical transformation,[14] and thus of inestimable significance in the practice of magic and is deliberately explored, encouraged, developed, exercised and celebrated.

Most religions denigrate Imagination as delusion and self-obsession but encourage contemplation or communion with the "outer" world or with other beings. Science is frequently understood to privilege "objective fact" over "subjective beliefs". Magic positively values the exploration of the inner world, refusing to disconnect it from the outer. "As without so within" might be a necessary counterpart of the traditional Hermetic phrase "As above so below". As with much of the magical enterprise this is applicable in Paganism more broadly: each person's self-exploration and personal growth are significant and celebrated. Self-denial and self-negation might sometimes be valued but only as temporary exercises engaged in to enhance other interests— they are far from the core of magic or Paganism.

Transmutation. Faivre succinctly notes

> If transmutation were not considered an essential dimension, the present discussion would scarcely extend beyond the limits of a form of speculative spirituality.[15]

The alchemical process of changing lead into gold is metaphorical, highlighting the importance of mundane, ordinary, seemingly valueless and unconnected things. Magical rituals aim at initiatory experiences which effect rebirth at a "higher" level. They are intended to result in a metamorphosis of the magician into one who knows their goal, is fully aware of it, and experiences it with immediacy. In short, magic aims at gnosis.

---

[13] See Sutcliffe (1996): 117. Cf. Imagination in Keats and other Romantic poets.
[14] Jung (1953): 262-7.
[15] Faivre and Needleman (1992): xviii.

A note on Gnosis

Gnosis is more than a synonym of Knowledge, or of a combination of Knowledge with Imagination. It transcends an understanding of facts, or a belief in unseen connections, realities and states. It is an immediate, intense, perhaps numinous, personal, revelatory and initiatory experience. After long preparation and study, the magician goes beyond the theory to a more mystical and mythic point. The magician "knows" and is known, "sees" the truth which things symbolise, is seen by that which is, "touches" reality and is deeply touched, "tastes immortality"—the inverted commas become necessary as metaphor, ecstasy and hyperbole intertwine. Gnosis is Enlightenment.[16] Sometimes a new word is required for such profound experiences and many have adopted Robert Heinlein's "grok", meaning "to intuit the 'fullness' of something from within".[17]

All this is not to say that magicians are necessarily Gnostic. It is more than possible to engage in magic without denigrating the mundane physical world, the body or ordinary reality. Pagan magicians celebrate gnosis—the intensity of ecstatic awareness—without feeling trapped by flesh or transmuting it into a symbol of sin and evil. I have heard a Pagan magician guide a visualisation which encouraged the "stripping away of flesh and the return to pure uncreated spirit", but my intuition is that this was only loosely rooted in Pagan experience. Paganism is not bounded by dogma and restrictions, but few Pagans are entirely comfortable with this contemporary form of Gnosticism.

What Magic Is

Faivre summarises magic as

> at once the knowledge of a network of sympathies or antipathies which bind the things of Nature and the concrete implementation of this knowledge.[18]

The magician is required to study the universal network, gain understanding of the connections and relationships between things, learn how they can be manipulated and what will happen if this is done. Various ethical systems can be brought to bear on this knowledge. Then the magician begins to put into practice the knowledge gained from observing the "theater of mirrors". Magicians serve an apprenticeship in order to learn how to practise the craft of magic and then they engage in "the work" of that craft or guild. Faivre asserts:

---

[16] See Sutcliffe (1996): 118-21.
[17] Heinlein (1961). See Adler (1986): chapter 10.
[18] Faivre and Needleman (1992): xvi.

More than practices proper, it is knowledge—in the sense of "gnosis"—which appears to contribute to the basis of an esoteric attitude.[19]

The following sections note that there are a variety of ways in which such "gnosis" is sought and a variety of practices which are engaged in. There are also various relationships between the gaining of knowledge or awareness and the attempt to gain results from the practice of magic. Not all magicians or all magic is concerned (only) with "gnosis"; much magic is an attempt to achieve something more mundane, self-benefit rather than self-improvement perhaps.

The Colours of Magic

The media and popular imagination are wedded to the idea that there are practitioners of "Black Magic" and that it makes sense to talk of "White Magic". These fantasies yield no interesting or useful contributions to the present discussion—even if the media parade the occasional self-styled "White Witch" at Halloween.

Isaac Bonewits distinguishes between various sorts of magic by colour associations.[20] Red Magic "has to do with matters of the body" and includes "healing and killing... blessings and curses, matters of physical strength and power". Orange magic "deals with matters of ego-strength and materialism, of pride and self-confidence, of courage and security". Yellow magic "is the magic of the mind and nervous system... learning, organization and theorizing". Green Magic is "the magic of agricultural fertility". Blue Magic is associated with the emotions and includes "religion, ESP, other psychic phenomena, spiritualism, fortune-telling, theology, and the social sciences". Indigo Magic "was originally the color of rain-making and weather control, and thus of meteorology". Purple Magic deals with "matters of love, lust, hate, fear, anger, and ecstasy". Ultraviolet Magic engages the "crackling flashes of pure power in the psychic realms" and "is often confused with black". It is the magic of "power and politics... strong emotions...[and] psychic power". Brown Magic is "the magic of the woods and glens, of animals and hunting, of the wilderness, and of the ecological sciences". Bonewits' primary motive here is to put some life back into magic, rather than the abstract and moralistic magic of some of his contemporaries.

These distinctions should not be taken too seriously; they have not generated different schools of magic or books on the subject. They are, however, affirmations of various focuses of magical practice and indicate at least some of the areas in which people "do" magic. For the

[19] Ibid.
[20] Bonewits (1974): 122-4.

most part they are indicative of what many magicians refer to as "results magic". Not all magic is engaged in as a quest for transformative knowledge, "gnosis"; much of it aims at transforming the "outer" world (e.g. healing sick friends) rather than the self. Nonetheless, the techniques used are comparable with those of the more philosophically-inclined magic. They are also indicative of the range of magics engaged in by Pagans and should be remembered when discussing the more elaborate ceremonial approaches.

Mention must be made of Terry Pratchett's addition to the magical vocabulary of another colour of magic, Octarine.[21] It is not particularly important that this is a "rather disappointing greeny-purple-yellow colour"—more interesting is Octarine's association with magic. In the Discworld ordinary light meeting a magical field splits into eight colours, those of the normally visible spectrum and this eighth colour, Octarine. Magical activity produces flashes of this "light fantastic". As with Isaac Bonewits' colour codings, this idea is suggestive more of the rich imagination integral to magic rather than of any serious codification of magical techniques or goals. More seriously, it might be taken to suggest that magic makes a difference to the world and the magician: they are changed by its exercise in various ways, not the least of which is re-enchantment.

Distinctions between different forms of magic of significance to Pagan magicians are discussed in the following sections.

Ceremonial Magic

Many magicians, only some of whom are Pagan, work within a tradition broadly identifiable as Ceremonial or Ritual Magic. With roots in the fifteenth century and continuous creative development and experimentation since then, the tradition provides elaborate techniques for self-discovery and personal growth. Much of the language, style and practice of such magicians is common currency among other magicians who might be seen as making the tradition more accessible—or as unnecessarily simplifying it. There is, of course, no guarantee that the techniques will lead to such growth, or that they will not be applied for other purposes, such as gaining authority over less adept magicians.

The most obvious characteristic of Ceremonial Magic is, not surprisingly, ceremony or ritual. Elaborately crafted, prepared and carefully performed ceremonies engage participants intellectually, spiritually, imaginatively, emotionally, physically and in every other way. They are hard to appreciate without some involvement or

---

[21] Especially see Pratchett (1985) and (1986).

experience and no description can hope to do justice to such essentially participative practices. The following summary only suggests the mechanics of a ceremony rather than describing an actual event.

At a time determined by astronomical and/or astrological phenomena, participants gather in an agreed place. This will usually be a room set aside as a temple or working space in someone's house (if this is only a temporary arrangement the furniture will be removed), but it might be in a secluded place out of doors, perhaps a wood or an ancient sacred site. The ceremony may have been written by someone proficient in crafting ceremonies or co-operatively by the group. Participants will have prepared to play their part—they might, for example, have been given a script to memorise. Improvisation is not a hallmark of such groups, but on the contrary a small mistake in a ceremony may be considered to invalidate it completely. More or less elaborate regalia will be worn and magical implements such as staffs, wands or daggers might be carried. The ceremony begins with the creation of a circular working space, usually thought to protect participants from unwanted intrusions or interference from outsiders— human or other-than-human. The various directions will be greeted with verbal invocations or chants, visualisation of symbols, colours or spiritual guardians, and appropriate gestures. For example, a pentagram might be drawn in the air while a particular musical note is intoned. Incense chosen for its affinity with the goal of the work or with those other-than-human entities being invited to participate will be burnt. The regalia, movements, incense and visualisations create a highly charged atmosphere in which the main work of the ceremony takes place.

The main part of the ceremony is a complex guided meditation or visualisation. This is typically called a pathworking. Jewish and Christian Kabbalistic mystics developed a complex model of the cosmos (seen and unseen) commonly called the "Tree of Life". In this diagram ten spheres represent the stages of manifestation of divinity or spirit in relation to matter or the mundane world. The spheres are arranged in a hierarchy beginning at the top with pure spirit and descending in three parallel columns to matter at the base. The spheres are linked by lines or paths. A pathworking is basically a meditation on the relationship between two or more spheres. In an imaginative journey up the Kabbalistic Tree the ceremonial magician seeks to meet the downward flowing spiritual energies which may then lift the meditater towards union with deity or spirit. Many magicians consider that Tarot cards carry representations of these paths, the spheres or those who journey. By contemplating these images the meditater gains insight, becomes inspired or empowered, or takes on the role of the particular traveller towards this form of enlightenment.

This is a necessarily brief suggestion of the actions and intentions of the participants in a typical magical working. It hardly touches the intensity and creativity with which magicians engage their Imagination. The most adept magicians aim to visualise not only shadowy representations of cosmic forces, psychological or psychic realities or esoteric ideals. They wish to encounter in profound moments of clarity (and sometimes tangible form) that which is most important to them: their deities, their "holy guardian angel" or their true self. Pathworkings aim to encourage personal growth and self-understanding which unites the practitioner with the cosmos as it really is. They unite the microcosm (the individual) and the macrocosm (ultimate reality).

There is a tension in these activities between the ordinary world and the world desired and reached for. This, of course, is of the essence in Kabbalah with its roots in matter and its crown in spirit. It is also productive of some of the other tensions which Tanya Luhrmann's study of London magicians explores: between spirituality and materialism, technological competence and imaginative playfulness, modernity and seeming irrationality.[22]

There is also a tension between the individualism of the quest for one's true self or the expression of one's own will and the socialisation of the practice of magic in orders, lodges, fraternities and other groups. A fuller description of magic would discuss the relationship between the individual's Will and Imagination and the group's collective consciousness, mind and creativity. Such tensions might explain the plethora of groups and literature offering magical teaching and advancement. They are also productive of the dynamism or the stagnation of at least some of these groups. The continuous transformation and development encouraged in the individual and often experienced (but not always welcomed) in groups should warn against any attempt to define "what magic is" in a complete and static manner. The impressionistic treatment attempted here certainly requires expansion and improvement but it is arguably better than any dogmatic codification which restricts creativity, transformation and development of what magic might mean or how it might be engaged in.

The majority of magicians in European history have been Christian. Mystically inclined Jews codified their experience in Kabbalah which was mediated to post-Enlightenment groups like the Golden Dawn through Christian Kabbalists. Little of this was Pagan. Much of it has slipped, consciously or otherwise, from a quest for gnosis, transformative knowledge, into a Gnostic quest for an ascent away from matter. Much of it has seen Earth as hiding more of reality than it reveals. Magicians naming themselves Pagan are frequently distinguishable from other magicians and from other Pagans. Their

---

[22] Luhrmann (1989).

magic is often more playful and more intimate with the Earth and the seasons. Their Paganism is often cloaked in elaborate costumes and more carefully crafted ceremonies than that of other Pagans.

Left-Hand Path Magick

The tension between Paganism and Magic is intense in discussions about Left-Hand Path Magick—the "k" is an important part of the self-identity of many magic(k)ians, not only left-hand path ones. In particular it distinguishes them from popular forms of magic as stage or TV entertainment, i.e. tricks. There are some Pagans who reject this variety of ritual magic. On the other hand there are Pagans for whom this *is* Paganism.

The term "Left-Hand" derives from the Tantric traditions of India. Instead of the asceticism, self-denial or, at least, self-restraint which are usually thought to be necessary to enlightenment in Indian traditions, Tantra includes a radical alternative. By indulging in exactly those things which are socially, culturally or religiously frowned upon or taboo, the practitioner breaks the illusion that some things are more spiritual, more powerful, more ultimate or more meaningful than other things. This is not an affirmation of enlightenment through negativity or "evil". Rather it is a denial of the dichotomy "enlightening" versus "deluding". Only ignorance, "non-transfigurative thought processes", makes us think that there is a difference between the world in which we live our daily lives and the ultimate reality of enlightenment.[23] In Western terms, Left-Hand magick is not "Black Magic" because "black magic" and "white magic", or "good" and "evil", are not productive distinctions or categories for practitioners who are certainly not trying to be harmful, corrupting, evil or satanic. Though magicians might identify certain actions as moral or immoral, magic(k) itself is neither moral nor immoral. Similarly, the Latin-derived word "sinister" is not useful here as its reference to "left-handed" is too deeply buried beneath its association with frightening wickedness.

Left-Hand magick tests boundaries and limits. If some practitioners of Ceremonial Magic work towards a model of self-improvement of which Christian moralists might approve, Left-Hand magickians reiterate the point that our supposedly "lower" or more carnal desires are also part of our Self. Self-development must be based on self-awareness and self-understanding and not on the rejection or repression of the more embarrassing or messy parts of our experience. Richard Sutcliffe explains:

[23] To paraphrase Lamb (1996): 5, himself quoting Nagajuna.

> In Left-Hand magick this knowledge [of one's true self] becomes possible
> essentially through an ongoing project of individual deconditioning aimed
> at the transcendence of everything which impedes the individual from
> becoming his or her 'true' self... [or] 'True Will'.[24]

This deconditioning is also applied to the magician's relationship with
Nature. Despite the broader Pagan movement's disquiet about Aleister
Crowley's influence on magicians, many adepts of the Left-Hand path
are clearly Pagan in their celebration of Nature, their animism and/or
their invocation of Pagan deities. Their rituals are as likely to take place
in ancient sacred sites, e.g. the landscape and monuments around
Avebury, or in natural surroundings, e.g. the banks of the river
Thames, as they are inside rooms prepared as temples or ritual working
spaces. Their magickal workings frequently embrace the body and
sexuality.

Three aphorisms from Aleister Crowley's inspired *Book of the Law*
(abbreviated as *AL*)[25] reveal the heart of the magickal enterprise of
Left-Hand magickians. (Crowley's magick is usually referred to as
Thelema, i.e. "Will", and is only one aspect of this tradition, albeit an
important one.)

> Do what thou wilt shall be the whole of the Law (*AL*.I.40).

> Love is the Law, love under will (*AL*.I.57).

> Every man and every woman is a star (*AL*.I.3).

The explication of these aphorisms and similar sayings in Crowley's
works constitutes a considerable part of the activities of ritual
magickians in orders, societies and other groups—not all of whom
value the existence of alternative groups. In brief, the first aphorism
should not be misconstrued—as it often is—as a licence or incitement
to self-gratification and debauchery. The importance of "will" is
central: the aphorism might be glossed as a call first to discover one's
true self in relation to the cosmos, to grow into being "what one is",
and then to live according to that discovered, uncovered true self. It is
an affirmation that the advice "Be true to yourself" and is *all* that is
required, it is the sum of all wisdom or of Law, understood to be the
full description of the reality of all things. Crowley's own explication
of the aphorism makes this clear:

> "Do what thou wilt" is to bid the Stars to shine, Vines to bear grapes, Water
> to seek its level; man is the only being in Nature that has striven to set
> himself at odds with himself.[26]

---

[24] Sutcliffe (1996): 120-1.
[25] Crowley (1983).
[26] Crowley (1973): 352.

Crowley goes beyond a vague assertion that humanity must rediscover its place in the cosmos and its true nature. His third aphorism roots Thelema in individual growth, individual value and individual experience. Every individual is unique, essentially divine and noble. No individuals have the right or authority to impose their beliefs or values on any other person, not even if they think themselves more aware of the nature of reality. Clearly, however, they can offer inspiration, encouragement, resources and contexts in which growth can take place. Many magickal (and magical) groups offer lectures, seminars, conferences, correspondence courses, books and leaflets concerned with their theories and practices. However, it is their rituals which provide the most explicit situation in which the individual (the "microcosm") can engage with the cosmos (the "macrocosm").

Left-Hand-path magickal writings, talks and rituals most obviously (though not solely) differ from other Ceremonial magical activities by including and exploring sex, rather than repressing it. Whereas Ceremonial magicians seemingly attempt to rise above or control sexuality and gendered bodily realities, Left-Hand-path magickians make use of the energies sexuality arouses and the change of consciousness it engenders. Sex magick illustrates the way in which the entirety of the practitioner is engaged in this form of magical activity. It also illustrates the transcending of a cultural taboo which considers spirituality and sexuality to be polar opposites—a taboo which prevents people from expressing their deepest intimations of spiritual fulfilment with their whole being. Ceremonial magicians and Left-Hand-path magickians might also be contrasted in the willingness of the latter to accord positive value not only to the sexuality of heterosexuals but also to that of Lesbians, Gays and Bisexuals. Finally, this celebration of sexuality allows the Imagination to be enriched rather than threatened (as it is in other spiritualities) by fantasy. The introduction to one of the more interesting books on sexual magick sums up all these ideas:

> Sex is a sacrament, and crossing-over into other modes of consciousness. It is the central act of the Great Work of transforming consciousness and, through consciousness, the world.[27]

Chaos Magick

Individual virtuosity in the techniques of magic is of the essence in this thoroughly contemporary and anarchic form of magick. These techniques are the standard tools of other magicians: invocation, visualisation, means of raising and manipulating energy, careful contemplation of desired outcomes (i.e. required changes in the

[27] Peter Redgrove in Shual (1994): v.

microcosm or macrocosm, the individual or the world) and equally careful absorption in self-reflection.

"Chaos" refers to two related themes: the application of recent scientific theories such as quantum physics to the exercise of magick, and the anarchic adoption of whatever beliefs seem appropriate to the desired outcome. Both of these can be summed up in the understanding that "belief shapes reality".[28] If the observation of scientific experiments has recently been discovered to affect the outcome of experiments, magicians and their actions have always been considered to be intimately connected to the outcome of their practice. Quantum physicists, Chaos mathematicians and Gaian ecologists might all be seen as supporting the magical intimation that the universe is radically interconnected in all its seemingly disparate parts. Meanwhile, if other sorts of magician attempt to bring their perceptions and beliefs in line with cosmic realities, Chaos magickians understand that beliefs, expectations and desires bring about different sorts of results and that perceptions of the universe are deeply affected by "inner" dispositions and moods. So Chaos magickians claim to adopt whatever beliefs seem appropriate to their desired outcome (e.g. more money, increased friendship, more self-awareness) and abandon those beliefs when no longer useful. This is summed up in a phrase commonly quoted by Chaos magickians, "Nothing is True, Everything is Permitted". The worldviews inculcated by Christians, Buddhists, Kabbalists, Odinists, Tolkien's Gandalf, Ursula Le Guin's Ged or anyone else can be useful and productive. What remains central is the "doing" not the "believing".

Chaos magicians seek an immediate experience of themselves and of the cosmos: an experience unmediated by beliefs and theories or by hierarchies and dogmas. This is more radical than the approach of other magicians but its goal is the same: self-understanding, personal growth, self-expression and/or gaining what is desired. Apart from the deliberate and playful adoption of beliefs, the techniques of Chaos magick are the same too, i.e. other magicians usually take their deities, holy guardian angels and spirits more seriously. Whether it is really possible to shift between competing paradigms of belief and practice at will—especially when each of those paradigms is meant to require many years of apprenticeship—is debatable. Perhaps it is enough for the Chaos magickian to act "as if" they have made the shift.

[28] Sutcliffe (1996): 129.

Signs and Symbols

One aspect of the magical tradition that Chaos has stressed is the use of sigils: the creation and manipulation of signs and symbols, e.g. the Kabbalah's Tree of Life and the tarot cards. Previous chapters have noted that Druids use ogham and coelbren signs and that Heathens use runes. Sigils are much the same as these in that they are symbols suggestive of a range of human desires, fears, characteristics, ambitions, sources of inspiration and so on. A typical example of the creation of a sigil is that the magician writes a phrase stating an intention or purpose, e.g. "I want £100 by Tuesday". The letters of this phrase are superimposed on each other, omitting any repeated letter (here "t", "y", "a"), making up a fairly pleasing pattern. The magician then ignores or forgets the phrase from which the pattern or sigil was formed and concentrates on the sigil. It is drawn, perhaps using bodily fluids, on a specially chosen piece of paper which might be passed through incense and chanted over. The symbol is given energy, power or effectiveness through visualisation, chanting and other magical techniques—but without conscious recall of its original meaning. Experience has suggested to magicians that things happen when you are not looking (an esoteric application of the general awareness that "watched kettles never boil"). It is also thought that for the sigil to be effective it must not be held too tightly, as it would be were the magician to concentrate on its meaning or purpose. The ceremony is intended to engage the practitioner's imagination, energy, creativity and, of course, will—without restriction. Once the sigil is fully potentised it is "sent" to do its work. Some place it in a place where it will be seen—perhaps only hardly, or subliminally—others prefer to burn it and thereby allow it to work unfettered by material form.

The inspiration for this practice derives from more traditional use of talismans as well as of runic symbols. Empowering, visualisation and "sending" are central to many magical acts, as is the idea that practitioners must not become obsessed with the result of their work. A degree of detachment is encouraged—obviously making spells for money, love and power exceptionally hard to achieve successfully.

Natural and Kitchen Magic

Pagans do not usually separate magic from their other interests and activities. It may not be as elaborate, as hierarchical, as Nietzschean (i.e. as ideologically individualistic) or as élitist as the practice of some of the magicians discussed above. Its ceremony may be less carefully prepared. Its circles may be cast not primarily as protection against outside interference but as a container for energies raised within. Magic is, however, a key part of what many Pagans do regularly within their celebrations. Other chapters in this book have noted the kind of things that Pagans do—and much of this can be called magic. Witches and Druids cast circles and invoke the directions. Heathens carve and cast runes. Eco-warriors hang symbols in trees and chant for their well-being and protection. Women light candles for healing. Men dance up their feelings. Imagination, visualisation, invocation, chanting and other aspects of the esoteric tradition have all been adopted and adapted by Pagans in the creation and development of a new archaic spirituality.

More simple magics, drawn from folk custom and popular beliefs about witches, also play their part in what some call "natural" or "kitchen" magic. Herbs are planted, tended, picked, preserved and prepared as remedies for a range of illnesses and injuries, and in attending to desires and fears. The phases of the moon, the seasons of the stars and the stations of the sun are observed—both watched and abided by—in all these activities. Healing, tending, encouraging, nurturing towards maturity or wholeness are all part of the simpler magics of many Pagans. Indeed, much of this book could be read as a discussion of the "natural magic" engaged in by the less structured, less philosophical or less esoterically inclined Pagan movement. A high percentage of Pagan publishing is concerned with such matters.[29]

Eco-magic

Among these general engagements with magic, there is a specific focused application in the drama of Pagan ecological action. Groups such as Dragon Environmental Group participate in "Green" protests and celebrations but also speak of "eco-magic". Their magic is rooted in the ecological understanding that every action has a range of effects, not all apparent even to the careful planner. Divination might suggest some of these hidden effects. Traditional methods such as gazing into water or fire, casting runic and other symbols, or the encouragement of dreams have all proved useful as means of gaining insight and, allegedly, foresight.

Dragon also uses a powerful symbol which combines a selected set of runes. Together these symbolise the health, healing, love, protection, growth and fulfilment of the Earth and harmonious relationships between this world and the various Otherworlds in which ours is rooted and towards which it reaches. This visually pleasing symbol has rapidly become a focus for Pagan eco-activists and eco-celebrants. It encourages joyful celebration and creative drama to balance the anger and dissipate the fear and depression suffered by many who attempt to

---

[29] For particularly clear examples see Green (1989, 1992) and Slade (1990).

counter the present seemingly global obsession with road-building, quarrying, tree-felling and other assaults on Nature.

Dragon and other eco-magical activists work with others, especially the *genii loci*—the spirits of place—inhabiting threatened areas. This is not only thought to be more effective, but is also based on the recognition that humanity is not alone—especially in being affected by environmental change and damage. Dragon ceremonies, in common with those of other magicians, begin with the casting of a circle and the invocation of the quarters and elements. This will be recognisable to those who prefer more formal ceremonial, but also to the increasing number of more anarchic or "shamanic" practitioners. Rather than verbal and verbose invocations, Dragon use dramatic and mimetic actions, for example fire is called by clapping sounds that imitate its crackle and weaving movements imitating the dance of flames. The central ritual may provide space and time for conversation with the spirit(s) of place. Eco-warriors are particularly energetic in raising energy, often using dance and drumming. They might visualise this as empowering the Dragon bind-rune or other chosen symbol, which can then be given to the place and its inhabitants to aid them in effecting their will, e.g. in protecting themselves from bulldozers.

The Web

Heathens have developed traditions of what elsewhere might be called chanting, talismans, visualisation and shamanism, i.e. *galdr*, *taufr* and *seithr*.[30] There is another theme of importance to Pagan and other magicians that is well expressed in ancient and contemporary Heathen traditions. Ecologists have adopted the name Gaia for the living, integrated environment within which we live. They have done so without always welcoming the idea that Gaia is personal, aware or autonomous. Although Pagans welcome this understanding, they could also offer a less personal image: that of the web. Heathen sources speak of a web of wyrd, a radically interconnected integration of all that exists. A similar image has been used for the computer information superhighway, the Internet or the World-Wide-Web. The exchange of information in the Internet is only a pale reflection of the dynamic image of the web of all things, the web of wyrd. Wyrd is more than "fate" (now associated with doom and disaster), it is the summation of all things, much like the cosmic "will" of ceremonial magicians. Some Heathens perceive the web to be like that of a spider, others as a trellis or lattice.[31] The runes can be seen within the intersecting lines of these

---

[30] See chapter 4.
[31] Butcher (n.d.).

patterns. The aim of a Heathen magician might be to achieve an immediate visual awareness of the web connecting everything in their surroundings: trees, clouds, hopes, fears and the energies flowing between them. This is sufficient for some, others aim to manipulate the threads of the web and so influence events in desired ways or to speed up existing movement.

The Ethics of Magic

Teachers of magic frequently hedge the practice with ethical warnings. Magic, they claim, demands responsibility and a high degree of maturity. For example, Dolores Ashcroft-Nowicki says:

> In the area of the occult, ethics are of paramount importance. Add to this self-discipline of the highest kind and a set of principles to act as a lamp on this the most difficult of paths, and all these must be thought about and accepted before anyone should place a single foot on the road to Adepthood.[32]

Almost all teachers and manuals of magic repeat this kind of advice. The Wiccan phrase "An it harm none, do as you will" and Crowley's aphorism "Love is the Law, love under will" are only two of the most commonly quoted examples. Tantric magickians can find considerable value in Utilitarianism with its concern for the "greatest good for the greatest number of people" and its rejection of immutable, divinely authorised codes of behaviour.[33] Eco-magicians allow environmental ethics to challenge purely internal or individualistic models of magic. For example, Barry the Expedant supports a holistic and ecologically focused magic in a booklet entitled "A Statement of Intent is not Enough".[34] Ursula Le Guin's powerfully compelling *Earthsea Quartet* provides a rich narrative framework to an ethical context for magic.[35]

Terry Pratchett honestly notes that anybody can do magic. His books reiterate the point that the problem is not doing magic, but understanding it and getting away with it. Various understandings are offered although none of them amount to a theory of magic in any sense useful to contemporary magicians. "Getting away with it" is a more productive issue. Victor Tugelbend, star of the silver screen at Holy Wood and perpetual student-wizard, explains that

> It was as if the human race was a field of corn and magic helped the users grow just that bit taller, so that they stood out. That attracted the attention of the gods and — Victor hesitated — other Things outside this world.

[32] In Butler (1991): 8.
[33] Shual (1993): 4-5.
[34] Patterson (1993).
[35] Le Guin (1993). For further examples see Luhrmann (1986).

People who used magic without knowing what they were doing usually
came to a sticky end.
All over the room sometimes.[36]

Usually magicians have more metaphorical "sticky ends" in mind for
those who do not engage in magic within an appropriate framework.
There are certainly those who believe that invoking deities, spirits,
daemons or elementals requires a correct ethical lifestyle—respect for
others, at least. Others suggest that correct etiquette is sufficient.
However, most magicians hold the view that every action affects not
only others but also the doer and that the considerable effects of
magical actions require care if they are not to harm the magician.
Magic may be as neutral as electricity, but both can be used harmfully
or improperly. Whether magic is seen as a means of personal growth or
as a means of helping or even influencing others it is rarely engaged in
without some careful direction, preparation or ethical framework. How
elaborate or binding this framework needs to be can vary considerably.
It is also the case that magic may be concerned with personal growth
and may encourage considerable individualism, but it most often does
this in social contexts. Magic is taught and practised in groups, and
groups require rules.

Attentive Scepticism

Magic is part of Paganism, as it is part of some people's Christianity
and other people's Judaism. It is not the whole of it nor does it form the
entirety of its roots. Magic means as many things to different Pagans as
it means to followers of other religious paths, and it can be more or less
central to those paths.

Magic requires a willingness to experiment and a degree of
scepticism. Much of it is an exercise in testing boundaries, methods and
procedures and trying out new experiences. As a set of techniques
magic can be used for a number of purposes by people with widely
different beliefs and motivations, but primarily it encourages personal
growth and self-awareness. Its exercise certainly changes people—if
only into people who find magical techniques effective—and, to that
extent at least, it changes the world. Deciding whether the changes
wrought in the individual by magic are real, lasting or positive depends
on the perspective of the observer.

Pagans have learnt some of their religious vocabulary and gained
some of their religious technology (casting circles might be an example
of both) from the esoteric tradition, i.e. from magicians. Some Pagans,
i.e. Pagan magicians, continue to use these words and things in ways

---

[36] Pratchett (1990): 150. (*1992): 189.

congruent with that tradition. Others have broadened their associations by blending them with more Earth-centred, more egalitarian and more open usage. There is a tension between Pagan Magicians and Pagans who do not define themselves by their engagement in magic. The more elaborate pursuit of self-understanding and fulfilment by the former may be matched by the occasional but no less committed attempts by the latter to change situations around them.

Margot Adler sums up some observations by Jacob Needleman:

> [M]ost people's entire lives are characterized by misdirection and suggestibility, the very traits that are manipulated so successfully by the stage magician. This passivity of attention, says Needleman, may be the most important human failing. In contrast, almost all who study real magic work vigorously to strengthen their attention.[37]

Perhaps this chapter's initial assertion that a gulf exists between stage magic and "real" magic is not the whole truth.

---

[37] Adler (1986): 155 quoting Needleman (1975).

7

SHAMANISM

Something picked him up and threw him into the air. Except that in another sense he was still sitting by the fire—he could see himself there, a dwindling figure in the circle of firelight that was rapidly getting smaller. The toy figures around it were looking intently at his body. Except for the old woman. She was looking right up at him, and grinning.[1]

Shamanism is a Humpty Dumpty word. During her journeys "Through the Looking Glass" Alice endured a bizarre conversation in which Humpty Dumpty claimed to be able to use a word to mean just what he wanted it to mean, "neither more nor less". If a word like "glory" or "impenetrability" is made to work hard, carrying unusual or idiosyncratic meanings, Humpty Dumpty says he "pays it extra".[2] "Shamanism" is now a hard-working word. A pedant might insist that the word can only mean whatever it meant to its original users, Siberian Tungus and their neighbours. Anthropologists might argue about its applicability to similar constellations of techniques, beliefs, traditional knowledge and authority in other cultures. They might also question its applicability to the activities of New Agers, Pagans or therapists in America, Britain and elsewhere.[3] Meanwhile, however, there are people who consider themselves to be Shamans[4] or to be doing "shamanic" things. This chapter notes anthropological discussions about "real" Shamans and disquiet about "neo-Shamanism", but concentrates on what Pagans mean by Shamanism, Shaman and Shamanic.

From Siberia with Power

The activities of Shamans are integral to many different societies around the world.[5] Because Siberian Shamans were the first to become wildely known to Western academics, a Siberian—specifically Tungus—word became attached to similar practitioners from other

---

[1] Terry Pratchett, *The Light Fantastic*. (1986): 83. (*1988): 97-8.
[2] Carroll (1872), quotation from 1962 edition: p.274-5.
[3] E.g. Johnson (1995) and Jones (1994).
[4] Originally a title applicable to both male and female practitioners. Some Westerners have borrowed a feminine ending from another Siberian language and invented the term *Shamanka*. This is as unnecessary as a feminine version of role titles like "builder".
[5] Invaluably portrayed in Vitebsky (1995).

cultures and lands. Shamanism has been appropriated from these societies (rarely if ever given or exported by them), distilled into a set of techniques and re-contextualised for modern urban societies.[6]

Mircea Eliade subtitled his book on Shamanism "Archaic Techniques of Ecstasy".[7] By doing so he firmly established the idea that Shamanism is not a religion but a way of achieving "Ecstasy": Shamans leave their bodies to travel in other realms. Eliade insists that they are different from mediums who welcome possession by spirits in that they commune with and are helped by spirits but they are not possessed or controlled. Ioan Lewis disagrees strongly with this, arguing that both the title and the activities of Shamans are those of possessed people. A Shaman is a "receptacle"—literally a "placing"—for the spirits who become incarnate in them.[8]

Shamans engage in magical battles against their enemies, who are frequently held responsible for sickness and disasters. Sickness is often understood to be the result of "soul loss"—part of the sick person has become detached and lost—and it is the Shaman's job to retrieve the "soul" and get it back into the person's body. Alternatively, the sickness might be caused by an unwelcome invasion by spirits which have to be removed. The Shaman might also escort the dead to their place among the ancestors. In short, a Shaman might be psychopomp, priest, healer, therapist, spiritual-warrior, spirit-controller, medium and/or powerful communal leader.

The techniques and technologies for these activities vary from place to place and culture to culture. They include rhythmic drumming, dancing, singing, chanting and ritual drama. Drums, rattles, kaftans or other ritual costumes, fans for wafting (smudging) incense herbs, bags for carrying incense, "spirit darts" or arrows, and objects used for divination are all part of shamanic technology. In some cultures drugs are chewed, smoked, eaten or snorted. Then the Shaman will need pipes for smoking, tubes for blowing or snorting, and containers for carrying drugs or lime to mix with the drugs. The acquisition of "power animals" and spirit guides who protect and direct the spirit-journeying Shaman are important in some shamanistic cultures. Parts of "power animals"—animals encountered on initiatory journeys or "captured" while in trance—including feathers, fur, bones and claws may be added to the Shaman's costume or other equipment.

Shamanic initiations vary according to their culture and environment. They typically include teaching by an experienced Shaman, a vision-quest or withdrawal to a remote place to fast and hold a vigil until spirit-guides or power-animals manifest themselves.

[6] Vitebsky (1995): especially 161; Johnson (1995).
[7] Eliade (1974).
[8] Lewis (1989): 43-50. Also see Hutton (1994).

Serious illness (e.g. epilepsy or smallpox) or spontaneous trance may mark an individual out as a likely candidate for initiation.[9] People are rarely considered by their community or themselves to be Shamans until they have been "killed, torn apart and put back together again" by Otherworld beings. This is not casually approached or lightly suffered: it is perceived to be a serious, dangerous and potentially fatal undertaking. Shamanism is not a technique available to anyone, but a calling which is not always welcome.[10]

Shamans are distinguished from their neighbours not by their beliefs but by the intensity of their experiences. Anyone can take the same drugs—in some societies non-Shamans take drugs to catch a glimpse of what Shamans see clearly without drugs; in others hallicinogens are administered to disobedient children to show them that adults know best.[11] Anyone can be possessed by spirits, go on a vision quest, be attacked by hostile spirits—though perhaps Shamans defend themselves better than most. Shamans share the same world-view as their neighbours, but travel to places which others only know by hearsay or in delirium or drug-induced vision or nightmare.

Shepherds in the Pennine hills of northern England live as close to nature as Shamans do. Both wear clothes suitable to their environment, unless they become impoverished. Both follow seasonal routines and have keen awareness of the weather, topography, flora and fauna of their surroundings. Both are important to the lifestyles of their neighbours—though the shepherd commands no special respect and no fear. Both shepherding and Shamanising are archaic and increasingly marginalised or abandoned lifestyles. The label "primitive" is equally applicable and equally inappropriate for both. It usually means "having few possessions" but says nothing of the potentially rich life—cultural, linguistical, religious, intellectual and so on—of those so labelled.[12] Yet the religion of that shepherd, probably Methodism, is not appropriated in the same way that the Shaman's is. People in Chicago and Oxford do not run workshops on shepherd's whistles[13] or on urban or Celtic shepherding, nor do they reconstruct Methodist chapels or meditate in search of the most significant animals of the shepherd's life: the sheep and the sheepdog. One cannot become a shepherd by correspondence course. No one braves the cold winters of the Pennines purely to see the world as the shepherd sees it. Shepherds' lives and their skillful

---

[9] Vitcbsky (1995): 57.

[10] Hutton (1995): 6.

[11] Harner (1972): 90.

[12] See Chagnon (1992): 100. "Primitive" has acquired such negative connotations that it is better avoided—along with words like "sect" and "cult".

[13] Though it is possible to learn to make shepherd's crooks at evening classes in some more rural areas.

control of dogs and sheep are celebrated by an entirely different group of (mostly TV-watching) people, perhaps as part of a nostalgic vision of "better days" or simple country life.

What is it about Shamans that makes them such potent symbols and role models today? It might be significant that non-European cultures are *perceived* to be closer to nature, simpler, more wholesome, more spiritual (but not dogmatic or God-controlled),[14] more ecological and more human than "modern", "civilised" life. Certainly the rise of interest in Shamanism coincided with experimentation with ways of altering states of consciousness—ways of seeing, experiencing and interacting with the world. It also paralleled interest in therapies alternative to the seemingly mechanical and impersonal medicine of rational science.

"Neo-shamanism" *can* be dismissed as nostalgic, and challenged as having reduced Shamanism to its lowest common denominators: essentially drumming, vision quests and Otherworld journeys. It is frequently marked by typically modern individualism, vague universalism and woolly psychologization.[15] It is also an expression of Western consumerism and commodification. However, Shamanism can also be seen as having affinities or resonances with other aspects of Western philosophies and experiences. Before anyone mentioned Shamans, Witches were already "raising energy", Heathens were chanting *galdr*, Druids were aware of the Otherworld and Magicians were inviting controlled possession. Pagans of all sorts already communed with other-than-human people, such as the faery, deities, trees and spirits. Freud and Jung had already begun to explore and map the inner worlds of individuals and cultures. Many people were experimenting with altered states of consciousness and hallucinogenic drugs. None of these are precisely equivalent to Shamanism but they did mean that when anthropologists described Shamanism people recognised similarities and resonances with familiar experiences and ideas. Anthropology gave people a name that could be attached to things they were already doing and added different techniques. More significantly, the name directed the growth of new constellations of experiential knowledge. Those who now learn from anthropologists' criticisms of Western "neo-shamans" will be taking

> certain claims of anthropology more seriously than anthropologists themselves. Twentieth-century anthropology has insisted that we have a great deal to learn about ourselves from the study of the other... This is the

---

[14] In fact many such societies are as "secular" as ours. Lerner (1995).
[15] The critiques by Jones (1994) and Johnson (1995) seem unquestionably accurate.

myth that justifies the anthropological enterprise, a myth that says that the study of the other leads to enlightenment.[16]

It would therefore be petulant to insist that modern or post-modern Westerners of European descent cannot legitimately call themselves Shamans. This is not to deny the accuracy and necessity of some anthropologists' criticisms. Pagans have much to gain from hearing and responding to anthropologists—just as they have learnt from ecologists, historians, botanists, folklorists and other academics.

Paganism has gained a transfusion of power, exuberance and experience—which are authoritative within the tradition if not elsewhere—from Tungus and Yąnomamö and other Shamanisms. Initially this has been mediated by anthropologists, more recently through more "enthusiastic" explorers who might not be so explicit about the benefits to the "donors". It is not only Pagans who have found the label "Shaman" applicable or who have learnt new ways from studying the phenomenon. For example, there are said to be "Shamanic elements" in the Pentecostal Church[17] and I have heard Shakespeare and Hitler referred to as Shamans. Many New Age counsellors now name their methods "shamanistic". The remainder of this chapter is devoted to exploring contemporary Pagan Shamanism. Some of the weaknesses, faults or errors to which anthropologists might point can also be seen as failures to integrate Shamanism with Pagan world-views. For the most part, however, the energy stirred up in Paganism by the discovery of Shamanism is acknowledged.[18]

Extra Pay

If Pagan Shamans are not exactly the same as Shamans elsewhere, this is not surprising. Their cultural context is different—more individualistic and fragmented. They have *chosen* to experiment with the "techniques of ecstasy" mediated by anthropologists, rather than being *compelled* by a powerful initiatory experience. The contrasts between the first, more ethnographic chapter of Michael Harner's pioneering resource book for new Shamans, *The Way of the Shaman*, and the later "how to do it" chapters are eloquent.[19] Harner is initiated in a series of arduous, frightening, dangerous, drug-induced and largely uncontrollable visions in which spirits deliberately try to mislead him. Both before and after these visions he is taught to see the world differently, otherwise his descent to "the Lowerworld" might have taken him to the more typically Western subterranean realm, "Hell".

---

[16] Eilberg-Schwartz (1989): 87.
[17] Horwatt (1988). For more ancient Christian Shamans see Melia (1983).
[18] Also see Adler (1986): 430-4.
[19] Harner (1990).

He notes too that other Shamans under the influence of drugs do antisocial and sometimes violent things for which they are not held accountable, i.e. they are not in control of themselves. Harner is, in short, "going native" and becoming integrated into Jívaro or Conibo culture. What his book advocates is tame by comparison with this description: a series of safe, simple, short "experiential exercises". The experimenters remain in control and face only aspects of themselves—worrying and perhaps frightening, but nonetheless safe and controllable. There is no need to adjust your beliefs or world-view if you are reasonably at home with Jungian ideas; nor do drugs play any part in this system. The only place where Harner suggests the possibility of danger and the use of drugs is in a short section on healing. Tobacco leaves are used to make "traps" for potentially dangerous and painful spirits which can them be removed to a safe place. No one drinks, smokes or snorts anything stimulating, including alcohol and tobacco. Harner also tries to divorce healing Shamanism from its more aggressive manifestations. Those who taught him in the rain-forests were careful to protect themselves from attack and were engaged in warfare against neighbouring groups, by shamanic and other methods. Most Pagan Shamans agree that violence is to be avoided, many being pacifists dedicated to non-violence. However, many neo-Shamans ignore the aggressive elements of Shamanism or treat them as something allegedly different—"sorcery"—as if the techniques, beliefs and experiences were of a completely different type.

If Shamanism has become an exercise in self-discovery and self-empowerment, such goals are not to be belittled in our age. But to consider this as the essence of Shamanism is to devalue the word and those from whom the original techniques were acquired. How then is Shamanism to be paid extra? What can be added or combined with lessons learnt from traditional Shamans that will not be merely Western self-therapeutic techniques by another name? I am not insisting that the only people entitle to call themselves Shamans are those who have painful quantities of hallucinogenic drugs blown up their nostrils, who experience terrifying visions, and who are able to heal or curse others. I am suggesting that the claim to be a Shaman would be more convincing if claimants were changed by their experiences in ways dissimilar to changes induced by Western psycho-therapies. Shamans might be expected to criticise the individualism and anonymity of modernity, rather than to re-affirm their self-centredness.[20] Shamanic journeys could be expected to change people's beliefs and not merely be an additional lifestyle accessory. Can Christians, Jews, Muslims, Buddhists and atheists really explore the same Otherworld geographies

[20] See Geertz's (1993) critique of Goodman (1990).

and talk with spirits without having their beliefs changed?[21] Despite Mircea Eliade's claim that Shamans are not possessed, they might be expected to have a relationship with "spirits" beyond the usual modern oblivious disregard for anything other than self. They might, in fact, be expected to be possessed.

Paganism has gained much from Shamanic techniques. Frequently, when they call something "Shamanic" Pagans mean that it is spontaneous, energetic, powerful, inspiring. Two sorts of event in particular are described in this way. One is drumming sessions, whether out in the woods or as the climax to an indoor conference or celebration. Everybody with an instrument joins in, picking up the rhythm from one or more experienced drummers. Others dance, clap, chant and otherwise participate in this style of "raising energy". This is certainly a way of inducing ecstasy and altering consciousness. It can be more than just a "send-off" at the end of an intense day of learning, networking and celebrating. It can, for example, be an integral part of festive celebrations or of direct action against motorway-building. In this context it can be used to shift people's awareness of the place and time, and to alter their mood and their consciousness of the place. It might help people contact the "spirits of place" or whatever other-than-human people may be thought to be nearby.

Visualisation, guided meditation or pathworking can also be called shamanic experiences. For example, solitary magicians meditatively contemplating the Kabbalistic Tree of Life and journeying between its various *sephirot* or spheres might consider this to be shamanic. Communal guided visualisations, led by someone with a drum or bodhran chanting and directing the journey, are more likely to be called shamanic. Many of these borrow vision-quests or quests for totemic animals from Harner style sources. People are directed to journey to some particular place within their "inner-world" which is sometimes identified as the Otherworld and sometimes seen as an internal, personal and individual echo of that outer realm. In a significant location they will meet, greet and perhaps become a particular animal. For many Pagans the animals of ancient Europe, of mythology, or of North American plains are more significant that those which can be met with every day in suburban environments. Some integrate the idea of power-animals with the heraldic beasts of European aristocrats, the "berserkers" (bear-warriors?) or the familiars of alleged witches.

Each of the major traditions of contemporary Paganism has aspects which it can associate with shamanism. Some of these are drawn from ancient traditions, e.g. the practice of *seidr* in Heathenism. Others, such as "raising energy" in the Craft, are more recent, though no less

---

[21] See Caitlín Matthews (1995): xviii.

significant or powerful for that. Both of these examples are methods of altering states of consciousness and of affecting situations beyond the practitioners' physical reach. The recognition that other peoples— perceived to be Earth-respecting and therefore kindred to Paganism— do similar things, has enabled Pagans to see their tradition in a broader light. They can also find new ways of explaining how such experiences fit with the world. The discovery of shamanic world-views has given new force and new expressions to the ecological imperative of Paganism. Each of these three things (ancient traditions rediscovered, new traditions revitalised and new imperatives) exemplifies the extra pay given to the word "Shamanism" in contemporary Paganism and deserves to be discussed in greater detail.

Ancient traditions rediscovered

Many Pagans go beyond Jungians in considering the Otherworld different from inner-worlds—though most consider them linked, i.e. the "outer world" is reflected in the "inner world", archetypes express "outer" realities, everything is radically interconnected. The places where the Æsir, Vanir, Elves and others live are not only poetic metaphors for archetypal forces within people. The faery and boggarts are not subconscious hopes, desires or fears within people. All these places and people might be echoed or remembered within the subconscious and may be expressive of archetypes, but they are portrayed in mythology and experienced now as "out there". The inner-worlds that Jungians visit might be closer to the Kabbalistic *sephirot*. Magicians, using Christian and Jewish Kabbalistic language and meditative practices, some of which were certainly ecstatic, attempt to climb the tree of life and enter the higher, upper realms—though not for the same purposes as Jewish and Christian travellers. Journeying to and from the Otherworld, as distinct from these inner-worlds, is portrayed in Western mythology as primarily the preserve of deities, the faerie and of those who come "here" from "there". Few humans enter the Otherworld, and none without danger: there are traditions about travellers who could not return to this world. More is said elsewhere about Pagan cosmology, this world, the Otherworld, those who live there and those who visit from there.[22]

Apart from the recovery of such cosmologies, other ancient traditions have affinities with shamanic themes. Chapter 4 notes the use of *galdr* and *seidr* by contemporary Heathens and their affinities with shamanic techniques. Chanting runes, *galdr,* with or without their associated postures, can induce a gentle alteration of consciousness,

[22] Especially in chapter 10.

perhaps a light trance, conducive to the celebration. *Seidr* is variously understood, but it is generally agreed that it should involve a complete shift of consciousness—perhaps even a loss of physical control: it is frequently glossed as "seething".[23] As with other shamanic practices this can be used for soul-journeying, healing, divining or cursing. The journeying part of a person might be called a *fylgia* or fetch.[24] Some Heathen groups have reinstated the role of *völva*, female seer, and are experimenting with these and other shamanic techniques.[25]

In Druidry too, various claims are made for the revival of ancient shamanic techniques and experiences. John and Caitlín Matthews have built up a library of works in which Welsh and Irish mythological sources are treated as guides to shamanic journeys.[26] As with Harner, so the Matthews introduce guided meditations[27] (which even include "spontaneous thoughts") taking travellers to the inner-worlds (possibly the same as the Otherworld). They meet guardians and totem creatures, discover sacred objects and lost wisdom, meet Gods, archetypes or energies, and learn ways to heal others and the Earth. Some of those met on these journeys are in "unregenerate forms" which might be "compulsive or obsessive" and which can be "unleashed" on the world, but should be "allowed to depart". Even welcome "contacts" should be "dismissed", but unwelcome ones can be "neutralised" by meditatively, "remaining emotionally objective", and placing them in a glass jar to be buried in the earth.[28] Readers are warned not to take "consciousness-changing drugs".[29] Leslie Jones criticises John Matthews' "shamanism" as dull and petulant in comparison with Irish invocations and native American shamanism.[30] The techniques of the "Western Mystery Tradition" or ritual magic, put through a New Age filter, predominate over more typically shamanic techniques. This is particularly clear from a comparison with Caitlín Matthews' excellent commentary and exploration of the *Mabinogion*, a collection of medieval Welsh stories possibly incorporating more ancient mythology.[31] Here the practical work is clearly a ritual drama, firmly within the "Mysteries" tradition. Taliesin, not properly part of the *Mabinogion*, is only very tentatively compared to a Shaman; he is more accurately identified as poet and

---

[23] See especially Fries (1993): 177-8.
[24] Düerr (1987).
[25] See chapter 4 for further discussion. Also see Metzner (1994).
[26] The most useful examples are John Matthews (1991a) and (1992), Caitlín Matthews (1995), and John and Caitlín Matthews (1987). The rest of the library tends to repeat material in these books.
[27] Contradicting Caitlín Matthews (1992): 15.
[28] Caitlín Matthews (1989): 101-2.
[29] Caitlín Matthews (1995): xx.
[30] Jones (1994).
[31] Caitlín Matthews (1986). Also see chapter 11.

bard—themselves important roles. This could have led to much more valuable insights and better poetry than the "shamanic" direction taken by the Matthews in their later books.

There is certainly much that is "shamanic" in Celtic poetry and mythology. The Otherworld and its sometimes very dangerous and never safe inhabitants are at least neighbouring countries to the Otherworlds of the Tungus, Yąnomamö and others. There are Irish and Welsh initiatory techniques and ways of gaining wisdom which are akin to those of Jívaro or Conibo Shamans. Some of these included the use of psychotropic plants.[32] Ancient Irish Druids used magical powers, shape-shifting and long-range curses to attack the enemies of their people and defend themselves. Human people speak with animal people, tree people and rock people, and even communicate with the weather.[33] The temptation, however, is to assume that all strange events and journeys in these sources are Otherworldly, especially if that is taken to mean "inner-worldly" or "into the Jungian subconscious realms". The quests for the Grail and for Mabon are portrayed as desperate journeys in this world, just as the Sidhe or faery-folk are met with primarily in this world during their incursions into it. There are people who take these things more seriously and contextualise them differently from the psychological models challenged by ˉPaul Johnson.[34] More is said about them after a discussion of the extra pay given to shamanism in the revitalisation of new traditions.

New traditions revitalised

The primary example here is "raising energy" in the Craft. Starhawk writes:

> Witchcraft is a shamanistic religion, and the spiritual value placed on ecstasy is a high one. It is the source of union, healing, creative inspiration, and communion with the divine—whether it is found in the centre of a coven circle, in bed with one's beloved, or in the midst of the forest, in awe and wonder at the beauty of the natural world.[35]

Paganism may be distinctive, among Western religions at least, in celebrating the natural, worldly and human as having religious or spiritual value, as being sacred. Awe and wonder in Nature and good sex are not, however, uniquely Pagan! More distinctive is the "cone of power" which is central to all versions of the Craft.[36] Witches "raise

---

[32] McKenna (1992).

[33] For ancient, folklore and contemporary examples see Naddair (1987).

[34] See p.112.

[35] Starhawk (1989a): 40.

[36] See p.47; Starhawk (1989a): 141-51, 236-7; Crowley (1989): 115-19; Jayran (1994): 41-7; Beth (1990): 63, 180.

power" by controlling their breathing, chanting, movement—especially in spiral dances—and visualising a spinning cone of energy. The effectiveness of this technique is what gives authority to those who established its centrality. The technique and experience itself is even more authoritative: directing the experimenter deeper into the world-view of the Craft or some other Pagan path.[37]

"Raising energy" is not new to the Craft; it is among the first things taught by Gerald Gardner. Shamanism has, however, provided a wider context in which to understand and celebrate it. It is clearly effective as a way of altering consciousness and is used, like shamanic techniques, to prepare for the real work. Energy is not raised for its own sake but so that it can be used for what can broadly be called "healing"—of a sick person, an endangered rain-forest, a meadow or a hill threatened by road-builders or a sick Earth. This aspect of Craft work can also be initiated using the Shaman's tools, drums and rattles in place of merely verbal invocations or chants.

Chapter 9's discussion of Earth mysteries will note that many Pagans find the existence of "ley lines" convincing. Explanations for these lines connecting places of power are many and various. However, one increasingly popular theory comes from the authoritative writer Paul Devereux who now rejects the idea that ley-lines are either "ancient symbolism" mapped in the landscape or lines of natural environmental energy. Instead, he argues, they are human artefacts created to image the shaman's out-of-the-body flight across the land.[38] This, at least, is evidence that the term "shamanism" is now being made to work hard to incorporate and give new explanations for existing beliefs.

While these existing traditions may have been revitalised by the discovery of shamanism, and while their practitioners may use the techniques of shamanism, there must be more to it than that. The words may be working harder but they may also be short-changed. Gordon MacLellan suggests that only when "people, land and spirit" are inextricably linked can something be properly called Shamanism.[39] When the discovery of shamanic techniques revitalises existing methods and understandings, perhaps it also moves these nearer towards being properly Shamanic. Then the word is paid extra: it is honoured as a force for change, an imperative in the growth and evolution of Paganism. Shamanism gives added impetus to move more Pagans out of their living-rooms-cum-temples and into the woods where some have always celebrated. It means that instead of candles they light bonfires and stay with them through the night. It means that

[37] Lamond (1993); Harvey (1996).
[38] Devereux (1992a).
[39] MacLellan (1996).

in addition to meditatively connecting to the Earth, Pagans are more likely to celebrate physical contact with the land, or places. Shamanism in this context is, as Gordon MacLellan goes on to say, "the grubby end of magic".

New imperatives

Paganism is finding new ways to express its ecological vision. Shamanism has provided a new imperative to do something about the land and its people, life and spirits. In camps formed to prevent motorway extensions or widening at the cost of complex living environments; in peace camps, anti-nuclear camps and in colourful dramatic events in cities and towns—this is where Shamanism is sending Pagans.

Few New Age Shamans inhabit or even visit the profoundly animated world that most Shamans of traditional societies live in. When spirits become archetypes or parts of the "self", Shamans become people who talk to themselves. A more primal and Pagan intimation is that the Earth is full of living beings, people. It is not enough to say that human people only sense these people while in "altered states of consciousness". Shamanism is part of these cultures' relationships and not merely a means of "sensing" other-than-human people.[40] Shamanism traditionally exists in cultures in which "everything that exists, lives". What you eat was once alive. The tree you cut down is alive and involved in complex relationships. You are related to everything, and the phrase "all our relatives" is not a piece of mysticism but summarises the nature of the world. Shamans live in communities of human people who are always related to all other life.

We can follow Gordon MacLellan again in noting three sorts of Shaman or shamanic practice among contemporary Pagans. All three are healers: the first helps to heal people's relationship to themselves, the second helps to heal people's relationships to one another and the third helps the community to communicate with its relatives in the other-than-human world.

Shamans as personal healers. Much of what is valuable in the new, Western shamanism is concerned with personal healing. Whether it be in freeing people from an inability to express their emotions—perhaps caused by a severe kind of soul loss typical of the modern world—or in dealing with conditioning or depression, these counsellors combine techniques learnt from Shamans with those learnt from Freud, Jung and

---

[40] Contrast the stress on "Self" in Meadows (1989, 1990 and 1991), e.g. (1991): 71 and 101, with the more relational stress of Naddair (1987), e.g. p.103.

others. Some claim that "there is nothing that cannot be healed", including rheumatism, arthritis, injuries, paralysis and operation scars.[41]

Pagans are also beginning to develop counselling methods with explicitly Pagan foundations. Not only welcomed life-changes can be marked and celebrated by Pagan rites of passage, but there are also rich resources for dealing with traumas. Victims of abuse, rape and violence can find considerable help in the journey towards healing and wholeness in Pagan contexts. If Pagans honour what is "natural", they can stand against what is "against nature". They can also say that not everything which happens is to be welcomed, accepted or suffered: it is as natural to escape from a hungry lion as it is to eat a potato. In such contexts, it can sometimes be useful to use shamanic techniques such as soul-retrieval.[42] It can also aid recovery to deal with the spiritual dimensions of an assault, just as Shamans remove the spirit-darts shot into victims by their enemies.

One significant aspect of healing in a Pagan context is that it encourages a change of perception. The patient or client and the healer are not alone but are intimately related to a host of others who are willing to help. Trees provide herbal, homeopathic or spiritual essences and wands or staffs. Otherworld guardians provide help in soul-retrieval. Time and place—temporality and spatiality, sacred festivals and sites—are involved in establishing the person in the context of a living world. This healing is intended to be holistic and a means of personal and relational growth. It gives people the eyes and ears to see and hear the living world, and the face to be known to those with whom they share life.[43] Healing not only removes "sickness" but tends towards maturity.

Shamans as community healers. In both close-knit communities and individualistic, atomised ones, people often need to be helped to listen to each other. Shamans are sometimes labelled "walkers between the worlds". Perhaps those who represent Paganism to non-Pagans, e.g. the police, the media or academia, might be thought of as undertaking a dangerous shamanic journey. Shamans traditionally work not for themselves but that their "people may live"[44]—which is a fine goal for contemporary negotiators and facilitators.

Pagan counselling in preparation for rites of passage such as birth, menarche, adolescence, marriage, divorce and so on can also be apt occasions for shamanic journeys. The couple getting handfasted, married, might gain considerable knowledge of each other with the aid

[41] Aziz (1992).
[42] See p.110.
[43] Compare the stories in Grace (1995), especially "the Sky People".
[44] E.g. Medicine Eagle (1991): 90.

of a Shaman willing to direct their shared exploration of inner- and
other-worlds. A shamanic counsellor—as one who listens to spirits—
might also be expected to be able to teach the couple how to listen to
one another.

   More common group experiences in Paganism, especially the camps
at which groups get to know each other better, could be included under
the heading of "shamanism with extra pay". Most of these are specific
to particular groups or traditions, some are more open. Shared rituals
and meals combine with guided visualisations akin to those already
noted. Many Pagan camps now include the opportunity to participate in
a sweat lodge. For those undergoing this intense experience it is
certainly bonding. However, some Pagans appropriate Shamanic
techniques without returning any benefit to the "donors", they appear
to be "playing Indians" and some even insult the "Indians" by
continuing to use the derogatory term "Red Man".[45] Healing between
communities should address the way in which people relate to those
from whom they "learn" shamanism. Pagans assert that their tradition
is one of respect for all living so this should not be too alien to them.

Shamans introduce people to the land. The most significant impact of
Shamanism on Paganism is in the imperative to listen to the Earth. The
real Shamans in the West are engaged in the difficult task of
environmental education, they enable people to find ways of relating
respectfully to nature. This rarely involves taking people out to the
woods and playing drums, but it recognises that cities are not separate
from Nature and that they are part of the environment, affecting and
being affected by weather, air, earth, water, animals, plants and "all our
relatives". Some of these new Shamans—Gordon MacLellan calls them
"Patterners"[46]—use contemporary environmental tools and locations.
There is Pagan input into computer-based environmental networks and
educational programs. Pagan motivations lead some into organising
tree planting or supporting city farms. Museum- and school-based
educational programmes in which ecological principles and practices
are encouraged can be natural contexts for such Patterners.

   Front-line environmental actions can also be educational, both for
the participants and for those who witness them, even on the media.
Such protests rely not only on those who set up camp in the path of
road-builders, but also on occasional participation by locals and
visitors. People often come with a concern that a particular road,
power-station or open-cast mine will affect their life and go away with
a new vision of the living, fragile, sacred Earth that is our home.

[45] Stafford (1990): 85.
[46] MacLellan (1996).

Eloquent speakers and colourful drama remind TV watchers that they too are participants in these matters of life and death. As Gordon MacLellan says,

> The future of the shaman lies in the road camps, or in city centre celebrations of people and place: a Tree Dressing day, a Kite Festival on Chinese New Year, a Beltane Dance in a country park. Shamanism works with and for the people: it does not belong in High Magic Lodges or in a Witches' Coven: it is rooted in people, land and spirit.[47]

The central job of Shamans in our community is to introduce people to the land and to help them find for themselves ways of relating to the living world.

If many neo-Shamans have made shamanism a safe and polite activity, some actions demonstrate that its the warrior aspect has its modern adherents too. Shamans participate in the struggles of their community against hostile outsiders. They lead their people's fight against Otherworld hostility, aggressive or disease inducing spirits and attacks by other Shamans ("sorcerers"?). Destruction of life in the cause of more and bigger motorways or life-threatening nuclear installations can arouse strong emotions and require more than letter-writing campaigns. Most Pagans are pacifist and all restrict the occasions on which they think violence is justifiable. Passive resistance is taught and practised in all Pagan peace camps, protests and actions. However, the shamanic struggle in defence of "Mother Earth", or of particular hills, trees, bat colonies, rivers or homes, can sometimes incorporate "aggressive magic". People play on the (irrational?) unspoken fears and taboos of road-builders in painting runic symbols or pentagrams, attaching talismans, or even daubing menstrual blood on trees. Some have invoked the Morrigan—an Irish battle Goddess—in times of stress or when the cause appears lost. However, other Pagans have challenged them in this: the general opinion is that such uncontrollable and aggressive other-than-human people should be left well alone. Groups like "Earth First!" are willing to damage machinery and thus impede the cutting down of trees or turning wood into planks, but they stress non-violence towards all life.[48]

Pagans too need these Patterners. They need to be taught how to "find your way in the woods" and practise the "art of conversation with the Genius Loci".[49] A Shaman can show them Pagan, i.e. Earth-centred, Nature-respecting, earthy and natural ways of listening to the Earth. Pagans sometimes borrow the individualistic, psychologized, universalistic approach of New Agers. They meditatively "strip away

[47] MacLellan (1996).
[48] Oliver (1992).
[49] Patterson (1991).

the human and return to pure spirit" in attempting to celebrate themselves or in "finding their power animal or totem". This gnostic honouring of "spirit" above "matter" is not in tune with the ideology Pagans profess; it dishonours Earth. Pagan Shamans can refuse this dialectic and re-introduce people to physical, embodied, material, spatial, temporal Earthly living. In doing so Paganism not only challenges New Age but also becomes an important part of the postmodern critique of modern society. It gives an important role to individuals and to their psychology, but refuses to remove them from the "here and now" realities of related living. Shamans remind people that it is not possible to be alone, everything that people do affects other people, human or other-than-human. It is not only butterflies in China which affect the weather in New York. Terry Pratchett writes

> One of the recurring philosophical questions is: "Does a falling tree in the forest make a sound when there is no one to hear?" Which says something about the nature of philosophers, because there is always someone in a forest. It may only be a badger, wondering what that cracking noise was....[50]

Philosophers, butterflies, Pagans, politicians, clouds, cities and forests are all related, all share life "in Earth".[51] Shamans remind them of this.

Raves in Cyberia

In contrast to Caitlín Matthews' workshop approach, there are more direct paths to the Otherworld and despire her authoritative "permissions",[52] people are journeying without passports. In Raves and clubs "technoshamans" are altering consciousness and taking trips in the web of connected, living reality—which is being called "Cyberia".[53] Consciousness altering drugs, rhythmic music, and colourful fractual patterns combine with the World-Wide-Web's information highway to provide an experience of "at-one-ness" with all things and access to (apparent?) omniscience. Mysticism and technology combine, as they always have. Perhaps wisdom cannot be gained in this way, but information and knowledge can. Cyberia can also be manipulated by the technoshamans just as their more traditional counterparts manipulate the information and technology available to them.

---

[50] Pratchett (1992): 6.

[51] Abram (1985): 96.

[52] Caitlín Matthews (1995): xix-xx and frequently thereafter. However the permissions are intended to be read, they forcefully evoke children's TV programmes in which parents must be asked for help in cutting "sticky backed plastic".

[53] For powerful, insightful introductions (without the music) see Rushkoff (1994) and the combined volumes 13 and 14 (1990) of the *Encyclopedia Psychedelica International*, entitled *Evolutioñ*.

Media coverage of Raves might suggest that they are solely concerned with drug-induced hedonism. They might be more accurately considered as egalitarian and communal arenas for achieving the experience of realising oneness with the universe. For participants it is important that this is a communal experience. There are

> no performers, no audience, no leaders, no egos. For the fractual rule of self-similarity to hold, this also means that every house club must share in the cooperative spirit of all clubs.[54]

The whole experience takes everyone to the awareness of "oneness".

Such mystical states are, of course, not necessarily Pagan—physical reality can seem to be illusory. However, many technoshamans do not decry the mundane in this way but see it as explicate order's manifestation of the implicate order—both are "real".[55] It would also be untrue to say that all Raves or ravers are Pagan. However, Cyberia is a postmodern Gaia. It a web of life and also a web of information. In it the consciousness of the world of work with its work-ethic and hierarchies is altered to an awareness of the interconnectedness of all things. There are several ways in which Pagans inhabit Cyberia. Just as everyone lives *in* Gaia, in the Earth—whether knowing it, or liking it, or not—so everyone lives in Cyberia, but some do so consciously, deliberately and willingly. The ultimate shift of consciousness here is to an awareness that all Otherworlds are parts of this world. Journeying or tripping around this world is just as important for traditional Shamans, technoshamans and Pagans as inner journeys or Otherworld explorations. It remains to note examples of recent explicitly Pagan journeys in Cyberia's Raves.

The Chosen Chief of the Secular Order of Druids, Tim Sebastian, asserts that Druidry has survived largely through its Bardic expressions: music, poetry and story-telling. His group has always been intimately involved with youth and counter-culture, especially its various popular musical manifestations. In a large indoor Rave in the English Midlands they recently proclaimed the Rave's organiser to be "the first bard of the dance of the modern age" and presented him with robes and an oak sapling, to be planted later. Megatripolis, a "House" club in London, opened with a Druid ceremony. The white robes of the Druids might have been created especially for the lights, colours and patterns of these events. Dragon Environmental Group have facilitated ceremonies at a number of clubs and other venues. Return to the

---

[54] Rushkoff (1994): 159-60.
[55] See ibid.: 167-9; and the works of David Bohm.

Source, a club in London, includes a regular and central chakra journey and trance dance among its dance events.[56]

One Chaos Magickian, who seems typical, told me that, apart from enjoying Raves, he goes when the energy is high and lets the momentum swing him higher in order to do his "work". When people's consciousness is already altered and connected to everything, it provides a context for making the changes "according to Will" that is understood to be the essence of magic.

Experimenting with Ecstasy

According to Feyerabend, "hardly any religion has ever presented itself just as something worth trying"[57] but Paganism influenced by Shamanism does exactly that: it encourages experimentation. In the Pagan forms of Shamanism there is continual interaction between alternative sources of information. Ancient mythology and contemporary science blend. Both the most carefully critical and the most popularly experiential discussions of Shamanism combine in new forms. Inner and outer visions glimpse new possibilities and discover previously untried potential in existing techniques. Such experiments encourage a search for "what works" which then becomes authoritative.

The results of experiments can of course be criticised. Pagans are eclectic but they have already established certain ground-rules. These are literally grounded, Earthed. An experiment or experience which encourages a belittling of the Earth, the body, the physical or the mundane—or an over-emphasis on "spirit"—can be seen as stepping away from Paganism. They may be fine for others, they may work in different contexts, but there comes a point when they cease being Pagan. At the time of writing Pagans are experimenting with shamanic experiences. They are rediscovering old traditions, revitalising more recent ones and hearing the imperative call to listen to the land, the Earth. Modern Western consciousness, especially religious consciousness, requires considerable alteration if it is to celebrate the Earth. The resources are available among other "listening peoples" and include secular scientists' careful observations of the ecology of the planet, anthropologists' careful observations of other societies, historians' careful descriptions of past agrarian cultures, and the traditions, songs, techniques and visions of existing shamanic practitioners. Therefore, Pagans are not only taking seriously the claim that studying "others" can teach us better ways of being human, they

---

[56] Partially replicated in a double CD: Return to the Source (1995).
[57] Feyerabend (1985): 19.

are also taking seriously the claims of "others" to have valuable ways of hearing the voice of the Earth and of all her inhabitants.

The word "Shaman" can be short-changed and used as a new label for doing whatever it was people did before. Adding a drum to the therapists' equipment does not define Shamanism adequately; also adding drumming to high ritual magic or spontaneity to Wiccan rituals does not make them shamanistic. Adding Jungian archetypes to "soul retrieval" certainly contextualises Shamanic techniques in Western thought, but it does not convincingly represent the richness of Shamanism. There is no need for the word to be paid extra in these contexts because, far from being made to work hard, it is almost redundant.

"Shamanism" works harder in the earthier context of Pagan eco-action and education, while doing similar work to that which it is accustomed to do elsewhere. When Shamanism—the word, the techniques and experiences—reminds or teaches people that they are part of the living Earth, that everything around them is alive, that everything they eat has a "soul", then it is working hard and being respected for it. Even closer to its heart, Shamanism "means something" when its techniques give people the experiences that are only taught in books. Pagans might also be asked to learn that traditional Shamans are not individualist virtuosi but community functionaries. If Paganism is to be truly shamanic it must revitalise communal values and struggle against the individualism and consumerism by which they are ravaged.

8

ECOLOGY

One of the recurring philosophical questions is: "Does a falling tree in the forest make a sound when there is no one to hear?" Which says something about the nature of philosophers, because there is always someone in a forest. It may only be a badger, wondering what that cracking noise was...[1]

What if I fell in a forest: would a tree hear?[2]

Paganism is a spirituality in which Nature—the Earth and the body—is central and celebrated. It is fundamentally "Green" in its philosophy and its practice, taking seriously the understanding that "everything that lives is holy".[3]

At their seasonal festivals Pagans regularly renew their relationships and deepen their intimacy with their environment, Nature. They are confronted not with the demands and claims of a "spiritual" after-life or deity, but with the significance of everyday life on Earth. Birth, growth, sexuality, fecundity, creativity, death, decay, vitality, beginnings, endings, joy, sadness and other mundane, everyday, ordinary affairs are found to be meaningful and sacred. It would be misleading to see these "themes" or a "quest for meaning" as the prime focus of the festivals. They are certainly significant, but Pagans celebrate the festivals with the much simpler understanding that they are honouring the seasons and the land. Pagan calendar celebrations are about time and space: this time—the present, now—and this space, here. They encourage and inculcate an awareness of being "at home" here and now in the mundane and therefore sacred Earth. The festivals teach ecology.[4]

Meditation and Bulldozers

Paganism has Green roots and encourages a diversity of ecological actions, none necessarily better than another. Some Pagans meditate for the good of the planet, some use the "energy" raised in ritual drama to benefit rain forests, some spike threatened trees, some lie in front of bulldozers. The following three sections look at different ecological

---

[1] Terry Pratchett, *Small Gods*. (1992): 6. (*1994): 6.
[2] Dillard (1974): 89.
[3] Blake (1793): plate 27 and (1795): 2.366. In Keynes (1972): 160,289.
[4] If theology is "talk about God", ecology is "talk about home".

expressions: meditation, membership of "Green" groups, and specifically Pagan ecology.

Meditation and Symbolic Action. Some Pagans meditate for the benefit of the whole planet. In the comfort of their own homes they meditatively radiate thoughts or feelings of peace and well-being to the planetary being, (Mother)[5] Earth. Some join together in guided visualisations, imaginatively seeing the Earth healthy and flourishing and then "send" these visions to affect the outer world. Some such people would have considerable reservations about participating in anything more public or political. Some may belittle this quietist meditation, but it should be understood that the people involved are acting in part on the principle that everything is connected—an intimation common both to esoteric traditions[6] and to chaos theory. What happens in the privacy of one person's mind is connected to every other part of this radically interconnected Universe. A change in understanding or motivation is already a change in the web of all things. Since this web and this Universe are full of life, the change is one of relationships. So, what begins as "thinking nice thoughts" begins to *affect* world-views and *effect* changes in lifestyle. "The personal is political"—so the slogan asserts—and using ecologically "friendly" washing-up liquid, biodegradable hygiene products, recycled paper and local products begins to affect wider economic and political realities. Supermarkets stock "Green" products, governments take note of voters' wishes.

Based on the same principle of the interconnectedness of all things, some Pagans go beyond meditations to symbolic action. If they cannot actually stand between a rainforest tree and a lumberjack, and they do not feel able to picket a business using rainforest timber, they can do something symbolic. They might plant a seed of the next apple they eat in the hope that not only will it grow, but that a rainforest seed will grow too. The action combines imagination, intention and a first step in the direction of a reforested planet—all significant aspects of a Pagan understanding of Magic.[7]

Membership of "Green" groups. Many Pagans are members of Greenpeace, Friends of the Earth and other groups that aim to preserve, protect and encourage the health of wildlife, or to protest its destruction. Involvement in these groups ranges from paying the

---

[5] The linking of Nature and women is of ambiguous value: it can be either empowering or disempowering. See Griffin (1984) and Bonds (1992). Also see Ursula Le Guin's provocative essay "Woman / Wilderness" in Le Guin (1992): 161-3.

[6] Faivre and Needleman (1992).

[7] See chapter 6.

subscription (a form of symbolic action?) to fund-raising and participating in marches and protests. No information is easily available on the religious affiliation of those Greenpeace members, for example, who put themselves between whales and whalers, but would not be surprised if some of them at least named themselves Pagan.

There are Pagans involved in groups whose primary interest is in the native mixed woodland of Britain, or in the wildernesses of North America. Groups such as the British Trust for Nature Conservation and the Woodland Trust are very attractive to many Pagans—which is not to say that these organisations or their motives are Pagan. Journalists are often interested in finding a "Green Party at prayer" among Pagans, but there are as many people of other spiritual traditions, or none, among such groups. If it is easier for Pagans to integrate their spirituality with their Green action, this does not mean that other people do not manage to do so. Almost all the religions and philosophies of the world seem to be vying with each other to be seen as ecologically sound or "Green". The spirit of the age is itself Green: green is the only colour in which to teach, preach, sell, electioneer, report, write or condemn. "It doesn't matter what religion or world-view you chose, just so long as it's Green", might be the advice of a latter-day, if somewhat New Age, Henry Ford.

Pagan Ecologists. There are, besides the above groups, more specifically Pagan ones with similar interests. Tree Spirit says it is "neither politically nor religiously biased", but it is clearly more Pagan than anything else. Robin's Greenwood Gang, a group interested in Free Festivals, camps and tree planting is also largely Pagan. Odinshof[8] has a Land Guardians scheme, and the Druid Orders are trying to buy land to plant trees. There is a Pagan Animal Rights group. *Hammarens Ordens Sällskap* encourages self-sufficiency by organic farming, small-holding or the use of city allotments. Extra produce can be bartered for things which cannot be grown.[9]

At the other end of the pole—the same pole of Pagan ecology, not some dualistic opposite—from the quietist meditators are groups such as Earth First! and Earth Liberation Front. "Such groups believe in direct non-violent action to prevent the destruction of the planet."[10] Earth First!, for example, damages machinery used for tree-felling, earth-moving and road-building; it inserts spikes into tree trunks to damage chainsaws, and blockades companies that use rain-forest timber.[11] Not all Pagans support such eco-vandalism,[12] although most

---

[8] See chapter 4.
[9] Harvey (1996).
[10] Ash (1992): 3. Also see Oliver (1992).
[11] Foreman (1987).

agree broadly with the motivation behind it.[13] Dragon Environmental Group is in the front-line of protests against the destruction of complex natural environments in favour of more or wider motorways and bypasses. In 1995 Dragon was also central to the flamboyant, carnival-style protests outside the French embassy in London against French nuclear tests in the Pacific.

These are some of the manifestations of Pagan ecology. No Pagan organisation demands of its members any particular action expressive of its ecological concerns. Indeed, many groups encourage their members to find their own level of ecological activity: the Order of Bards, Ovates and Druids encourages "Personal Environmental Responsibility" without codifying how this is to be expressed. It encourages action by, for example, participating in tree-planting on Arran's Holy Island, owned by Samye Ling Tibetan Buddhist monastery, and providing recycling bins at its summer camps.

A later section looks beneath the ecological actions in which Pagans are involved to attempt to discern the roots of Pagan ecology, and asks about Paganism's contribution to environmental thought and practice. However, that it preceded by a closer look at an explicitly Pagan ecology.

Somatic Ecology

Adrian Harris, a founding member of Dragon Environmental Group, argues eloquently for a Somatic (embodied) approach to ecological action and knowledge.[14] That people "know" through their bodies is obvious, common sense, to many people: we "know" because we see, smell, taste, touch, hear things. We "know" people most intimately in "good sex". Religions tend to offer experience, perhaps moulded by belief, as the final authority: people "know" their religion is "true" because their experiences confirm its veracity. The problem is, of course, that almost every belief is "provable" in this way—experiences seem to confirm everything! Nonetheless, experience and sensed knowledge are vitally important. This is not negated, but only made difficult, by the fact that this sort of knowledge is not valued as highly as "rational" intellectual knowledge.

What is it that bodily knowledge and experience teach people about ecology? Harris links such profound "knowing" as that experienced in

---

[12] E.g. the editor of *Deosil Dance* felt it necessary to "disclaim" the previously cited article by Ash.

[13] They might be disturbed by Churchill's critique (or exposé?) of the "eco-fascism" of some American Earth First! leaders; see Churchill (1992): 195-7, 209.

[14] Harris (1996).

"good sex" with that experienced in "good ritual" and especially in ecological-ritual:

> In our rituals we reconnect with ourselves, healing the rift between body and mind through ecstatic dance, chanting and the drama of ritualised myth. We lose our ego-centred selves and achieve that somatic knowing of the unity of everything. It is in these moments of spiritual ecstasy that we know the wisdom of the body.[15]

Pagan ecological protest against road-builders draws "courage and inspiration" from the practice of this somatic knowledge. The Dongas—anti-road protesters whose experience united them into a tribe at Twyford Down, with its then threatened, now destroyed, ancient earthworks which gave them their name—and Dragon engage in colourful drama and celebration, not just angry opposition and eco-vandalism. They live in threatened trees, sleep on threatened ground, build relationships with the "spirit" of threatened places, often perceived as a dragon. Some of these places are not ancient woodlands, hills and water meadows but urban environments. Shamanism, combined with ritual magic, gives a "grounded strength" empowering campaigners.

Many of these continuing experiments with ways to protect the Earth, protest its pollution or desecration, and celebrate its diverse but interconnected life derive from (continuing) involvement with cultural, ancestral, sacred locations such as Stonehenge. They have also inherited many of their approaches, members and interests from the peace camps. The festival movement which began in the 1970s and the peace camps combined all the features now seen in Pagan eco-dramas (a more inclusive term than "protest"): joyful celebration, music (including "shamanic" drumming), ritual, anger and sorrow at opposition. The Secular Order of Druids combines both long-term involvement with Stonehenge campaigns, eco-protest (e.g. against extensive quarrying in Somerset) and encouragement of the spreading (counter-) cultural movement of Raves and road-protests. They have established a Bardic Chair at Bath in the context of the Solsbury Hill action and created a "Rave Bard" during a large inner-city Rave in Coventry. Festivals, peace camps, raves and road-protests also meet similar responses from the authorities: heavy police presence, razor-wire barriers, and particularly the drafting and enforcing of laws designed to curtail such events (first the Public Order Act and now the Criminal Justice Act). Most important for this discussion, however, such events have rooted Pagan ecological action in particular places, particular problems, particular relationships. Pagans participate in acts

[15] Harris (1996): 153. Also see LaChapelle (1989).

of neighbourliness rather than in (New Age?) mystical, salvational "pseudo-connectedness" with some numinous, nebulous "All".[16]

Although Adrian Harris stresses the experience of knowing the unity of all things, his examples show that this does not negate the honouring of particular places, diverse experiences and pluralism in knowledge. On Twyford Down, Solsbury Hill[17] and Jesmond Dene the trees did not fall without being heard and the ground was not dug up without being mourned. Protection of London's last remaining ancient woodland, Oxleas Wood, continues—successfully so far. Pagans continue to plant trees and remove tyres from ponds. They continue to experiment with ways of "recognising Gaia from within", experiencing "communion between ourselves and the living world that encompasses us".[18] Ecstasy in ritual may reveal the interconnected unity of Gaia, but bodily experience also teaches that the "all" is made up of "many", each part of which can be hurt or healed. Individuals join groups like the Dongas and Dragon and begin to find themselves forming new relationships with themselves, with places and with people. Somatic ecology does not overwhelm the individual and submerge them in some greater unity, but builds relationships between those who celebrate life. This might be why Pagans frequently use trees as logos for their groups or newsletters, rather than the ubiquitous but "ambiguous modern icon" of the Earth seen from outside by astronauts and satellites.[19]

Ecological Roots

The following sections note four roots of Pagan ecology: the endangered Earth; Blake and Gaia; understandings of deity; and shamanism.

The Endangered Earth. Western religion at its best teaches that human people are stewards of the Earth. This is a "light Green" ecology, the "conservation" of the great landowner's gamekeeper looking after grouse and their habitats so that the "great and good" can shoot their prey for which they might pray their gratitude. For anything more than these Green tints we must look to secular scientists like Darwin. Their careful look at the world has enabled us to refuse the human-centred and even the God-centred vision of the world. Humanity is not the "pinnacle and goal of creation" but one part of an elaborate and evolving community of living beings, a web of life, an ecosystem. The

[16] See Cheney (1989a and 1989b).
[17] Made famous by Peter Gabriel.
[18] Abram (1985).
[19] Sachs (1994).

continuing work of ecologists and other such scientific observers of the planet shows that humanity is part of Nature, though such *observation* can obscure participation.[20] It is this secular activity and not religious responses to the world that has *enabled* both popular concern about the ecological crisis and the articulation of that concern. Religions might, however, motivate people to *do* something beyond being concerned. To do so it must be more than an opiate which allows people to believe that concern or attitude is sufficient.[21]

Paganism encourages people to develop their spirituality according to their experiences, intuitions, desires, dislikes and thoughts. (Christianity insists on the opposite: experience and moods must be brought in line with authoritatively revealed and taught "truth".) People seeing the Earth in danger recognised Paganism as a spiritual ground to stand on, and have brought that deep ecological concern with them. Perhaps the linking of the name Pagan with honouring the Earth was all that was required for the initial attraction at least. Paganism has not had to tell people to change their attitudes towards ecological concerns. It has encouraged them to explore and express their concern because ecology is of the essence of Paganism as a spirituality of Nature. Its celebration of seasons and other natural phenomena—sunrises and the lunar cycle being the most obvious examples—have suggested hope to many people. Paganism seems to them a chance to explore different ways of relating to the environment which might lead to a healthier relationship or balance between humanity and other living beings. Some people are satisfied with expressing ecology in scientific research projects or in political protest. Others require a spiritual underpinning to their involvement. Discovering in Paganism a celebration of Nature, they recognise a way of exploring a spiritual context for ecology. Pagans are "at home" in an endangered Earth and are trying to find ways (all ways, any ways) to put things right for all life. In other words, there is an elective affinity between Paganism and ecology. The "spiritual world" of Paganism is the same as the physical world. More helpfully than perhaps it intended, the Ordnance Survey has mapped sacred places and revealed the lineaments of the Goddess. As the sacred is polluted and the Goddess is sick, Pagans are impelled to try to do something about their actual locations and the condition of the Earth.

Blake and Gaia. Paganism has heard the widespread desire for a Green Spirituality and answered, in the words of William Blake, "Everything that lives is holy". It has enabled the celebration of the experience of

[20] Ibid., which warns that observation of the planet reinforces managerial models.
[21] Cp. Bordo (1992).

being participants in Nature or Gaia as opposed to being divinely appointed caretakers at best or tyrants at worst. This experience and celebration are closer to the heart of Paganism than the worship of a divinity, however immanent. Nature/Gaia includes everything: divinities, seasons, weather, animals, birds, insects, fish, the human body, flu viruses and "everything that lives".

Perhaps to understand "everything that lives" we need to learn from children. To many children, perhaps all of them before they are taught otherwise, the world is profoundly alive. Trees speak, rocks move, there are giants beneath the hills and the clouds have faces. Asked "when did you become a Pagan", many people assert that they have "always been Pagan but did not always know it". Some mean that at some point they discovered that "Pagan" was the word for their feeling that everything is alive, which they had forgotten since childhood. Their adult vision of the world gains impetus from the Gaia hypothesis, ecology, anthropology,[22] feminism, eco-feminism, fiction and non-fiction writers and many other sources.[23] Its strongest root is, however, their own experience of the aliveness of all that surrounds them. Their world view is one in which everything that lives deserves honour and rights not normally given to other-than-human life.

That "everything that lives is holy" does not mean that Nature is a rose without thorns. The Earth is a dangerous place to live, as full of death as it is of life.[24] It is of course human to search for a meaning in the seemingly senseless violence and pain. Perhaps in these "negative" or "shadow" things we encounter the Earth as it really is: disinterested and indifferent to humanity and the petty clinging on to individual life. Perhaps. Paganism somehow acknowledges that here too is holiness.

Theology, thealogy, theoilogy. The third root of Pagan ecology is its beliefs about divinity.[25] Since Pagans most often refer to either Goddess or to Goddesses and Gods, this deity-talk could be labelled the*a*logy or the*oi*logy: the feminine singular and the plural of theology. However, the worship of divinity, of whatever gender or number, is not the primary experience of Paganism. Celebration of Nature is more central, especially as it is experienced as Earth and body. These, though, are precisely the locations in which divinity is manifest and met with. Pagan deity-talk tends to use the language of either pantheism (deity underlying and manifest in Nature) or polytheism (many deities, themselves as closely and as distantly related to the original cause of

---

[22] For an example of anthropological writing about ecology see Milton (1993), including Luhrmann (1993).
[23] See chapter 11.
[24] Dillard (1976).
[25] More fully discussed in chapter 11.

existence as humans, hedgehogs and any other living being), or to combine the two.

Deities are not "out there" waiting for prayers and praise. They are within physical matter, reinforcing but not revealing the importance of ecology and of the body. If the Earth is threatened, it is "our home", "our mother", life-giver and life-taker that is threatened and all life, including ourselves, is threatened with her. A living being who enfolds the lives of "all that live" in her life is being assaulted. To permit this rape and blasphemy to continue is to invalidate the celebration of seasonal festivals and the choice of the self-designation "Pagan", "one who loves the Earth".

For many people it is an ecological vision that attracts them to Paganism. The deities, in sending them back to Earth-ly life, reinforce ecology. There is nothing unique or singular about the deities: there cannot be singularities in Nature—single things are one step from extinction—and Pagan deities are part of Nature. Some Pagans are attracted to Paganism by its polytheism. They find that honouring deities leads swiftly to the celebration of the Earth.

Those attracted by the immanent Goddess of the Craft and of Goddess Spirituality also find that this connects them immediately in relationship with all that lives. Starhawk eloquently describes the "three core principles of Goddess religion": "immanence, interconnection, and community". For example,

> Immanence calls us to live our spirituality here in the world, to take action to preserve the life of the earth, to live with integrity and responsibility... Interconnection demands from us compassion, the ability to feel with others so strongly that our passion for justice is itself aroused... Community includes not only people but also the animals, plants, soil, air and water and energy systems that support our lives. Community is personal...[26]

Pagans invented theology,[27] but did not practise it in the same way that Christians do.[28] Whether in mythological poetry or philosophical prose, theology to Greek and Roman Pagans was part of an account of the nature of the universe. Pagan theology is a part of Pagan ecology. The Natural is more important than the Supernatural or spiritual.

Shamanism: Eating and Being Eaten. In addition to Blake's phrase "Everything that lives is holy", Shamanism[29] largely depends on the intimation that "everything that exists, lives". Gordon MacLellan claims that one significant role for the Shaman in Western society is

---

[26] Starhawk (1989): 10-11.

[27] Jones (1996).

[28] See, for example, Deane-Drummond's (1992) critique of Moltmann's use of ecological language in his theological writings.

[29] See chapter 7.

that of "Patterner—one who helps people listen to/relate to the world around them".[30] He also explores the implications of life in a living world—a world in which people must eat living things.

Wiccans assert that the phrase "An it harm none, do as you will" adequately summarises their ethics. The statement encourages development of a mature Pagan understanding of the world and of the individual's place within it. "Will" encapsulates this understanding and suggests effective thinking based on correct knowledge. Initiated Wiccans are therefore encouraged to make changes in the world according to their best understanding of the ways things are... as long as "it harm none". "None" here is frequently discussed in the context of other human affairs and rarely in relation to other-than-humans. In other words, this is not really an ecological ethic, more a rule about the practice of magic[31] and perhaps a social ethic. It would, in fact, be hard to "harm none" unless perhaps one became a Jain ascetic.[32]

Shamanism and many traditional cultures are more realistic, recognising that in order to live it is necessary to take life. A Maori writer, speaking from within his people's tradition, says that religion is "doing violence with impunity".[33] It is absolutely wrong to take life but it is also wrong to leave your guests unsheltered and unfed. So you must go into the forest and cut down a living tree to make a shelter, you must dig up a tuber to make food. These violent acts deserve a response and a recognition. That they are necessary does not negate or mitigate their violence. So the tradition or religion provides ways of enabling the "doing violence with impunity". Western Pagans cannot simply adopt Maori ways but can see this phrase as encapsulating, for example, their traditions of asking permission before cutting holly and ivy for midwinter decorations and making offerings afterwards.[34] They can consider ways to approach what they eat in the knowledge that life has been taken, perhaps given, and the way this affects relationships with "all that lives". In everyday life human people eat those other-than-human people with whom they share life. Paganism is truly ecological in that it is grounded in the ordinary and in earthy matters of what is eaten and the relationships affected by the transformation of living things—cows or carrots, trout or tomatoes, pheasants or plums—into "food".

---

[30] MacLellan (1996). He skilfully fulfils this role himself.
[31] See chapter 6.
[32] See Dundas (1992).
[33] Tawhai (1988): 859.
[34] Patterson (1991).

Shades of Green

Paganism does not come ready-made with an ecological dogma or an environmentalist agenda. Nothing is finalised, everything is being worked out in encounters between people and environment. If Pagan ecology is moulded by seasonal festivals, it is fired in the more difficult meeting between Pagans and those who build, control and use roads, power-stations, weapons, mines, agribusinesses and so on. In looking (not always systematically or deliberately) for ways to understand and express human relationships with the Earth, Pagans draw on other Green agendas, approaches and thoughts.

Deep Ecology is attractive to many Pagans. It encourages deep thinking about human interrelationships with the rest of Nature and provides a necessary critique of dominant ideologies of the West that permit—perhaps demand—the mastery and exploitation of Nature. However, its critique is flawed by both a dualistic alienation from Nature and "a heavily masculine presence".[35] People remain dominant over Nature because they are exhorted to see the Self as enlarged beyond the physical reality of the body, its spatiality or embodiment,[36] and encompassing everything. Threatened rain-forests are no longer either "It" to be exploited or "Thou" to be related to, but are revealed as actually being "Me". While an appeal to self-interest will certainly encourage many people to use more energy-efficient light bulbs, this is an inadequate response to the problems the Earth faces because of human activity.

Many Pagans would recognise, and have to some degree anticipated, the value of Plumwood's suggestion that

> a different and improved basis for environmental politics and philosophy might be constructed by taking better account of the ethics and politics of mutuality as developed by a number of feminist thinkers.[37]

While many Pagans do talk about "connecting with" and "tuning in" to something in Nature, this radio language better represents the New Age. Talk of "Harmony" with Nature is an improvement but might again suggest the merging of the individual's lived reality with some greater, more real Reality. Such a loss of identity is disrespectful both of the individual's own bodily self and of the multiplicity of those with whom they relate. "Mutuality", however, brings us firmly within the realm of relationships[38] and ordinary experience and is thus more fundamentally Pagan.

[35] Plumwood (1993): 2. Also see Cheney (1989b), Bonds (1992) and Le Guin (1992): 161-3.
[36] Jung (1988).
[37] Plumwood (1993): 2.
[38] Grey (1991).

Paganism is concerned with expressing, encouraging and developing intimacy between human people and all other-than-human people. It values all these people as "beings in their own right" with their rights, relationships, responsibilities, significance, agency, autonomy and meaning.[39] While many Pagans do consider that all things are manifestation of deity, often of "the Goddess",[40] this usually goes beyond the valuing of things only as manifestations of deeper spiritual realities to a more polytheistic celebration of the multiplicity of living things. Paganism, especially in its most feminist-influenced branches, encourages intimacy with oneself, with other human people and with other-than-human persons.

While rejecting the dualistic separation of "spirit" from "matter", the Pagan stress on the countryside as a location for significant encounters with Nature and with "the sacred" could be decried as "mere Romanticism". It is, however, a more positive experience and vision. Many Pagans do regularly and easily celebrate seasonal festivals in their urban environment; the city too is part of Nature, but the countryside is a place of greater bio-diversity. There are more types of living being, more life, "out there" in the woods, moors, rivers and hills of the countryside. There may be no wildwood, no wilderness, few remaining areas of semi-natural woodland left in Britain, and American wildernesses may be threatened by clear cutting, river damming and tourism. But even in city parks or working woods (perhaps this does not include plantation forests) it is possible to encounter a less human-centred, more varied manifestation of the profligate abundance of life.[41] Life survives in the margins: motorway verges, bits of hedge, wood, marsh or pond ignored by industrial agriculture and road-builders. In these margins it is possible to "speak with" and "listen to" trees and hedgehogs, flowers and trout, robins and snakes. It is possible also to listen to oneself. Erazim Kohák argues that a philosopher and a tree can converse, neither exchanging information nor "decorating a putative harsh reality with poetic gingerbread" but communicating respect and exploring a

> manner of speaking which would be true to the task of sustainable dwelling at peace for humans and the world alike, a manner of speaking that would be true in the non-descriptive sense of being good.[42]

Perhaps the trees have taught philosophers what they have been teaching Pagans and children for many years: the virtue of respect and

---

[39] Cf. Plumwood (1993): 128. See also Kohák especially (1993) but also (1991) and (1994).
[40] Long (1994).
[41] Dillard (1976).
[42] Kohák (1993): 386.

the pleasure of intimacy. Many Pagans, however, assert that trees are willing, and able in some way, to communicate things that they would otherwise be unaware of, and therefore the "speaking with" and the "hearing" may also pursue information. Sadly, children are soon removed from tutelage of trees by adults—perhaps because of a deeply suppressed and feared knowledge that

> we are not bounded objects in orbit around each other, but we create ourselves in relationships with each other. We are the outcome of the intersections of our conflicts and cooperations and the influences we exert on each other.[43]

What would happen if children continued to have significant relationships with trees and hills, rocks and ponds?

Pagans, who already celebrate the gendered, embodied character of human-nature, can become open to experiences which enable them to celebrate the diversities of life. They can perhaps do this more easily than some other religionists. Not only "mystical experiences", which are themselves intimately related to gender and physical reality,[44] but also ordinary, everyday experiences empower such celebrations which are integral to polytheistic and feminist-influenced Paganism.

The Earth's ecological problems are not abstract and distant philosophical problems. Nor are they only economic or technological problems. They are not to be left either to politicians, scientists or even philosophers. Just as such problems are largely caused by everyday life (the cars we drive, the trucks which deliver our foods, the forests destroyed to make way for our fields, etc.) so the responses must involve everyday life. They are problems of relationships.

Gnostic Temptation

As has already been noted, no description of Paganism will be entirely applicable to all Pagans. Although almost all Pagans talk about the honouring of Nature, which would seem to demand the valuing of matter, some adopt the language or ideology of Gnosticism which sees the body as imprisoning the "soul" or "spirit".[45]

At Pagan events it is not unknown to be invited to follow a guided visualisation in which the body, "human condition" or "human conditioning" can be stripped away leaving the "spirit" free. Numinous experiences are sometimes thought to be glimpses of what "Reality" is "really" like when the accidents of bodily nature are stripped away. There are (uncommon) occasions when the Goddess of Wicca leads to

[43] McKay (1993): 287—quoting Linda Gordon.
[44] Raphael (1994).
[45] Also see Jayran (1996).

such a stress on the unity of "the All" that the physical world begins to look merely apparent. Although Paganism is rarely centred on deity, it can occasionally suggest that the Earth is only important as a mask (revealing *and* hiding) the divine Reality behind it.

The Gnostic temptation is the attempt to transcend the physical world, to experience unity with the ultimate and original "spiritual" creative forces or being. As Paganism gained a large amount of its ritual structure (e.g. the quartered circle, initiations, magical techniques) from the hermetic, esoteric tradition, it is not surprising that some Pagans do or say things which denigrate matter. In recent years such "mystical" states have been inaccurately labelled Shamanic, and the techniques of soul-journeying have been hijacked in a quest for moments of "transcendence" intimating personal immortality. Perhaps this Gnostic temptation expresses a form of schizophrenia in which the celebration of Nature is assented to while disembodiedness is sought. Counter to these ritual occasions in which Gnosticism intrudes into the celebration of nature, the following section says something about Pagan lifestyles which thrive in the mundane realities of matter.

Hedgehogs, vegans, hunters and prairies

Ordinary human living threatens ordinary other-than-human living. Sometimes it does this intentionally, e.g. fox hunting, meat production, whaling, pest-control, leather production, badger baiting, vivisection. Equally often it does so unintentionally and just by the way. Our cars frequently run over hedgehogs, for example. I do not intend to give "meaning" to this unnecessary slaughter but it can help us to understand the relationship between ecological thinking, animist Paganism and neighbourly living. Other Pagans express their ecological vision equally powerfully by hunting animals for food.

If drivers stop their cars to move a hedgehog from the middle of a road, this is not because the hedgehog was praying for salvation. Nor would the rescued hedgehog go on to develop a religion praising and thanking that human or all humankind. It would simply carry on with its ordinary life. This is much the same approach as an animist Pagan might take to those other-than-human people which, tradition teaches, are more powerful than humans, i.e. deities and the Faerie. It might be encouraging to know that such beings share a Pagan's delight in certain places and times. Their presence at festive occasions is sometimes invited but is not necessary or central to the celebration of that festival. Usually humans get on with their lives, hedgehogs get on with theirs, deities with theirs. Sometimes paths cross and this can be dangerous. This is not necessarily because humanity is thought ill of, though that might be understandable, and only sometimes because, so tradition teaches, the Faerie do things which are harmful. What "They"[46] consider to be entertaining is, for humans, as dangerous as our relaxing drive in the country is dangerous to hedgehogs. Awareness of these dangers can enable people to adjust our lives to be less dangerous. They can become more ecological by enhancing the diversity of life. However, it will never be possible to live without taking life, doing violence to those with whom this planet home is shared.

Not all Pagans are vegetarian, let alone vegan. A few consider that hunting for food is more ecologically justifiable and more expressive of relationships with other-than-human people than buying pre-packaged food in supermarkets. The prairie-sized mono-cultural fields of grain now dominating agricultural industry are ecologically worthless, and worse when they depend on chemicals to destroy the diversity of life that Nature prefers. Hunters are able to draw on traditions in which the hunted is addressed and asked to give up its life, receiving honour for doing so. Pagan hunters might consider that the current imbalances between species require "culling" of "vermin" for the benefit of other life. It is arguable, however, that such language is not a "good" way to express honour of living beings.[47]

If "everything that exists lives" and "everything that lives is holy", eating becomes a problem. What is eaten has been killed. Even vegans eat things that were once alive, once participated in more or less complex relationships with their neighbours, had rights, meaning and value. In the contemporary world it is perhaps not possible to go into a supermarket and address a can of beans in a way that expresses the recognition of the violence done and the need to do violence, or the mutuality, relatedness and neighbourliness of our shared lives. Some other means—perhaps ceremonial, perhaps mystical—must be found to address this problem. What remains clear, however, is that choices of lifestyle affect "all our relations" and express views of the world. Paganism does not impose a particular diet or any other lifestyle, but it does encourage people to consider their impact on the environment. Ecology is not just a matter of the activities of chemical companies, oil refiners, road builders, nuclear power generators, quarriers and agri-industrialists. It is about what people do at home and at work. Conversely, it is not just a matter of private and personal action: picking up litter beside a power station, a chemical factory, a quarry or a motorway is as valuable as putting an Elastoplast on a severed arm.

---

[46] It is traditional to avoid naming such people too often—various circumlocutions are available.

[47] Kohák (1993). Meanwhile, one reader of an early form of this chapter suggested: "The vermin most in need of culling is Homo Sapiens."

Ecology demands concerted public action and active changes in society of benefit to the Earth.

Listening Neighbourliness

We did not choose to be neighbours with those "others" with whom we share our planet home. Yet here we are, surrounded by many neighbours, only some of them human. If other religionists are passing through this place on the way to some more spiritual afterlife (heaven, nirvana, enlightenment), Pagans are discovering that they are "at home". They therefore agree with their more secular neighbours that something must be done to halt the devastation and to increase the diversity of life. This needs to be done, not on behalf of some deity or because it will benefit each individual's "deep green" Self, but primarily as an act of neighbourliness.[48]

Paganism discourages the phallic view that humanity is dominant on Earth and therefore entitled to exploit its resources. It does not permit the equally phallic though potentially less damaging view that humans are stewards of God's Earth, caring for it while ruling over or managing it. Paganism is not a phallic quest for a place in the world. Some Pagans do celebrate a more uterine view, chanting:

> The Earth is our Mother, we will take care of her.
> The Earth is our Mother, she will take care of us.

On the other hand, Paganism encourages people to go beyond the return to a womb for comfort and nourishment. It certainly refuses to give a rebirth which is in any way discontinuous with embodied, gendered, temporal and spatial reality. Paganism is not a uterine rebirth into connected harmony with the cosmos.[49]

Paganism has a more ecological view. This is the clitoral affirmation of life in its physicality, its ordinariness, its diversity and its excess.[50] This *celebration* of being at home in our bodies and in Nature is Paganism's greatest contribution to ecological debates today. The Earth is humanity's only home and the only home of our many neighbours whom we must learn to respect and live peacefully alongside. To do so, Pagans can find their closest companions among ecofeminists who also link celebration with committed ecological action.[51]

---

[48] Finn (1992).
[49] Again see Cheney (1989b): especially 307-12.
[50] Spivak (1987): 82. Also see Bell (1992): 199.
[51] See Caldecott and Leland (1983), Griffin (1984), Plant (1989), Plaskow and Christ (1989), Diamond and Orenstein (1990), Plumwood (1993). Also see Dickens (1992).

A common metaphor for religions is that of a path, a journey from an imperfect "here" to a perfect "there". Paganism does demand changes in human relationships with Nature and expects people to act on what they learn from listening to Earth's voices. But the journey metaphor has its limits. This is, first, because, as Nelle Morton says,

> Maybe "journey" is not so much a journey ahead, or a journey into space, but a journey into presence. The farthest place on earth is the journey into the presence of the nearest person to you.[52]

Secondly, it is because Earth is already "Home"; there is nowhere else to go. Paganism is less a path than a sitting among the trees. There is a journey to get to the woods, of course, but this is not the primary activity of Pagans. Paganism is about the respectful living of ordinary lives "here and now". Among the trees Pagans are a listening people because the Earth speaks. Pagan deities too are not "*telling* us to be, and what to be"[53] but "hearing to speech",[54] listening until all people— human and other-than-human—have found their voice to say what is wrong, what is needed, what is hoped for.[55] Such listening typically begins in the seasonal festivals in which Pagans learn to hear—and see, smell, taste, touch and celebrate—the Earth. It is in response to the ecological needs of the planet that Paganism and Pagans are tested: will all the fine words about respect lead to more participation in real action on behalf of "all our relations", or will there be a retreat into the fantasy that right attitude or intention is sufficient? It is also in relation to the environment that Paganism will have most impact on the rest of society. At this point it offers its most radical challenge to the consumerism and individualism of contemporary culture. There are those who would like it to be part of the mainstream and resent the tree-dwelling Pagan eco-warriors, but the counter-cultural flow in Paganism is its lifeblood.

---

[52] Morton (1985) and Keller (1988).
[53] Keller (1988): 63.
[54] Morton (1985): 54.
[55] Compare Le Guin (1992): 161-3.

9

EARTH MYSTERIES

> People have asked: how does the Disc move on the shoulders of the elephants? What docs the Turtle eat? One may as well ask: what kind of smell has yellow got? It is how things *are*.[1]

The world which Pagans inhabit is at once the same as and different from the one inhabited by other people. This is true also of other religionists, whose worlds are different again from the world of Pagans. Religions typically assert the existence of two worlds: a world of ordinary perception and daily life and a spiritual world entered by special means at special times and in special places, and especially after death. This chapter says more about the Otherworld(s) of Pagan traditions, and notes that the spiritual world of other religions is also not just a single place with or without connections to the everyday world. It explores another sense in which Pagans inhabit a world which is different although it appears to be the same as "this world", the ordinary world inhabited by most people.

Pagans are at home in Earth, in the world of daily life, of eating, drinking, making love, conversing, working, playing and suffering. They do these things much as others do them and are not distinguishable from the rest of the human population by age, gender, class, occupation or preferred entertainment. Only some are distinguishable some of the time by what they wear. During ceremonies they might dress differently, or even undress, and they might wear jewellery identifiable to others as Pagan, Wiccan, Odinist, Druidic, Magickal and so on. Otherwise they disappear within the mass of humanity living unexceptional lives. However, unlike other religionists, Pagans are spiritually at home in Earth too. They are not looking for a means of escaping the material world or bodily life and gaining spiritual enlightenment or salvation. For Pagans there is no heaven or nirvana; thus the world which they inhabit is the one inhabited by other religious people, but with the first major difference being that they celebrate this world for itself and not only as a testing ground or preparation for somewhere better. Daily life, employment and leisure do not necessarily distract from spiritual, sacred concerns—the two things are part and parcel of each other. This is not to say that all Pagans enjoy their work or that they are fulfilled in their leisure. It

[1] Pratchett and Briggs, *The Discworld Companion*. (1994): 32.

is only to assert that Paganism finds "sacredness" inextricably linked with what others might consider "profanity".

A second, related difference between the world as seen by Pagans and by many other people is that Pagans consider the Earth to be alive. For most of them the distinction between "animate" and "inanimate" is not entirely certain. For others it is irrelevant or false. Not only do humans, animals, birds, fish and insects have life, but so too do trees, clouds, rocks, fire and water. Pagans approach these inhabitants of the world in ways which suggest that it is possible to communicate with them and equally possible that this communion is mutually desirable. Pagans may hug trees, but they also say that it is worth listening to trees. Rocks are not only greeted in honour, but are also offered gifts and present them in return. Much of this reiterates the matter of the previous chapter. It stresses once again that Pagans acknowledge, to one degree or another, that humanity lives as one part of an intricate, intimate, inter-related, ecology of souls. There is more, however. This chapter does not merely expand a discussion of Pagan ecology, but is required because ecology is only one aspect of Pagan cosmology. In other words, to understand the world Pagans inhabit it is necessary to explore not only ecology as others would understand it, but also to combine this with the insights of magic and shamanism. The full portrayal of Pagan cosmology requires discussion of the various deities and other-than-humans who also inhabit the world. This, however, can wait until a fuller picture of this inhabited world has been painted.

Gaia

We humans and our neighbouring living beings live in a small blue-green planet. The word "in" is not a mistake. We do not live "on" Earth, crawling over its surface as a spider might crawl over a kitchen work-surface away from its normal habitat. Earth is our ecological niche, our home, our environment. There are those who think that the space age has liberated us to become citizens of the cosmos. When the Earth was first viewed from spacecraft and from the moon—and especially when the first pictures were seen and disseminated—the idea that humanity was somehow separate, some sort of observer looking in from outside, seemed to justify, but this is a false vision. Astronauts and cosmonauts cannot separate themselves from "mother" Earth, they take with them all that Earth provides as life-giver—especially air, food and water. There has been no "coming of age", no leap into independence—this is merely an adolescent and, perhaps, Freudian fantasy. Humanity remains a child of Earth and kin to all others who share those gifts of life and especially the gift of the only possible space in which to live: the Earth herself. Despite their delight in Future Fiction (Science Fiction),[2] Pagans are happy with this state of affairs, and in their regular festivals they celebrate the Earth's seasons, climates, ecosystems, geography and geology.

There are those who think the original and true home of humanity is somewhere more spiritual, less physical: for example, heaven or nirvana. Others assert that space-aliens have told them of the origins of humanity or of all Earth's life in the manipulations and gifts of visitors from other planets or other dimensions. Such matters of belief, hope and intense contemplation and striving remain unprovable and unfalsifiable. Those who assert that they have undeniable proof of the correctness and absolute veracity of their belief or vision face only limited acceptance and considerable implausibility. Most of the world's population (of humans, let alone other intelligent species) continues to disregard divine interventions, angelic visitations, miraculous cures, strange manifestations and curious signs. The soul and the spirit may be of vital importance to artists, but they have not yet been isolated scientifically. Heaven and similar post-mortem destinations remain elusive, especially in comparison with the solidity of our Earthly existence. Such utopias may inspire the kind of altruism that some religions require, but they have not inspired the kind of respect for the Earth necessary to the current age of ecological degradation and potential disaster.

Pagans are usually happy to assent to scientific accounts of the origins of life. Something *in* this planet led to the conditions responsible for the way things are. The many and varied deities to whom Pagans relate may have an interest in the weather, the crops, fecundity, spiritual insight, children's growth and well-being, and any one of a million concerns, but they are far too involved and implicated in the world to be responsible for its creation. Even Pagan theologies in which there is a transcendent deity do not dissent from scientific narratives which claim to explain the origins of time and space. Pagan myths and stories may speak of the origins of this or that in the activity of a deity or hero, but Pagans do not entertain dogmas that assert a divine first cause of the cosmos.

The Gaia hypothesis is particularly attractive to Pagans. This does not pretend to be an explanation of how things came to be, but is an observation of how things continue to be. Lovelock and other scientists apply to the global environment ecological understandings that ecosystems are integral wholes. Just as removing snails from a river's ecosystem affects all other living beings and even the river itself, so changing the chemical blend in the atmosphere by the addition of

[2] See chapter 11.

exhaust fumes affects the entire planet's systems. The label Gaia was not intended by Lovelock to imply a belief that the Earth is a conscious and personal being, but only that Earth appears to act as if it were a single living being.

> I am sorry that my enthusiasm has unintentionally given to some readers an erroneous belief in a sentient Gaia that looks after us like a nannie. She is in fact as I described her on page 152 of Gaia, a self stabilising system comprising all of us living things and the environment as a single dynamic entity.[3]

Few Pagans consider Gaia to be "nanny"—not a natural image for most Pagans who know of such characters only from Disney films and period dramas. They are aware of the complexity of human relationships with the Earth. Some might veer to the opposite extreme and see humanity as an infection or irritation only being temporarily suffered by Gaia whose self-healing immune system is beginning to destroy us. This is sometimes said to explain phenomena as diverse as Sydney's bush fires, Los Angeles' earthquakes, AIDS, the ozone hole and African famine.

Whatever scientists may have intended by linking the name Gaia to their hypothesis, and to whatever uses and abuses it might be put by popular imagination, the name does powerfully evoke a deity. Pagans were already discovering (or uncovering after years of neglect) the power of evoking and communicating with Nature as a living, personal, autonomous being. Experience suggested that such a being was more than an anthropomorphic personification or a strongly projected archetype. The Goddess was manifesting herself in her fullest, most essential form: the Earth. The scientist's Gaia resonated with Pagan intimations about the nature of deity and seemed to suggest appropriate means of building relationships. Gaia would not respond primarily to calls for salvation or expressions of praise, but responded better to life-styles expressive of ecological commitment: recycling, down-shifting, simple living and "Green" co-operation with the environment. Doing, not believing, seems a more adequate response to Gaia.

If Gaia is revealed as a single living entity, then perhaps her planetary body has more than metaphorical circulatory, reproductive and other systems. If so, Pagan magicians can use her name for that macrocosm of which the individual is the microcosm.

Micro- and Macro-cosmos

Magicians have long held that

---

[3] Lovelock (1985). Also see Lovelock (1982), Hughes (1985) and Abram (1985).

"magic" is at once the knowledge of a network of sympathies or antipathies which bind the things of Nature and the concrete implementation of this knowledge.[4]

This network goes beyond the confines of the Earth and includes the stars and planets in their courses. Astrology, alchemy, herbalism, music and an intense engagement in observation and theorising rooted magicians in experience of the physical and metaphysical world. The individual and the cosmos are considered by magicians and by scientists to be made up of the same material—though scientists may not agree that "soul" is a useful term for one part of this shared essence. Human beings can communicate with Nature because they are already of one essence. Their material forms relate to one another: human bodies (even in spaceships) require the water, air and physical sustenance that are provided by Earth. Their "soul" is also a shared one. What affects Nature (drought, flood or ozone depletion for example) affects magicians. What an individual magician does also affects Nature. Simply digging the garden changes things. Digging quarries makes more widespread changes—the water-table is altered, the rock forms are spread around in the form of roads or houses. The "energies" or "light" that are perceptible only to magicians are scattered but continue to affect people healthily or detrimentally. Magicians on a quest for transforming-knowledge, wisdom or enlightenment make considerable changes to the world they inhabit. In meditation and ritual they experience themselves as microcosm in relation to the greater macrocosm. Making changes in consciousness enables a resonance with global energies or entities.

The idea that the Earth has a "subtle body", a chakra system or a series of "power points" akin to those of the human body has been linked to beliefs that the Earth is a living being, Gaia or macrocosm. Just as rivers echo blood-vessels and the water-cycle echoes the circulatory system, so the Earth and the human body are thought to share other, more mystical energy systems. When the blood does not flow adequately or the nerves become trapped, doctors or therapists aid the suffering human body to recover. Human interference in the way that water flows within the Earth—from clouds to ground water, lakes, streams, rivers, seas and back to clouds—can be damaging to life. Human technologies can counter these damaging changes, getting the system flowing again. Magical technologies might be employed in ways sympathetic to these more scientific but not necessarily more rational or secular technologies. When the "subtle" energies of the human body do not flow, an acupuncturist might help to get them moving again. When the Earth energies get sluggish, polluted or

---

[4] Faivre and Needleman (1992): xvi.

diverted, other magical technologies might be employed. To understand these energies and technologies it is necessary to explore beliefs and practices surrounding ley-lines, dragon-lines and other networks or manifestations of Earth energies.

Ley and Dragon Lines

There is a theory that lines of some sort connect places of significance. For example, a line drawn between two ancient sacred sites, two medieval churches, two ancient burial sites or an ancient well and the summit of a hill, and then extended in either direction will be seen to link several or many more such sites. A classic and popular example is a line drawn between churches dedicated to St Michael from Cornwall north-eastwards across southern Britain. This connects not only several such churches but also Glastonbury and Avebury. These are presented as objective facts for which it is possible or even necessary to find an explanation. Both claims for the veracity of such lines and their explanations, and arguments against them, are far from objective or neutral. The present discussion is not interested in whether such claims can be scientifically proved or disproved, or in the adequacy or accuracy of the complex metaphysical systems built around acceptance of such lines, but focuses on the nature and role of such understandings in the wider practice of Pagan living in a living planet.

"Ley lines" or simply "leys" became part of the currency of the English language after 1921 when Alfred Watkins

> stood on a hilltop in Herefordshire and suddenly perceived the beautiful English landscape before him as newly laid out in a web of lines linking together the holy sites of antiquity.[5]

Watkins himself thought of these lines as ancient trackways or mundane roads. Those convinced by UFO stories have thought of ley lines as the navigational flight paths which direct space aliens around our planet.[6] These theories are less important now, except as the initial cause of considerable interest in alignments of sites and in the lines themselves.

Theories about ley lines can be divided into two broad groups: those which hold that the lines occur naturally and those which hold that they are human artefacts. Some theorists understand ley lines to be cognate with the natural channels along which positive and negative energies flow in Chinese geomancy or Feng Shui. These are frequently named "Dragon Lines" and carry beneficial energies just as river courses carry beneficial water. Just as water can stagnate, so natural energies can

[5] Leviton (1993): 246.
[6] Devereux (1992a): 20-8.

become negative. Ley lines have also been compared with the "song lines" of Aboriginal Australian cultures. These are paths along which creative, Dreamtime ancestors walked giving shape to the land (or walk—this creative activity does not belong to the past because all time in the Dreaming is synchronous). They rest and a rock forms, they dig for water and a stream flows, they sleep in the land and there is a hill, they emerge and there is abundant and healthy life and further creativity. Those initiated know the songs which express, reveal, respond to and honour the land, the ancestors and life. They sing the land as they travel it and as they sing the land arises to meet them. Whether this is an accurate portrayal of Aboriginal traditions, or another chapter of the noble savage myth is less significant here than the point that Westerners are trying to find resources for a vision of the Earth which inspires respect and engenders celebration and ecological responsibility. Of course, myth and religion can provide the illusion that the land is being respected while the reality is that people are entertaining each other with songs and stories as a quarry is destroying another hill just around the corner. However, many of those convinced of the existence of leys see them as strong incentives to do something about the state of the environment. If the Earth has a "subtle body" with channels along which its own life energy or perhaps its spirit flows, then we may be able to work with it, or stop interfering with it, to the benefit of all life. Going beyond mapping the lines, spotting the intersections, waiting for the mysterious lights which seem to appear over sacred sites and dowsing the energies around standing stones, the ley-initiate might have a powerful role comparable to the acupuncture therapist. Just as acupuncturists manipulate the "subtle body" of the sick human, so it is said to be possible to promote the healthy flow of positive energies in the sick body of the living Earth.

This is true too of those who think that ley lines are human artefacts. Rarely if ever are they considered to be simply ancient trackways along which cattle may have been driven, messages carried and trade conducted. For such mundane purposes there exist winding paths like the Ridgeway of southern Britain which, as its name suggests, largely follows the ridges at the edge of the chalk downland connecting settlements from the south coast to the Wash. Evidence from all round the world suggests the ubiquity of both winding paths respecting local topography (bio-regional tracks perhaps) and straight lines connecting special places. These are illustrated in every book and magazine concerned with "Earth Mysteries" or ley lines.[7] Some might be conceived of as pilgrimage routes, others as changes to the landscape to

---

[7] See especially Devereux (1991, 1992a, 1992b); Pennick and Devereux (1989); Michell (1988) and Dames (1992).

mark the direction from a centre towards significant sunrises. Paul Devereux, who has been a key figure in the Earth Mysteries tradition, now argues that the lines and the sites they connect are a result of the interaction of human shamanic activity and the Earth's natural but as yet little understood energy fields. Humans have perceived the Earth's energies or a universal force, e.g. in the form of strange lights and electro-magnetic fields, and marked the sites of these experiences, e.g. by erecting standing stones which themselves store and emit strange effects of the energy. At the same time, Shamans in their out-of-body experiences flew across the landscape in the most direct manner possible, "as the crow flies", i.e. in straight lines. Returning to ordinary consciousness they directed their people to mark these "spirit" flight paths in such ways that we have inherited standing stones, notched hillsides, artificial pools and all the rich cultural artefacts into which initially simple markers have been elaborated, e.g. cathedrals.

Before discussing the point and purpose of all this interest in seemingly arcane mysteries of lines across the landscape, there are three other issues to be noted: sacred sites, terrestrial zodiacs and sacred geometry.[8]

Sacred Sites

Many people are aware of differences of mood between one place and another. While some buildings, hills, springs, forest glades and other places are pleasant to be in, others can appear to resent human intrusion and others seem to require special preparation and polite greeting before access is permitted. Pagans are adept at creating space in which to perform rituals. In spare rooms, living rooms, waste ground, city parks, deep forest, sea shore and open moor they make circles in which to celebrate the seasons and the living of life. Although the whole Earth is sacred, it has special places and powerful places. Some of these have been marked by the ancestors who formed stone circles and avenues, temples and cathedrals, groves and shrines. Others appear to have gone unnoticed or unaltered, but have been recognised as places where powerful experiences are more common than elsewhere.

To some Pagans these are simply places where the potent life of Earth is obvious, clearly manifest and easily experienced. To others they are places where the life-force of the Earth wells up. Whether they consider this force cognate with the Chinese *chi* or gain insights from other cultures,[9] they see that it is integral to the health of the entire

---

[8] The following chapter contains further discussion of sacred sites.
[9] See Swan (1993).

planet and of all the inhabitants of Earth—city-dwelling humans and "wild" animals.

It is not unusual around the world for access to some of these sacred sites—both ancestral and recently recognised—to be difficult. Sometimes this is because the place itself is considered to manifest a strong will against casual or regular visits. Just as Mount Shasta and Mount Saint Helens are said to demand particularly careful approaches by rare individuals, shamans or medicine people,[10] so some Pagans experience Stonehenge as a difficult, even temperamental place requiring careful preparation and respectful approach. More often sacred sites are hard to approach because they are "owned" or controlled by those to whom they represent "ancient", "archaeological" or "heritage" sites rather than by those to whom they are sacred. In this age of consumerism and leisure, money is required more often than respect by the custodians of "heritage". Cameras are more appropriate signs of a "good reason" to "visit" than offerings of food or drink. Archaeological preservation is a more central concern than celebration. The "original context" of a site is of more value than any contemporary vision or affection. Such places are large-scale museum artefacts or installations rather than living sacred centres or celebratory venues. All visitors to a place are treated equally and without distinctions by those who "care for" it. This seemingly democratic and secular affirmation would be admirable if applied to many other social institutions, and it is not hard to defend in the terms of modern state administration of public access sites. Why should someone who claims that a stone circle was a Druidic temple be any more privileged than someone who thinks of it as a UFO landing pad? On what grounds should access be allowed or denied to holy ground? What evidence can legitimately be required of those who think they should be allowed access? Perhaps these questions of heritage management are entirely the wrong ones, and the fundamental question is, instead, whether the claim to ownership is valid. In answering the question, "Who owns Stonehenge?" Christopher Chippindale, Peter Fowler and their fellow disputants conclude not only "no one" and "everyone" but, also and more significantly, "arguments about who owns this or that begin to pale into insignificance".[11] This is a problem with which archaeologists and the heritage industry will have to continue struggling. Their difficulties will be made more acute by the knowledge that any decision they make will affect and be responded to by a considerable number of people who have interests in access to places they consider vital (i.e. both important and life-giving). Their deliberations should take into account

---

[10] Lake (1993): 50-1.
[11] Chippindale & Fowler (1990): 171. The other contributions are also significant.

that they are not alone in discussing issues of access and use of sacred sites. Nor do they themselves hold a privileged, unfalsifiable, disinterested or objective view of the places of which they consider themselves the custodians, protectors or managers.[12]

Terrestrial Zodiacs

In addition to interest in ley lines and sacred sites, some Pagans are interested in terrestrial zodiacs: alleged replications or reworkings of the zodiac signs in features of the landscape. The first and most famous is mapped out in hedgerows, watercourses, hillsides and tracks surrounding Glastonbury, and was first noticed by Katherine Maltwood in the 1920s.[13] Since then terrestrial zodiacs have been identified or claimed in many other places. Once again, these are sometimes seen as human artefacts (as they clearly are at Glastonbury) and sometimes as natural outworkings of some more mysterious relationship between the living Earth and the great powers of the sky. This obviously supposes that the zodiac is more than a human imposition on the seemingly random scatter of stars in the night sky. While such significance and refusal of randomness or chance are alien to the materialism and scepticism of modernity, they are deeply rooted in Western esotericism, and attributable also to the synchronic and interconnected nature of reality as a manifestation of the relationships of living beings or the great web of all things.

Given the importance of Glastonbury in the revelation of these massive zodiac figures, it will be no surprise that interest in them is more obvious in New Age than in Pagan circles. There are certainly overlaps between New Age and Paganism, and some people accept both designations. However, there are also enough distinguishing features to make an encounter between them comparable to a meeting between two religions. What Pagans might do with the understanding that such features might be discernible in the landscape will be considered after a discussion of sacred geometry.

Sacred Geometry

Every land has a centre. Every town has a centre. Every house has a centre. Every place can be defined by its centre, its boundaries and the connections between its centre and its boundaries, its entrances, exits and pathways. Some places have been carefully designed by those who believe in some form of harmony, proper relationship or proportion.

---

[12] See Bender (1993), especially her own chapter on the contested landscape of Stonehenge.
[13] Maltwood (1964). For a concise summary and critique see Ashe (1990): 63-5.

Others simply exist as ways of getting as much into a given space as possible. Thus high-rise buildings are rarely pleasant to look at or to inhabit, unless they are the corporate headquarters of a company that wants its building to advertise an image of artistic merit or civic pride. If the principles of Feng Shui are meant to be applied to the design of "good" places in which to live, worship, learn, be buried and so on, it might be thought that modernity is sadly lacking in comparable traditions.

Among those writing about ley lines and other more or less esoteric landscape features, John Michell is prolific, and in addition to his observations, mapping and discussion of alignments of sites,[14] he has devoted considerable energy to more geometrical studies. His work, as is especially clear in *The Dimensions of Paradise*,[15] argues that sacred places are positioned in relation to regional, national and/or geographical centres. They encourage a round or progression of festivals for the celebration of proportion and harmony. Geography, geometry, planning, musicology and spirituality combine in a vision of perfection or perfectibility—both human and planetary. Both the dimensions of sacred sites and the relationships between are significant. Stonehenge, for example, is revealed as a model of the dimensions of the Earth and the Moon, of the distance between them and of other cosmic relationships. It is also part of the wheel of sites geometrically marking the sacredness of Britain. Michell and similar writers[16] are not solely interested in Britain, nor is Britain privileged in their works as a unique land. This is a vast enterprise exploring all lands and all sacred sites.

Geomancy

In discussing sacred ecology, the previous chapter should have established that the more esoteric vision of "invisible worlds"[17] is not an opiate preventing engagement with the "real" world. On the contrary, it can enhance and stimulate engagement with the physical realities of the everyday world, not only in radical eco-action but also in the rejection of dualist and gnostic denigration of that world and of "the flesh". Discussion of cosmology and sacred places continues in the next chapter which explores the belief and experience of the intersection, at certain times and in certain places, between the world of everyday life and the deeper life of the land: the Greenwood and the Otherworld. The present chapter has already noted that some Pagans

---

[14] E.g. Michell (1974).
[15] Michell (1988).
[16] Pennick (1994) is an accessible and excellent example.
[17] Flood (1993).

are interested in the related fields of sacred geography, sacred geometry and sacred sites. Its main focus is the relationship between the geomantic visions of those interested in ley lines (often called ley-hunters), terrestrial astrologers and geometrical geographers and the earthy eco-passions of Pagan celebration of the mundane environment (whether it be in homes or in the woods and other "wild" places).

Geomancy can be defined as "divination by figures on or of the earth",[18] but this is only useful if "divination" is understood as analogous to the activities of geologists. Geomancy is less an attempt to discover the future or gain advice about fortunes than a seeking of information about the state of the land revealed by its forms. A geologist working for a mining company might survey a landscape and suggest that a particular place would be good to dig for coal or oil. Something about an area's topography, the surface details of the hills and valleys, indicates the underlying constituents of the land. The more esoteric geomancer looks across the same landscape and discerns the flow of energies that are creative and supportive of its particular forms.

Why do they do this? Why seek lines and shapes expressive or generative of the kind of "earth energy" which goes unnoticed, unremarked and untapped by more secular viewers of the land? The simple answer, of course, is that people seek energies in order to use them. Geomancy is distinguishable from more exoteric pursuits not by degrees of rationality and secularity, or conversely by degrees of fantasy or spirituality, but by the kind of energy sought and its intended manipulation. It is a technology, like other forms of magic. In some cultures it has respected and expert practitioners; in the modern West it is the preserve of eccentrics and visionaries. Its nearest kin in the respectable economic world are town and country planners and architects—people who are paid to find or produce pleasant living, working or leisure environments for others.

Richard Feather Anderson defines geomancy as

> an ancient, holistic, integrated system of natural science and philosophy, which was used to keep all human activity in harmony with natural patterns—from seasonal cycles, to the processes that maintain the balance of nature, to the universal geometrical proportions found in the way all organisms grow.[19]

Underlying this and all planning is an understanding that the Earth has energies and rhythms which are good or bad, healthy or harmful, exhilarating or enervating, relaxing or exhausting, pleasant or disturbing for people who live or work in them or merely visit them. The geomancer as planner finds places in which "abundance and well-

---

[18] *Chambers 20th Century Dictionary*: 524.
[19] Anderson (1993): 192.

being, optimum health and a fullness of life" are not only possible but also natural. For example, in the northern hemisphere a south-facing aspect and shelter from cold north winds are desirable. It is better to live away from noisy and smoky places like industrial cities.

The geomancer goes further and meets the shaman in being concerned not only for human well-being but also for that of the planet. The planner can treat the land as an object to be manipulated, re-formed and altered for the benefit of clients. From a geomancer's point of view this is part of the problem of the contemporary world and its threatened ecosystem. Rather than seeking to live in harmony with the Earth, humanity has imposed itself, dominated, subdued and not so subtly altered natural systems and cycles. Anderson says:

> Geomancy's overall purpose is to maintain the web of life and keep the Earth Spirit alive and vital... The intent of geomancy is to affect how we live on the planet so that we adopt lifestyles and habitation patterns that keep us in harmony with all creation.[20]

This is perhaps more interesting to Pagans than notions of auspicious places in which to live. Few Pagans are affluent enough even to dream about designing a perfect home in an auspicious location and even fewer run businesses which generate enough income to make the design of a work space affordable. Reading about Feng Shui or other forms of geomancy might influence them to re-arrange their furniture or to try and make some sort of "hearth" more central than a TV in their home. They might try to make a home out of the anonymous boxes so typical of the buildings of modernity. More commonly, however, geomancy is part of wider Pagan interest in outdoor places and landscapes, places in which to celebrate rather than live. It is also part of their concern with the Earth's health.

Geomancy seems to support the Pagan understanding that the world is a single living being, perhaps divine, perhaps "the Goddess" or "Mother Earth". It suggests that just as the human body has energies ignored or untraced by the dominant medical approaches of modernity, so the Earth has not only wind and water systems but also more subtle or esoteric energy flows. In some places these energies are strong, in others they are polluted, dammed or diverted by industrial processes. The former places are beneficial to those who visit or inhabit them. A festival gathering at an ancient sacred site can draw on naturally available energies to enhance the occasion further or be directed to the benefit of the wider community of living beings. Where the energies are polluted, dammed or diverted, the analogy with the human body can suggest approaches to a cure. Herbalism, homeopathy and acupuncture are useful in the treatment of sick humans. Some attempts

[20] Ibid.

have been made at adapting these to the treatment of the ailments of a landscape or of the whole Earth.

Earth Healing

Pagans frequently express the idea that the Earth is sick, and in their belief that it is a living autonomous subject, they take this as more than a metaphor for pollution or habitat destruction. They also view some landscapes as sick: the digging of quarries, the diverting or polluting of rivers, the destruction of forests, woods and hedges, the industrialisation of agriculture with its monocultural fields and its chemical sprays and the building of super-highways can all be seen as assaults on life-rich habitats and environments.

Pagan participation in tree planting and "grass-roots" conservation movements might be seen partly as an application of herbal remedies to a sick planet or landscape. A degraded landscape might benefit from an increase in trees as much as a weary human might benefit from an invigorating cup of peppermint tea or a sun-burnt traveller might benefit from the application of St John's Wort ointment. The metaphor, of course, must not be stretched too far; it only suggests that a general "greening" (including that of medicine and therapy) might be of more holistic value to humans and the Earth.

Homeopathy has been applied not only to sick humans and other animals, but also to polluted rivers. An almost infinitesimally small quantity of a carefully prepared substance has effects far beyond its apparent potency. Homeopathic arnica deals with bruises with amazing efficiency—and not only for those who "believe" in its efficacy. There is anecdotal evidence that pure spring water dripped into a badly polluted stream or river has amazing purifying effects. That it is not specific enough for the validity of the claim to be tested is less significant that the fact that Pagans are willing to try it.

Dragons and Rituals

More commonly than this application of the principles of homeopathy, Pagans engage in rituals which some claim are cognate with acupuncture. A needle inserted into the correct part of the human body affects another, not immediately connected part of the body. The subtle energies are encouraged to flow properly and balance is restored. The Earth's body is sick because its physical body has been cut up with environmentally unfriendly roads, mines, cities, power cables and other paraphernalia of modernity. It can allegedly be helped back to health by the insertion of metaphorical needles, some of which (e.g. standing stones and metal-tipped staffs) are visually similar to those of the acupuncturist. Even rituals without such "needles" are thought to have similar effects. If a ley line is prevented from carrying energy because of an intervening quarry or road system, it can be aided by a ritual which boosts the energy over the gap, or by one which diverts it around the problem. If the energy is not flowing because a power centre is damaged, it can be stimulated to function properly by a ritual which raises a standing stone in either the apparent or the subtle aspect of the world.

Pagans often see the Earth's energies as represented by dragons. Some engage in "raising the dragon" rituals in which, for example, the dragon is called upon to provide the energy required to confront the assaults of road-builders and tree-cutters. The medieval legends of St George and the dragon have the hero defeat the demonic beast to save a town. (The saving of the princess is only the occasion of the deed and not its motivation, as is indicated by the saint's continuing journey in search of occasions for further noble deeds.) While some Pagans assert that dragon-slaying is a heinous crime and a patriarchal assault on Nature, others see the event as an annual ritual in which the Earth's chaotic energies are "pinned" (as if by an acupuncture needle) and thereby directed to the benefit of all life. Instead of spring growth being random and diffuse it is channelled to the good of particular places, entire ecosystems. In the autumn the dragon's energies decline and need to be directed again in case everything goes with them—this time the legends speak of St Michael.

Paolo Uccello's painting "George and the Dragon" can be interpreted as the portrayal of a spring ritual in which the Earth is represented not only in the form of landscape but also personified as the maiden Goddess-priestess-princess and as the wild dragon. The princess is far from threatened by the dragon, she holds it and appears to be introducing it to St George. Meanwhile George emerges, young and innocent, from the Greenwood to meet the Goddess as lover and devotee. His lance channels the energy of a vast spiralling storm into the throat of the elemental dragon outside its cave pool lair. If the princess and the dragon are usually nameless in the telling of St.George's story, Uccello's painting might remind the viewer of the two very different epics: those of Marduk and Tiamat or of Perseus and Andromeda. The background in Uccello's painting is also meaningful to Pagan viewers: the drama takes place just before dawn in a maze beyond the fields and distant houses of the city. This dragon ritual is a May Day event in which "green" celebrants direct the wild energies of the Earth before making love (privately, with neither Uccello nor any other observer present) and then returning through the fields to the town, leading the celebration of summer's abundance. This is not to claim that Uccello intended this in his painting, but only that what he painted can be seen as an evocation or inspiration of an aspect of Pagan engagement with the Earth and geomancy.

The Sound of What Happens

Paganism is a spirituality in which Nature (the Earth and the body) is central. Ecology is not a fringe interest but an integral part of this eco-spirituality. Pagans consider the Earth to be more than an object to be manipulated or used with some degree of respect, but rather as a person with rights, responsibilities, desires and dislikes, problems and pleasures. In the language of philosophy, it is an autonomous subject. Just as humans are sometimes thought to have both body and soul, both physical and subtle bodies, both body and mind, so the Earth can be considered to share this same nature. If this is true, environmental problems are analogous to sickness in the human body and can be treated in the same way(s). The symptoms can be tackled with disregard for underlying dis-ease, un-healthy lifestyles and unfulfilled potentials. Therapies which aim at eradicating the obvious signs of the problem (e.g. oil spills and quarry holes) can be employed without challenging humanity's continued addiction to petroleum products and roads. Alternatively, Pagans share a wider interest in the application of more holistic approaches to the health of the planet and of all individuals who make up the ecosystem. In addition to protecting threatened woodlands (or supporting those who are willing to do so), Pagans are likely to value some form of geomancy. They draw on the Earth's energies just as they draw on the waters and the air, and engage in rituals to aid the flow of those energies, especially where they appear to be diminished or dammed. Paganism is not escapist encouraging avoidance of the contemporary world or rejection of the benefits of "civilisation" or even of modernity. It does, however, consider these to be open to criticism and in need of balancing with more "harmonious" ways of human living.

While "all the Earth is sacred", not all places are alike. A respect for the diversities of life as well as the unity of the Earth allows a celebration of particular places and requires the healing of other places. Ancestral sacred sites are sometimes viewed as parts of a complex geomantic system which requires respect and the remembering and practice of rituals, chanting or other "good" human activity. There are certainly Pagans whose views of the world include the full complexity of geomantic vision (geometry, alignments, zodiacs and so on). In general, however, Pagan interest in these areas is less evident than that of New Agers. It might enhance Pagan appreciation of sacred sites and it might encourage some to explore new locations, but on the whole Pagans seem to hold a less technical and more animated view of the Earth. They celebrate and use the energies of particular places but are not as concerned as their New Age counterparts with the precise geometric or magnetic properties of those places. Pagans are at least as likely simply to hug a standing stone as they are to approach it with a pendulum or dowsing rod. Paganism celebrates a more active and less theoretical or abstract approach to places. Rather than questing after the music of the spheres they are more likely to agree with Oisín, Fionn mac Cumhaill and the Fianna that the best music is "the sound of what happened", the sound of that which is.[21]

---

[21] Heaney (1994): 170.

10

GODS AND HEDGEHOGS IN THE GREENWOOD

Most witches don't believe in gods. They know that they exist, of course. They even deal with them occasionally. But they don't believe in them. They know them too well. It would be like believing in the postman.[1]

The Earth has been seen from the moon. It has been surveyed and mapped from high vantage points—hills at first, satellites more recently. Places are viewed through a bus window or a TV set. People and "wildlife" are observed by surveillance cameras. Fine Art has taught us to see landscapes: bounded, defined parcels of land. Humanity watches. Those who are not just passively watching are engaged in presenting or packaging the spectacle. They include landscapers, heritage managers and TV producers, acting as lenses through which vision takes place. Builders of roads and diggers of quarries employ other manipulators of the land to direct sight away from "eyesores" or to soften the edges of the aftermath of their work. In these and other ways humanity has become a voyeur.

Meanwhile, this Earth and these places are inhabited. They are home to someone, even if that someone is "just a badger" or "just a snail". The last two chapters have explored aspects of the land as inhabited and seen by Pagans. They have stood on high hills gazing across lines and figures in landscapes. They have looked over the shoulder of those who peruse maps looking for connections. They have climbed trees and blocked roads and gates with those who say the Earth's diverse inhabitants come before its economic exploitation or its military control. They have attended to the food eaten by those who seek ways to respect the life of those who become food, whether they be animal, vegetable or mineral. In such ways previous chapters have explored the ways in which Pagans live in the world. Without ignoring the romantic roots of Pagan vision and without denying that some Pagan geomancy can seem like "ley spotting", Paganism encourages more than a visual engagement with life, Nature and "all our relations". This chapter explores another facet of Pagan intimacy with the other-than-human people with whom the world is shared. It introduces various Pagan ways of talking about deities and their place in the scheme of things. Deities are not alone or divorced from the web of

[1] Terry Pratchett, *Witches Abroad.* (1991b): 17. (*1993): 20.

relationships enmeshing other living beings, so they are not alone in this chapter. After an aside on the relative insignificance of deity-talk in Paganism, the discussion of Pagan relationships with their deities begins properly with an exploration of the Greenwood.

Religion and Theology

It might seem strange to some religionists and some observers of religions that it has taken until chapter 10 to devote a lengthy discussion to "theology". Many people, after all, consider beliefs or talk about deities to be the defining characteristic of religion. When people ask "Are you religious?", they usually mean "Do you believe in God?" In fact, there are religions without deities (Buddhism and football, for example) and religions in which belief is less important than practice or lifestyle (Judaism and the traditional ways of most small-scale societies). Both "religion" and "spirituality" are notoriously difficult to define in such a way as to include everything people refer to by these words. Dictionaries refer to deities, beliefs, ultimate truths, "the Sacred" (a strange amalgam of all those things, places, moods, actions, affections and hopes to which the adjective sacred is more properly applied) and to the meaning of life. People might also think of dogma, hierarchy, powerful experiences, inspiring times, visions, uplifting songs and terrifying encounters. However, it is problematic to apply approaches appropriate to one religion or spirituality—if there is a difference between these—to any or all others. I am happy to assume here that Paganism is a religion among others, and to state that it need not be a religion like or unlike all others.

Paganism is not *centred* around the worship of deities. Pagans may have invented theology[2]—and some are deeply concerned with feminist thealogy[3]—but a concern with correct and fervent belief is not common in Pagan discourse. Seasonal festivals are more indicative and formative for Paganism than the names or nature of particular Goddesses and Gods. Ask Pagans what is most important, attractive, enjoyable, profound or Pagan about their Paganism and they will not begin by describing their beliefs about deities. Equally, Pagan ceremonies do not focus on particular creeds or dogmas. No one is excluded who has an affinity for one particular deity rather than for another. It would be unusual, but not entirely impossible, for a Celtic deity to be honoured at an Ásatrú gathering, though it is no longer rare for Saxon deities to be honoured by at least some Druids. Deities, however, are far from the main focus of attention. Pagans frequently,

[2] Jones (1996): 32.
[3] I have not yet been able to persuade anyone that the plural "theoilogy" might be useful.

easily and without malice translate the God-talk of their Pagan
companions into their own language. In a circle in which someone has
just spoken of "the Goddess" some will hear this as a reference to the
high Goddess of their tradition, others will hear a reference to their
favourite Goddess or Goddesses, and others will envisage "the Goddess
and the God". Not all Pagans enjoy the company or the thought of
every possible deity ever invoked, but theology and belief are not the
prime cause of diversity or disagreement among Pagans.

The Greenwood

The basic concern of this chapter is cosmology: the study of the world
and the relationships of its parts. A cosmology is a world-view—a way
of seeing the world, the cosmos, life or things around us—and such
points of view are intimately related to "where you stand" or "where
you are coming from", i.e. viewpoints, perspectives, vantage points.
Too often humanity has tried to observe the world as if from outside.
This false sense of distance (even superiority) has caused considerable
difficulties to humans and others living in the integrated living
ecosystem of the Earth. Pagan ecology and geomancy—the subjects of
the previous chapters—are significant aspects of Pagan cosmology
because geography, geology, ecology and other disciplines are
concerned with what is most sacred to Pagans: the Earth. They are
rooted in Pagan cosmology which is fundamentally a sense of being "at
home", being intimate with and part of Nature.

Religious cosmologies often suggest that the physical, sensual world
is only one part of reality. Usually it is said to be the least important
part, something as temporary as a waiting room or an examination hall.
There are "higher" places to which people wish to go and "lower" ones
they wish to avoid. Not all religions share this hierarchical ranking of
space, but most concur with the idea that "this world" is not the only
one. There are other, less frequently sensed realms. All these "invisible
worlds" can be mapped by religious specialists like writers of icons,
carvers of statues, mystical poets and eloquent preachers.[4] People
describing a spiritual experience or a religious hope can be said to be
"mapping their invisible world".

The centrality of the Earth, or Nature, in Pagan spirituality suggests
that a map of its cosmology, its perception of the world should bear
some relationship to the landscape mapped by secular cartographers,
like the Ordnance Survey. Ley lines and terrestrial zodiacs can indeed
be marked on such maps. But this is also true of the more mundane and
ordinary places which are even more significant in Paganism: ancestral

---

[4] Flood (1993).

sacred sites, woodlands, hills, rivers, springs, seashores and wilderness. What Ordnance Survey maps do not show is that these and other locations have life and relationships. A map to accompany a walk through a nature reserve or National Park may represent the animals, plants and birds that can be encountered en route. A child's map is perhaps more likely to animate the trees and rocks as well as involving people in the scene. A Pagan celebrating a landscape might appear to be on no more than a nature-ramble or childishly animating the world around them.

Although they believe that "all the Earth is sacred", Pagans are likely to have a special place or places to which they return often, especially at seasonal festivals. Increasing intimacy with these places permits a richer experience of the changing seasons and moods of the Earth and, Pagans assert, a deeper appreciation of the aliveness of the cosmos. While not everyone agrees that the Earth is sacred, it is increasingly widely held that the "Earth is one". Pictures from space make this clear, as do the availability of bananas in countries where they do not grow, wars between distant nations, world music and the seemingly global enjoyment of TV soap operas set in very narrowly defined communities.[5] Eating a banana or watching a soap opera may be ways of celebrating the unity of the Earth, but Paganism offers others. It suggests that experience should be rooted not in nebulous intimations but in concrete, tangible experiences. It encourages a sensuality beyond the voyeurism of the heritage and entertainment industries. In a chosen special place within the one, sacred and living Earth, a Pagan experiences and pays attention to a particular moment and place. It is all very well knowing that when it is midsummer in Australia it is midwinter in Finland, but it is hard to experience this except in the imagination—important though imagination is.[6] Pagans and other "earthed" people (ecofeminists for example) might question an attempt to do so. The life and seasons of the Earth, and in them its sacredness and its life, are better celebrated in the particular place and time where the celebrants find themselves.

These particular and special places in which Pagans celebrate can be named "the Greenwood". This name is meant to be enchanting, evocative of leafy glades inhabited by abundant "wildlife" and danced through by elusive, beautiful and powerful beings. It is an echo of those "Once upon a time" days of faerie. It is also a reference to the "Once upon a time" when forests covered many lands. Only a small proportion of woodland now survives the ravages humanity began in the Neolithic, if not immediately after its first ancestors came down

---

[5] In am indebted to Jon Davies of Newcastle University for this realisation of the significance of bananas.

[6] Sutcliffe (1996): 117.

from the trees. In the remaining semi-natural woods of Europe and the richer but still threatened untouched forests of North America, Pagans enter a less human-centred world. This is true too of other "wilderness" areas and places on the margins of human control. "Greenwood" alludes to the ecology of the temperate zones and the myths and psyche of the peoples of north-east Europe. Other evocations of bio-diverse lands might be found elsewhere, e.g. marshlands, arid outback and also areas where secondary growth is reclaiming what humanity has discarded as "wastelands" or "barrens". The Greenwood is a place where we are visitors and can encounter Life in all its many dimensions, with all its relationships and in all its profligate abundance.[7] It is entered not only in woodland or wilderness: the "special place" of some Pagans is a single tree in a city park, perhaps encountered as the World Tree, Yggdrasil. Ancestral artefacts like stone circles, burial mounds, cathedrals, grottoes and enclosed pools are also places where the Greenwood can be strong. In the circles in which rituals take place, even though they may be cast in someone's living room, time and space are experienced differently. In them Pagans step "between the worlds" and into the Greenwood.

Although "Greenwood" is a mythopoetic word, its purpose is not primarily to entice people away to a fantasy, never-never land. It invites people not only playfully to re-enchant the world, but also to engage with the political, social and economic realities which are destroying life, species by species, and those far from abstract or anonymous forces which are restricting people's access to, and encounter with, the diversity of both "natural" and socio-political life.

The Greenwood is a place full of Life: a community of plants, insects, animals, birds, fish and the teeming bacteria of the soil. These other-than-human persons have their own lives to live. They usually live without interest in our human lives, although we often disturb them, sometimes fatally. In terms of the Earth's life or ecology none of them is less significant than others. Beauty or ugliness, wildness or tameness are no indicators of importance in the cycle of life. Some Pagans relate to trees but are only minimally interested in the other plants and have no interest in building friendships with insects. Others pay attention to the minerals on which the Greenwood depends.

The Greenwood is also inhabited by those other-than-human persons who are named variously according to the tradition or choice of different Pagans. Some 'talk of "Gods and Goddess", others of "Elementals", "the Faeries" and other beings. There is a diversity of opinions on the nature of these beings. Some say that they are as real as humans and hedgehogs. Others believe that this is a poetic way of

---

[7] Dillard (1976).

speaking about natural phenomena, for example personifying storms or growth. Some prefer to think of them as archetypes, existing "inside" people (as individuals or groups) which can be evoked by a walk in the woods or in meditation at a chosen special place. Others are happy to be ambivalent in their attitude to these people, addressing them as if they exist "out there" but believing that "all deities reside in the human breast".[8] More will be said about Pagans and their deities and other inhabitants of the Greenwood and mythology after an excursion into the Otherworld.

The Otherworld

The Greenwood is an integral part of this world, the ordinary world that everyone lives in. It is not a post-mortem destination like heaven or hell. It does, however, intersect at certain times and in certain places not only with special places, ancestral or contemporary sacred sites, but also with the Otherworld. This is a dimension of the Earth accessible to those able to alter sufficiently their consciousness or perception. For some this is possible only in elaborate ceremony, with rhythmic drumming, dancing and chanting. Others are more visionary, and are predisposed by nature or training to enter the Otherworld. Yet others believe that the Otherworld is accessible in dreams and guided visualisations. It might also be entered through some special place in the Greenwood at some special time in the Pagan calendar. Others do believe that the ancestors, if not all who die, live in the Otherworld. This is not entirely separate from this world, but part of the same Earth, as if France or Tasmania were sometimes accessible from places not spatially proximate. It is beside you but not always perceptible or tangible—as near as your shadow, but requiring the ability to slip between the bark and the tree or enter an ancient mound at the right time after careful preparation.

Some Pagans consider the Otherworld to be the true home of deities, the faerie folk and others. While deities are at liberty to interrupt people while they wash the dishes, and the faerie are liable to distract people walking across fields so that they arrive in the Otherworld, their natural habitat is the Otherworld and that part of the Greenwood which it borders.

Pagan deity-talk

In the Greenwood, the less human-centred parts of our world (where paths to the Otherworld are more easily found), Pagans regularly meet

---

[8] Blake (1793): plate 11. In Keynes (1972).

their deities. They rarely describe their approach to deities as worship, which they often see this as a form of self-denigration and servile dependence. They honour their deities, and respect them for their more-than-human abilities in some area, or for their care, concern and guidance. Pagan deities, however, do not have to be "nice", compassionate or ever provident. They are not necessarily projections of human wish-fulfilment always ready to provide another special experience or another message. Even Pagans who consider deities to be archetypes existing only "in the human breast" (mind or spirit) treat them as real beings. All real beings can be pleasant and accommodating at times and aggressively unpleasant at others. Just as no one expects hedgehogs to have much concern for human attitudes, whether of respect or dislike, so Pagan deities can be allowed to live independent lives.

In the early phases of their modern renaissance, Druids tended to speak of a single deity, God. Now that Druidry has become a more Pagan movement (except where it continues to be primarily a cultural or charitable institution), it has found inspiration in the polytheism of the pre-Christian Celts or the rich mythologies of high medieval Christian Celts. The "prayer which unites all Druids" no longer begins "Grant, O God, thy protection" or envisages a Masonic-style Great Architect, but "Grant, O God/dess". Since it is impossible to recite this "/", most Pagan Druids chose to say either "God" or "Goddess" or, more frequently, say "Grant, O God and Goddess". In other parts of their ceremonies Druids refer to a wide range of Celtic deities, the most popular being Ceridwen, Lug (or Lugh or Llew), Bride (Brigdhe, Brigit or Brigantia), Epona and Cernunnos. Characters from history and mythology are also important, especially those from the epic cycles of Arthur, Finn, Cúchulainn, Taliesin and the branches of the *Mabinogi*. Individual Druids may discover an affinity with one or more particular deities, but will have no difficulty honouring other deities alongside them.

Witches tend to speak of "the Goddess and the God", though the former is mentioned more often than the latter and some Craft traditions have no interest in the God. A long list of names for these deities can be used, especially those drawn from Celtic and Saxon traditions but also some from Roman, Greek, Egypt and West Asian traditions. Some even draw on Christian tradition, e.g. honouring Aradia who seems to derive from Herodias (Mark 6:17), who in medieval Christian demonology epitomised evil women .

Similarly, Goddess Spirituality focuses on "the Goddess" who, like the Goddess of the Craft and Apuleius' Isis,[9] embraces all Goddesses,

---

[9] Apuleius (1950): 228.

for "all Goddesses are one Goddess". But in another way, the Goddess manifests herself in a multiplicity of forms, many recognised as distinct Goddesses. Thus all Goddess names, stories and representations concern the one Goddess. Alternatively, ever more people prefer to see things the other way around: the Goddess is just a shorthand for any and every Goddess. There is no need to argue about the correctness of someone else's naming of a deity; all the Goddesses exist and are cordial enough not to be insulted if another Goddess is thanked for help. All the Goddesses co-operate in divine activities and are happy to be summed up as a community under the label, "Goddess".

Heathens honour the pantheons of north-eastern Europe, especially those of Scandinavian, Germanic and Anglo-Saxon peoples. The Æsir and Vanir are particularly prevalent, especially Odin and his kin. Festivals in which these various deities are honoured, or their activities celebrated, structure the year for those Heathens who have not adopted the eight festivals of other Pagan traditions. There is a growing movement to re-balance the seeming predominance of male deities by explicitly stressing the many powerful Goddesses of the tradition— though this is far from feminist in motivation. Again, particular affinity with one or more deities does not preclude honouring the rest of the pantheon. Ásatrúar are usually explicitly or radically polytheistic. Pagans from beyond the Celtic and Teutonic areas are also rediscovering their ancestral deities and exploring ways of relating to them now. Kati-ma Koppana, for example, describes Finnish deities for English-speakers. Although she says that "they are really only personifications of various forces, activities and emotions", she describes them more traditionally as if they were real beings in their own right.[10]

In less organised Pagan gatherings an array of deities will be named, depending on the predilections and experiences of the individual or the group. Under the growing influence of Shamanic understanding and experience, many Pagans are (re)discovering the value of totemic or companionable animals. Alongside the invocation of deities in Pagan ceremonies there has always been invocation of elementals, earth, wind, fire and water—sometimes seen as autonomous beings in their own right, sometimes as archetypal constellations of natural phenomena. Shamanism has added a new depth to this, developing what was sometimes an elaborate symbolic system into a more profound participation in the community of a living world.

Is Paganism, therefore, a monotheistic or a polytheistic religion? Or is it possible to be an atheist Pagan? Is animism a better label for Pagans than theists? It will be no surprise by now that Pagans can

[10] Koppana (1990).

affirm all these options and more. Indeed, they can affirm several of them at once. There are certainly Pagans who reject monotheism and atheism as inherently un-Pagan. But there are also some who speak of a single deity and others who deny the real existence of all deities (though they may find some use for them as metaphors or symbols). Without denying these diversities (or the importance of diversity itself), it is possible to assert that Pagans are polytheistic, basing this on an understanding that number is the least significant aspect of this discussion, and that the nature, character and activities of deities are more interesting. If it is insisted that monotheism primarily refers to one deity and polytheism to many, then there are apparently Pagan mono-, duo-, heno-, poly- and a-theists. This is unproblematic for most Pagans, first because deities are not central to these traditions in the same way that they are for the monotheistic religions, but also because Pagans can and do accept the kind of diversity that has caused bloodshed in other religions. This is made particularly clear by one of Margot Adler's informants who celebrates the diversity of experience, saying

> This recognition that everyone has different experiences is a fundamental keystone to Paganism; it's the fundamental premise that whatever is going on out there is infinitely more complex than I can ever understand. And that make me feel very good.

As Adler comments,

> What an uncommon reaction to people's differences and how unlike the familiar reactions of fear and hostility![11]

It may be an "uncommon reaction" because polytheism is uncommon in the West. It is also true that monotheism can be incorporated into polytheism ("Yes, your one God exists, he's the son of one of our Goddesses"). Alternatively, polytheists can easily affirm the honouring of one deity among the many ("Which Goddess do you feel most inspired by?").

However, the heart of this discussion is the assertion that polytheism envisages or experiences its deities differently from the way monotheists do. Pratima Bowes argues that contrary to the opinion of most Western commentators polytheism and monotheism are not incompatible; "they embody two different outlooks on the divine, the one sees the many in the One, while the other sees One in the many."[12] Deirdre Green comments:

> If our purpose is to adore the many as manifold expressions of the splendour of the divine—particularly as these impinge on what we value in

---

[11] Adler (1986): 36.
[12] Bowes (1977): 103.

life as matters of immediate concern—we use the "language" of polytheism. If we wish, on the other hand, to seek the one principle that permeates all, we use the "language" of either monotheism or monism.[13]

Polytheism (to summarise both Bowes and Green) celebrates our everyday concerns and immediate interests, concerns and values, "such as our physical environment and social relations".[14] Monotheism evinces a concern with salvation, especially after death, and with the increase of human virtue (whether perceived as holiness, righteousness, enlightenment or moral improvement). Polytheism admires and adores ordinary life—or ordinary things as part of the glory of Life or "the all"—perhaps as a gift from deities, perhaps as important parts of the way things are and people relate. Sometimes overwhelming, unexpected and unwelcome divine interventions take place in polytheistic traditions (e.g. Greek and Hindu narratives of deities who overwhelm humans they desire sexually). Polytheistic deities can become angry if they do not receive the honour they feel they deserve or if humans seem to overstep the mark set for them. Generally, however, polytheistic deities send people back into their ordinary lives better able to live with the way things are, or more empowered to do something for themselves and their companions. Monotheistic deities tend to speak of salvation, rescue from the ordinary (not always unpleasant) world or of a system of obedience. Polytheistic deities tell us that this is our world, monotheistic ones try to take us into their world. In polytheism sacredness, value, beauty, spirituality, power and life reside in ordinary, everyday things and events as well as in strange or unusual ones. The divine is manifest more clearly in physical nature than in supernatural ways.

These generalisations are certainly true in contemporary Pagan deity-talk. Pagan deities are not intervening to give Pagans access to a more perfect world, they are not taking Pagans to a more spiritual unearthly home. They are empowering Pagans to consider themselves and their place in the web of things, to honour the richness and enhance the diversity of life. They do not demand worship and obedience though they might invite the expression of relationship, community and reciprocity in the form of gifts, offerings or, in "religious language", sacrifice. Gifts of objects (threads of wool in trees), shared food (mead poured and bread crumbled to the Earth), music (a chant, song, tune or clap to greet the spirit or guardian of a place) and posture (head bowed or raised, arms outspread, touching ground or stirring water) are common examples among different sorts of Pagans. Some Pagans

---

[13] Deirdre Green (1989): 8.
[14] Ibid.: 9.

might offer a strand of their own hair or a drop of their own body fluids (blood or saliva) as part of a ceremony. In short,

> The basic relationship between god/esses and humans is one of gifts given by each to the other.[15]

Animists and Atheists

In addition to being polytheists—however many or few deities they speak of—many Pagans are animists, asserting that everything that exists lives.[16] Words like "soul" or "spirit" are not always useful but are attempts to say what it is about something which makes it alive. Rocks do not breathe, trees do not speak English, hedgehogs do not preach sermons, mosquitoes do not seem to theorise, clouds do not seem to aspire to immortality. So what does it mean to say that they are all alive?

Animists assert that it is possible to "speak with" and "listen to" trees and hedgehogs, flowers and trout, robins and snakes, rocks and rain. The "speaking with" and the "hearing" may not be a pursuit of information, though some Pagans assert that trees are willing to communicate *in some way* things that we would otherwise be unaware of. Erazim Kohák argues that a philosopher and a tree can converse, neither exchanging information nor "decorating a putative harsh reality with poetic gingerbread" but communicating respect and exploring a

> manner of speaking which would be true to the task of sustainable dwelling at peace for humans and the world alike, a manner of speaking that would be true in the non-descriptive sense of being good.[17]

Perhaps the trees have taught philosophers what they have been teaching Pagans and children for many years: the virtue of respect, the pleasure of intimacy and the vital importance of eco-responsibility. Sadly, children are soon removed from tutelage of trees by adults— perhaps because of a deeply suppressed and feared knowledge that

> we are not bounded objects in orbit around each other, but we create ourselves in relationships with each other. We are the outcome of the intersections of our conflicts and cooperations and the influences we exert on each other.[18]

---

[15] Gundarsson (1993): 59.
[16] The *Oxford English Dictionary* misleadingly includes an insistence that there are such things as "inanimate objects" in its definition of "animism".
[17] Kohák (1993): 386.
[18] McKay (1993): 272, quoting Linda Gordon.

Like other aspects of Paganism, animism should not be considered a belief but an exercise or way of life. It is a theory which is acted on and tested out, an approach or path which is walked. Pagans act "as if" the story they tell is true: as if their deities exist, as if magic works, as if nature is worth celebrating. In doing so, they might find that the intuition or hypothesis fits; things do work this way and life is enhanced by this approach. Acting as if everything is alive and related tends to lead away from an obsession with deities and towards an interest in a wider diversity of other-than-human persons. Sometimes this can also permit a projection of human temperament on to other-than-human people. Is a hurricane "angry" or is it merely doing what hurricanes do? Were bush fires around Sydney a warning from Gaia that she is running out of patience with humanity? Rather than such discourses negating animism they should be viewed as part of the problem of finding "good" ways to relate to our environment.

Some Pagans explicitly avow the non-existence of deities, seeing them as illusory projections of human desire or insecurity. This Pagan Atheism in no way diminishes the celebration of those things in Paganism which seem to be more central than worship and theology, i.e. the celebration of nature, the land and festivals.[19]

The difficulty with Pagan animism and atheism is not with the theory but with finding adequate ways of "speaking" and "listening". More will be said about these means of communicating after further inhabitants of the Greenwood have been introduced.

Ancestors and Animals

In Pagan and other polytheistic traditions deities and ancestors are frequently indistinguishable: ancestors might become deities, and deities might act as ancestors. The dead may inhabit the Otherworld and visit this world at particular times—particularly at Samhain according to Pagan tradition.

Many Pagans share the experience of other nature-respecting people that animals form intense relationships with them. Some Pagans, for example, express a particular reverence and affinity for wolves, bears, herons or eagles and they support groups that protect or care for them. They are excited whenever they see their chosen animal, collecting emblems of it: bits of feather, tooth or fur, or representations of it in carvings or paintings. In ceremony, meditation and dreams they "become" their chosen animal. This ritual experience clearly shades into the "shamanistic" experience of animal companions, guides and totems. A "spirit" form of the chosen animal is encountered and asked

[19] Collins (1995).

for support and guidance in spirit journeys and healing. Pagan celebration is not obsessed with humanity or deities but frequently aims to include "all our relations". In introducing Circle Sanctuary, Selena Fox shows slides not only of Pagans engaging in ceremonies but also of the trees and animals which she avers are part of that community.

Faeries, Elves and others

In addition to such more or less mundane other-than-human people as herons and badgers, the Greenwood is also inhabited by those drawn from folk and faerie tales, myths and legends. These include those named faeries (by various spellings and circumlocutions) and elves. Most Pagans consider these to be inhabitants of woodlands and hidden special places. Although a few say they can be encountered in cities and towns, most agree that they have withdrawn into less human-dominated places, i.e. the Greenwood. The Victorians almost persuaded us that such beings are diminutive and cute. Tolkien permitted a grander, more noble vision of proud and powerful if elusive inhabitants of the twilight and fringes of the world, but his elves are not at home in human-centred Middle Earth, and there is always a poignant sense of homesickness and loss about them. Even while celebrating they observe places and people who they aid in a lordly, indulgent and even condescending way. These are not, in the end, the elves of earlier tradition, native to their forests and fringe lands. They are not the tricksters and kidnappers of Irish folklore, of Thomas the Rhymer and Tam Lin or the hidden arrow firing human foes of Scandinavian and Anglo-Saxon tradition. Tolkien opened the way to a revalidation of belief in faerie (whether as literature or as dwellers in the land), but he also sent people back to the traditions of Ireland, Norway, Britain and elsewhere to find more ancestral understandings.

Beliefs and intuitions, expectations and desires lead to experiences or the understanding of experiences. Stories not only narrate events, they also create them. Pagans often say that they know of places where these denizens of myth actually live. In the Greenwood strange things happen: well-known woodlands become maze-like labyrinths, conjunctions of bough and branch reveal and hide watchers, candles cast light like bonfires, incense billows like mist, hares and owls trace meaningful paths, flutes are heard, sudden breezes reveal the passage of unseen travellers and some have seen the faerie folk dance. While Pagans celebrate these things, they do not say that it is always pleasant to be misdirected through a wood or that being certain of the presence of faerie is a safe thing. Terry Pratchett has reminded his readers of a more ancestral understanding:

Elves are wonderful. They provoke wonder. Elves are marvellous. They cause marvels... Elves are terrific. They beget terror... No-one ever said elves are *nice*. Elves are *bad*.[20]

This "badness" is not conceived by contemporary Pagans as moral evil, or implacable antagonism to humanity or anyone else. It is rather that, as in Pratchett's story, "they" (it is traditional not to name them too many times) are not us. Their difference manifests itself in a carelessness about what is good for us. Just as we treat hedgehogs badly—running them over on our roads in appalling numbers without malice or intention—they, "the lords and ladies", treat us badly. They are one indigenous European version of the trickster: doing antisocial and dangerous things. Sometimes, however, the tricks result in an increase of wealth, health and happiness: gold is found at the end of the rainbow in stories, Pagans find they are not alone in honouring the land in festivals.

The elves or faerie are not alone in the Greenwood. They encounter not only trees, insects, animals and visiting humans, but also innumerable other people known to us in folklore, myth and legend. There are dwarves and trolls below the ground, and mermaids and selkies in the water, unicorns tread the whirlwinds, and dragons manifest all four elements. Whether these people have "real" existence or are "just" characters in enchanting stories depends on which Pagans you ask, the experience they have, and your ability to tell the difference between stories which entertain and stories which empower. For some Pagans there is no difference, and the distinction between "Reality" and "Imagination" is a false one.

Hobgoblins and foul fiends

Tolkien followed a common Western theme in dividing the world into competing light and dark halves, represented by his "good guys" (elves, hobbits and most humans) and "bad guys" (orcs, dragons, spiders and some magicians). Despite the power of this narrative and accusations of Satanism, Pagans do not share this kind of ontological dualism. The faerie may not be "nice", deities may not be "nice", but no one said that they should be. Humans are not "nice" either. These divisions and the attachment of degrees of animosity and moral superiority to the neutral fact of difference are unnecessary projections.

What is wrong with the world is not that there is something demonic out there perverting what is good and sowing seeds of destruction. Nor is it that the world is too material, or a trap for pure spirit. Pagans explain the wrongness either as a lack of balance—primarily in human

[20] Pratchett (1993): 169-70.

activities, especially their exploitation of the land—or as a breakdown in humanity's relationships with the rest of the web of life. The former of these views may be cognate with a form of Taoism, the latter with the "flower sharing" (or related reciprocity) of Yaqui tradition.²¹ What is certainly true is that Christian dualisms are being shaken off and should not be imposed again on those who do not have a place for a devil or for sin, salvation, grace, worship and heaven in their cosmology.

Pagans in the Greenwood

What do Pagans do in the Greenwood? What, in other words, is the point of Pagan deity-talk? It is not to determine or impose correct belief or even correct practice, but is best seen as a threefold process of enchantment, etiquette and exuberance.

Pagan cosmology re-enchants the world. Pagans talk about deities and faeries not because they "believe" in them but because they take seriously the intimation of many cultures that the world is inhabited not only by animals, vegetables and minerals but also by less commonly seen people. The world is an exciting and sacred place to live.

In Pagan cosmologies the role of these other-than-human people who are seen only rarely by either human people or hedgehog people is not to receive praise and thanksgiving but to relate. They live independent lives, much as any other species does, with their own unique abilities and inabilities. They have a niche in the scheme of things. Part of their relationship with humanity is to remind us that we are not alone and to show us that just as moles might lead excellent mole lives and Goddesses might lead excellent divine lives, so we should lead excellent human lives. This would mean doing what we do well within the web of life, perhaps living up to the aphorisms "Love and do what you will" or "An it harm none, do as you will". It might mean recognising that current human lifestyles do too much violence to those with whom we share the Earth and that we must find more respectful ways of relating. The violence of eating so many living beings must be reduced. The violence of destroying habitats to make economic life simpler or transport marginally swifter must be ended. Divine beings might educate humanity in the etiquette of sharing a densely inhabited small planet. Unlike the visiting deities of other religions they might remind us that we are at home in Earth.

Deity-talk in Paganism encourages an exuberant celebration of human living. Rather than rejecting the body and its gendered realities for a more "spiritual" existence, Pagans experience their deities and

²¹ See Morrison (1992b): 217.

other companions as revitalising and revalidating imagination, intuition, sensuality, sexuality and many other human characteristics. This, rather than wickedness or stupidity, explains why Pagans and other polytheists can image their deities in material form and expect them to "take up residence" in that image. As the physical is the manifestation of divine life, it would be foolish to denigrate matter.[22]

Similarly, this exuberant affirmation of life might also explain why blasphemy is not recognised in the linguistic currency of Paganism. If Pagans usually speak with deep reverence for their deities, totems and others, they can just as easily tell salacious and comical stories about them. Pagans still enjoy old Norse stories of Thor's drunkenness and Irish stories of the sexual and gustatory prowess of the Daghdha. Deities are honoured for their involvement in life, not only for displaying their pre-eminence in revealing the truth behind things.

Theology within Ecology

The world is inhabited not only by human beings but also by a vast variety of other beings, e.g. hedgehogs, oaks, trout, mosquitoes, potatoes and flu viruses. Folk tradition suggests that there are also a number of other species, not known to science, who share the planet with us. The names given to these beings vary from tradition to tradition, but include the faery, dwarves, elves, trolls, land-spirits, boggarts, brownies, genii loci and others. Then there are those beings accorded the status of deity. Some religions have experts (i.e. theologians) who insist that there is only one deity who, they claim, is "beyond gender"—but then give the game away by insisting that God is "he". Others claim to have experience of many deities, both male and female, Gods and Goddesses. Typically, a singular deity maintains some distance from Earth, occasionally intervening in "miraculous" (i.e. non-natural) ways or perhaps verbally. Polytheistic deities are distinguishable not only by number (and gender) from these monotheistic deities; they differ also in kind and habitat. These plural Goddesses and Gods can best be seen as part of the natural environment. The distinction between transcendence and immanence (distance from or proximity to matter, Earth or humanity) is again of little value in polytheism or Paganism: deities can be immanent in as much as they are experienced in the full array of life experiences and at the same time transcendent in that they are autonomous people in their own right. Sometimes they get involved with other species and sometimes they withdraw into their own private habitations. Therefore, in addition to labels like polytheist and animist, Pagans might accept

[22] Cp. Miranda Green (1989).

names like pantheist or panentheist.[23] They will rarely fit into neat categories or tidy boxes, but this is a familiar scene in the study of religions even if it causes problems to theologians.

A contemporary myth might suggest that deities evolved along with all other life on the planet and are equally threatened by the ecological devastation many humans fear and deplore. Polytheists do not deny the underlying unity of life, or the singularity of the planet which itself can be seen as a (or the) Goddess or, more rarely, the God. Polytheism is not fundamentally a question of numbers of deities or of their distance from non-divine life. It is, rather, a concern with the many and varied relationships between living things. It is an affirmation of the importance, beauty and absorbing engagement with ordinary everyday life. It allows both presence and absence, approach and distance, privacy, intimacy and mystery, companionship and detachment.

If ecology is the study of the home in which we and other Earth-dwelling species live, we might be reminded that our name, "humanity", is rooted in the organic, life-giving earthy *humus*. A *humanus* is an "earth-dweller".[24] Presented with the spectacle of ecological devastation and species extinction, people often say "What can I do?". This is sometimes said with despair and justifies passive voyeurism. Religions can function as opiates distracting people from engagement with the difficulties, realities and pleasures of their situations. They can also provide powerful inspirations, influxes or flows of spirit, life, vitality or energy. They can powerfully engage the desire and will to do something. Talk about deities in Paganism does not function to direct attention away from earthly reality but sends people back to engagement and intimacy. Talk about deities does not take place in an ivory tower—there are no professional Pagan theologians, few who would wish to take on that role, and fewer still who would accept them if they tried. Deities are not the centre of Paganism as they are of some religions but one of the many species of living being inhabiting the Earth. Although they may not be *seen* as often as the postman, Pagan deities are equally commonplace. Starhawk speaks for many Pagans in saying,

> People often ask me if I believe in the Goddess. I reply, "Do you believe in rocks?".[25]

As deities are part of the ecology of the Earth, so Pagan deity-talk (theology, thealogy or theoilogy) is a category within Pagan ecology.

---

[23] Carpenter (1996): 50-3.
[24] Buttimer (1993): 3.
[25] Starhawk (1989): 91.

11

HISTORY, SOURCES AND INFLUENCES

Things just happen, one after another. They don't care who knows. But
history... ah, history is different. History has to observed.[1]

Paganism draws inspiration from many wells. It has created and
developed an identity from many threads which it has woven into
patterns at once original and familiar. This chapter does not present the
true history of contemporary Paganism, but is interested in history as
one important source among others from which Pagans derive their
spirituality and self-understanding.

In developing this interest in history as one source of identity it
resists the temptation to treat history as a source of legitimacy. Some
people believe that a religion "founded" a long time ago is acceptable,
one "made up" in this century is not. Roots "deep" in the ancient past
are boasted of, whereas ones entwined with the concerns of the
contemporary world are an embarrassment. Some Pagans have
accepted this fallacious view of history, authority and legitimacy and
have bolstered their claims to be a "real religion" by stressing alleged
continuities from antiquity rather than celebrating the many aspects of
their traditions which address issues of great interest to their
contemporaries. It is more than likely this approach to the issue of
legitimacy derives largely from a response to challenges from
"outside". Christians and the media have at times seemed particularly
concerned with "historical" validity in religious traditions. Sometimes
the academic label "New Religious Movements" has been taken to
mean that groups identified in this way are less serious, respectable,
spiritual or valid than longer established traditions. I will note later that
conflicts between Pagan traditions, Odinism and Wicca in this case,
often express themselves in terms of "we are the old religion and you
are not". Without such misdirected attacks on self-identity and self-
development by particular religions and groups it is unlikely that
anyone would have thought that the passing of time alone could bestow
legitimacy. There are many Pagans for whom history is only one
among many wells from which to draw refreshment, inspiration, vision
and wisdom. Other sources include archaeology, anthropology,
literature, science, politics, ecology, folklore, imagination, intuition,
experience, personalities, festivals and films. Such a rich diet has
nurtured a profligate growth and diversity of traditions, groups and

[1] Terry Pratchett, *Small Gods*. (1992): 6. (*1994): 6.

characters. It is this growth which is of interest here. While origins are interesting, they are rarely the most significant aspect of a religion's formation, identity or character.[2] The fruits of a tradition are found not in its roots but at the end of its many branches and present manifestations.

To discover how Paganism became what it is today this discussion explores some of the experiences, predispositions, events, groups, books, traumas and ambitions commonly cited by Pagans when asked "What led you to become or to identify yourself as a Pagan?" Further detail arises from more specific questions about choices among particular Pagan paths: Druid, Witch, Heathen, Shaman or Magician.[3]

History and Folklore

Ronald Hutton has identified four "direct lines of connection" between ancient Paganism and the present. These are

> high ritual magic, "hedge" witchcraft, the general love affair of the Christian centuries with the art and literature of the ancient world, and folk rites.[4]

This disciplined exploration of the links between the Paganisms of the past and the present contrasts with the earlier prevailing academic wisdom which provided a major impetus to the rebirth of Paganism.

In 1921 and 1933 Margaret Murray presented, in elaborate detail, what was really happening in the early modern witch trials: a confrontation between Christianity and the last surviving members of a pan-European rural fertility cult. Her vision of Paganism was built on the works of James Frazer and his contemporaries, which in turn drew on a long-cherished theory that folk customs and rituals derive from the ancient Pagan past. Her book *The God of the Witches*[5] clearly resonated with something in the spirit of the age. The first Wiccan covens can be described as embodying Murray's "carefree and natural" pre-Christian religion of northern Europe.[6] Such groups were not content to leave the "information" about such religions stored away in academic literature. Folk customs (as ancient survivals) could be revived and combined with more modern manifestations like naturism, in which communal nudity expressed both self-respect and harmony with nature. When blended with initiatory or Craft traditions akin to Freemasonry, Rosicrucianism, Druidry (not Pagan at this time), Woodcraft Chivalry

---

[2] Smart (1993).
[3] See chapters devoted to these traditions.
[4] Hutton (1996a): 4.
[5] Murray (1933).
[6] Hutton (1996a): 12.

and Kibbo Kift, these once academic imaginings became the earliest forms of self-identified contemporary Paganism.[7] At around the same time, in the same geographical area and in the same kind of groups, others discovered the importance of their Saxon ancestry and began the revival of Heathen tradition. The Nazi sympathies of some significant people in the inception of this tradition, such as Alexander Rud Mills, are well documented.[8] Ásatrúar continue to struggle with ideological racism, some trying to root it out of the movement, others presenting it or re-visioning it as a celebration of natural human racial diversity, i.e. as "race-love" not as "race-hate". Jeffrey Kaplan discusses the usage by white supremacists of aspects of the tradition, but notes that Christianity is far from immune to these problems.[9]

The academic disproof of the thesis that early modern witches were Pagans has begun to change the story most Pagans tell about their antecedents, but it has not destroyed their identity or their sense of connection to earlier generations. Perhaps the myth sustained the emerging spirituality until it reached the mature position of being able to survive without claiming direct and continuous descent throughout the ages. This is not to disguise the fact that a significant number of Pagans do still assert that the "witches" were Pagans, that there is an unbroken chain of tradition through particular families or clans from Neolithic, Celtic, Saxon or Norse settlers in Britain to today. Some angrily dismiss requests for evidence, and dismiss historically based arguments as prejudice. The evidence offered by others is questionable, for example, the use of a forked staff or stang which is claimed by some to be a sign of a real hereditary Craft tradition seems to derive from Arkon Daraul's 1962 description of the North African Dhulqarneni tradition.[10] Others have accepted that while Paganism is a new religion, it revives more ancient ways of living and believing. They can then explore history in a far more disciplined way.[11]

If a particular constellation of beliefs about folklore and witchcraft provided the impetus for the rebirth of Paganism, the development of the religion made considerable use of various literary sources.

Mythology, Archaeology and Anthropology

Ancient and medieval literature is particularly important among the sources on which Pagans draw for the building of their identities and the creation of their rituals. Druids read ancient writers such as Caesar,

---

[7] See Hutton (1996a) and Kelly (1991).
[8] See Kaplan (1996) for discussion and bibliography.
[9] Kaplan (1996): especially 208.
[10] Baker (1996): 187.
[11] See Jones and Pennick (1995).

and are aware of what historians say about them. They read archaeological reports on ancient sites and finds from the pagan past. They might visit these sites as pilgrims, erect stone circles in their gardens and incorporate reproduction jewellery or musical instruments such as the Bronze Age dord, or more recent harps and lyres, into their ceremonies. They invoke deities whose names have long been buried in the rubble of ruined temples. Many Pagans understand the medieval Welsh *Mabinogion* as a record of pre-Christian Iron Age myths and life. They re-tell these stories, enact them in seasonal dramas and portray episodes from them in illustrations for their magazines. Most Heathens are well aware that much of the literature on which they draw, especially the Eddas and Sagas, was written by Christians. This does not invalidate it as a source of pre-Christian understandings about deities, fate, the structure of the cosmos and so on, but it does require careful and critical reading. This can lead to a diversity of interpretations which are not always compatible. For example, some Heathens consider Odin's epithet "All-father" to be a late Christianisation of his role in a complex pantheon and therefore deny him pre-eminence among the deities they honour. Even more than the Druids, Heathens explore the potential for producing costume and liturgy out of this literature. Hammers replicating Thor's tool/weapon, mjölnir, were used in weddings, funerals and house dedications and as pendants. Heathens have revived the traditions of using hammers as eloquent symbols in their ceremonies and of wearing pendants to advertise or celebrate their identity.

A particularly close relationship exists between academic literature and those to whom Matriarchy is empowering. Both those who present "Herstory" and Matriarchy[12] as historical facts and those who understand them to be empowering myths for now and the future, rely heavily on academics such as the archaeologist Marija Gimbutas and a host of feminist thealogians and scholars of religion. Archaeologists recover material not seen since pre-history, interpreters argue about the cultures in which it played a role and such work is made available to those who are concerned with finding alternatives to prevailing male dominance. Alongside artefacts there is ancient Goddess literature to be recovered, interpreted and applied to today. One popular text is that of the descent of the Sumerian Goddess Innana into the Underworld.[13] However this myth functioned in its original context, it has now been re-contextualised to enable women to "face their dark side" in therapeutic contrast to their devaluation in patriarchy.[14] It also performs

---

[12] See chapter 5.
[13] Wolkstein and Kramer (1983).
[14] Perera (1981).

a major role in Starhawk's more openly political exploration of this theme.[15]

For information, inspiration and expression of beliefs about life after death, the Otherworld, deities, faery and elven folk and the workings of fate and nature, Pagans refer to Celtic, Norse and other ancient literatures. Pagans also make considerable use of anthropological sources to make up for the lack of Nature-respecting traditions in Western thought and lifestyle. This is most obviously the case with Shamanism, but anthropology books and TV documentaries are also significant in providing inspiration for new or alternative ways of doing ritual, greeting other-than-human people and developing healing techniques.

First Nations

Understandings gained directly from indigenous peoples have also affected the self-understanding of many Pagans. As Paganism abandoned medieval witches as ancestors or forerunners (though sometimes continuing to honour them as victims of religious and/or male violence),[16] they increasingly looked to existing First Nation peoples as close kin. Many of the themes and techniques evident in the revitalisation of such communities are also evident among Pagans, and their development perhaps follows a similar chronology. As North American First Nations were making use of gatherings (or pow wows) and sweat lodges to recover and encourage a sense of self-worth and celebration, so Pagans were developing a round of festivals. Sacred fires and drumming, albeit in very different styles—Pagans seem to prefer a more African style of drumming—are only the most obvious similarities between the two types of gathering. These gatherings also provide one context in which Pagans and First Nation peoples encounter one another without the mediation of academics or the media. Although there are still considerable tensions about White appropriation and consumerism, real friendships and mutuality have emerged from such encounters.

Fantasy and Future Fiction

Academic literature is undoubtedly important in the construction of Paganism, but Tolkien's *Lord of the Rings* and other Fantasy writings are more frequently mentioned by Pagans. Fantasy re-enchants the world for many people, allowing them to talk of elves, goblins, dragons, talking-trees and magic. It also encourages contemplation of

[15] Starhawk (1990).
[16] See Barstow (1988).

different ways of relating to the world, the use and abuse of power (especially as expressed in and by magic), and issues of race, gender and sexuality. It counters the rationality of modernity which denigrates the wisdoms of the body and subjectivity. Alongside Future Fiction, the genre explores new and archaic understandings of the world, and of ritual and myth, and attempts to find alternative ways of relating technology to the needs of today.

Tolkien's works are not Pagan in intention or ethos and their resolution of the "good" and "evil" dualism does not fit easily with Pagan visions of the world. His writing remained Christian and patriarchal, but led beyond typically Christian myths and encouraged others to go further. For example, Guy Gavriel Kay, who was partly responsible for completing Tolkien's work, produced his own trilogy, *The Fionavar Tapestry* (*The Summer Tree, The Wandering Fire* and *The Darkest Road*), in which less omniscient and therefore more Pagan deities meet with dragons, unicorns and a diversity of human cultures in a more recognisably Pagan tale. Many Pagans have found these books more emotionally satisfying. They also appreciate Kay's exploration of different sorts and sources of magic and power; for example, there are tensions and co-operations between magicians, priests, shamans and seers as well as between warriors and pacifists. Similarly, many of Ursula Le Guin's works explore themes of importance to Pagans, especially to those who engage in magic.[17] They inculcate responsible use of power, rather than purely self-centred motivations, and reinforce the idea that, far from being destructive, fears faced and darkness explored can lead to considerable personal growth. Le Guin's writings are more holistic than Tolkien's, and explore more radical social and personal alternatives to contemporary life. Issues of gender and sexuality are an important part of her writing: it is telling that there are more significant women in Le Guin's works that in Tolkien's.

Margot Adler explores the impact of Ayn Rand and Robert Heinlein on many Pagans and especially on the formation of the Church of All Worlds (CAW).[18] What was gained from these writers—apart from the general romance and heroism of an alternative vision or even lifestyle—was the importance of a libertarian blend of individualism and communitarianism, and of personal responsibility, life-affirmation and especially of intuitive and empathetic knowledge for which the term "grok" was coined.

Fantasy writers have frequently taken traditional folktales as the centre of their new storytelling. For example, Alan Garner's earlier

---

[17] Especially see her Earthsea Quartet: Le Guin (1993).
[18] Adler (1986): 283-99.

writings, *The Wierdstone of Brisingamen* and *The Moon of Gomrath*, combine Cheshire folklore, the larger mythologies of Britain and north-west Europe and the magical and geomantic imagination of today. His *The Owl Service* is perhaps the most powerful contemporary re-telling of a *Mabinogion* story, "Math son of Mathonwy". To these books which many Pagans read as children and rediscovered again as adults, even visiting the locations of the tales, he has now added *The Strandloper* which links Cheshire folk-custom and Aboriginal Australian ways of evoking and singing the land. This might be seen as the fruit of the contemporary fascination with Aboriginal ways of relating to places and is likely to inspire further Pagan celebration of chanting and ritual approaches to nature.

Every generation finds new ways to tell the tales of King Arthur, the Matter of Britain. Pagans frequently refer to Marion Bradley's *The Mists of Avalon* and John Boorman's film *Excalibur*. Neither of these is entirely consistent in keeping to one historical setting, but both evoke worlds attractive to Pagans. Bradley's version is especially important as an expression of a women-centred, perhaps feminist-inspired, spirituality.[19] It is almost unique in focusing on the roles played by women in these tales. The central character Morgaine, elsewhere known as Morgan Le Fay, is portrayed as a priestess of the Goddess struggling against rising patriarchy and Christianity. She also struggles to affirm herself, her vision and her embodiedness. Boorman's film is especially noted for its portrayal of Merlin and his powerful description of the dragon as Earth,

> a beast of such power that if you were to see it whole and all complete in a single glance it would burn you to cinders. Its scales glisten in the bark of trees, its roar is heard in the wind and its forked tongue strikes... like lightning.

In many Fantasy works nature can be passive or nurturing. In others, and especially in some Future Fiction, nature is an aggressive alien presence to be fought against or resisted. Merlin reveals that although the coils of the dragon/nature can be dangerous to humanity, they are also our home, source of our life and vitality.

Going far beyond Tolkienesque derivatives, Robert Holdstock's *Mythago Wood*[20] and its sequels take readers deep into the shadowy and sometimes terrifying labyrinth of the Greenwood. For Pagans these books resonate with experiences in which woods become maze-like and things glimpsed at the edge of sight, tricks of shade and light, and meetings of branch and bough transmute themselves into elusive woodland spirits. There is also a quality in Holdstock's storytelling

[19] See Leonard (1990); Harvey (1993) and Grey (1992).
[20] Holdstock (1984).

which is evocative of tales told around Pagan festival fires. Although some Pagans (re-)enact Tolkien episodes and name festivals (e.g. Lothlorien) after locations in his epics, his work rarely strays far from a book-lined study. With Holdstock there are terrors to encounter, enchantment to be entranced by, and a journey to be made in Imagination which forcibly affects journeys in woodlands and river-valleys.

These books, a small selection of the Fantasy genre of importance to Pagans, join the mythopoetic works of previous generations as resources for the Pagan renaissance. They are quoted or alluded to alongside phrases from Kipling's *Puck of Pook's Hill*, Graves' *White Goddess*, Wagner's operas, and earlier evocations of the Moon and other manifestations of deity from Romantic poets, Irish, Welsh, Norse and Finnish epics and Scottish or Breton poetry. It is significant that the primary literature of Paganism is neither theology, textbooks nor "how to do it" manuals but fiction. For example, Gerald Gardner's first Pagan publication, *High Magick's Aid*, and Dion Fortune's *The Sea Priestess*, may not be "great literature" but they evoke Paganism more adequately than later more didactic works. They suggest the kind of thing that these foundational figures thought Paganism should be, describe the training and use of Magic(k), and portray the kind of deities honoured and re-enchanted the world for their readers. Similarly, Brian Bates' *The Way of Wyrd* and William Gibson's *Neuromancer* have been as influential in the varying Pagan understandings and practice of Shamanism as anthropological treatises.[21]

Reading these works encourages the expression of imagination and creativity, diversity and humour. This is linked to the playfulness of most Pagan ritual drama and deity-talk which is alien from the seriousness and doctrinal correctness of much religious liturgy. Pagans are well aware that much of the literature that inspires and entertains them is fictional and even blatantly fantastic. Those who do rituals inspired by *Star Trek* or the comic strip *Bloom County*, now *Outland*,[22] celebrate such playfulness. Paradoxically, perhaps, this playfulness has a serious dimension: it enables the development and expression of self- and group identity. Of course, the line between this playful entry into Imagination and escape into "mere fantasy" is thin. It would be naive to assert that Pagans are never escapist, and do not sometimes retreat into cosy romanticism rather ' than face unpleasant facts of late modernity such as the continuing rape and abuse of women and nature. It is equally unrealistic to expect anyone to refuse to turn aside from

[21] Bates (1983); Gibson (1995).
[22] Magliocco (1996):107-8.

stark and disempowering scenes at least once in a while. The anti-nuclear and road protests combine exceptional artistic and joyful expression with focused confrontation and direct action. Healing rituals drawing on a wide array of therapies combine powerful theatrical drama with sympathetic tenderness. Fantasy and fiction can allow people to find a vision and a voice and bring the whole of themselves to fuller participation in life, rather than merely intellectual or emotional political engagement. It does not offer facts for consideration but truths to inspire or beauty to appreciate, and thus subverts the dominance of the modernist idea that everything is given, set and bounded. Fantasy says that things are not always as they seem and can change, and that this is especially true for readers and hearers of these tales.

Discworld

It would be inexcusable to attempt a description of Paganism without referring to Terry Pratchett's Discworld series. Not all Pagans enjoy Pratchett's humour but most recognise his portrayal of Pagans as bearing similarities to themselves or their friends. A thoroughly Pagan world is frequently evoked in the Discworld—with its deities, its ordinary magic, animism, frequent synchronicities and meaningful encounters, its general earthiness, enchantment and diversity, the literalness of its metaphors, its personified Death, and countless other details. However, more than all of this, it is the style of Pratchett's writing that is most Pagan. There is an easy shift between seriousness and humour, ritual and play, profundity and profanity, that is recognisable among other nature religions, as anyone who has heard masters of ceremonies at First Nation pow wows will know. Deities can be invoked in a ceremony in which they are expected to take no more part than the human participants. Jokes can be made about them without the thought that this might be blasphemy. People are encouraged to experiment with different ways of doing things, with different approaches to deities, festivals, stories and the whole complexity of tradition. Other religions encourage firm commitment, and discourage "dabbling", being unable completely to accept experimentation in religion or the ease with which many people now make up their own spiritual traditions. Paganism not only accepts this but it encourages it.[23] Among the sources of Pagan identity, imagination, intuition, experimentation and experience are central.

[23] Feyerabend (1985): 19.

Pratchett is not unique as a comic source. Some Gallic Druids observed roaring at the sky were at least partly inspired by the hearty Paganism of characters from *Asterix the Gaul*.[24]

Nature

What attracts most people to Paganism is the recognition that it is a nature spirituality. Some have been creating an ecological lifestyle and now want to bring their spirituality into line with it, or they want a spirituality which will better express their environmentalism. Others have been finding that they feel most "at home" or most spiritual, inspired, alive or aware while in the forest, by the sea or among the hills. Then they discover that they are not alone in this and are part of a large family of people who name themselves Pagan. Thus Paganism functions as both an expression and an incitement to greater environmental awareness and action.

More than this, Nature itself is formative of the character of Paganism. The cycles of the seasons and relationships between all the related inhabitants of the Earth dictate regular occasions on which Pagans celebrate and contemplate the life of their environment, of the whole Earth, of particular places and of themselves in relation to them. The emotive aspect comes before the intellectual, the celebration before the contemplation, the ceremony before the meaning. The festivals reveal the cyclical nature of time and the facts of life—change, growth, maturity, breeding, decline, decay—and provide the context for explorations of the joys and sadness of embodied life. Pagans are directed to fit their individual and social lives into a "scheme of things" dictated by what the planet, the moon, sun and stars are doing. The individual human life encapsulates Nature's life: they are respectively microcosm and macrocosm.

Intimacy with the land directs the Pagan's experience of nature. It is also insistent that Paganism earths itself in the physical, that it does not become Gnostic but celebrates embodied life. It reveals the "place" of humanity as part of nature, and refuses to offer the Earth to humanity as gift or as responsibility. It regularly, easily reminds Pagans that they are not the sole inhabitants of the planet, but are linked physically, emotionally, spiritually, ecologically and in every other way with "all our relations". If celebrating the seasons inculcates understanding of the "temporality" of life, the celebration of the land teaches the "spatiality" of life.[25] Fundamentally these encounters with the land, its

[24] Andy Letcher, personal communication.
[25] For an important discussion of spatiality and temporality, see Jung (1988).

seasons and its inhabitants teaches the centrality of relationship and mutuality.

Embodied reality is authoritative in Paganism because it is the location in which people explore "reality". Models of divinity, "the meaning of life" and religion are worked out in everyday life. Birth, menstruation, eating, drinking, making love, getting angry, being hurt, growing older and growing old, learning, forgetting—these and all other aspects of people's ordinary lives are not divorced in Paganism from the lives of other-than-human people (however exalted they might be). They are also significant as manifestations of the divine. Deities and humans share similar experiences, similar cycles, similarly authoritative lives.

Paganism is not a revealed, scriptural, priestly, supernatural or dogmatic religion. Its chief sources of authority are in Nature: the observable cycles of the planet and the experienced cycles of the body. Paganism is formed by Pagans observing and experiencing these things and then evolving forms in which they can be celebrated.

Christian writers have alleged that honouring Nature is an insufficient foundation for religion or life because Nature includes violence and brutality. C.S.Lewis alleged that

> confronted with a cancer or a slum the Pantheist can say, "If you could only see it from the divine point of view, you would see that this also is God". The Christian replies, "Don't talk damned nonsense".[26]

Harold Wood politely calls this a "misunderstanding of the nature of pantheism". Pantheism is

> simply a religious teaching which does not separate humans from nature, nor the divine from natural processes.[27]

Such "processes" include eating and other forms of violence—including cancer (though perhaps not slums). To honour nature involves finding a place for such things in an understanding of the world—but not necessarily a passive acceptance, pleasure or celebration. Mary Oliver's poetry and Annie Dillard's prose provide fine examples of finding meaning in these unpleasant facts of life.[28] Having observed life (including death and violence), Pagans are not encouraged or commanded to imitate anything or anyone else. They might accept that something is part of life or nature but cannot therefore say "And I can (or should) do the same". Pagan ethics are not derived from theology (or thealogy) but from relationships with "all

[26] Lewis (1943): 33-4.
[27] Wood (1985): 161.
[28] Oliver (1986); Dillard (1976).

our relations". Nature is authoritative not as a model to observe but as a web of relationships in which to engage.

Experience and Intuition

A Pagan sitting on a hillside, gazing into a fire or a pool, walking in a forest, swimming with dolphins or living in a threatened tree is likely to have similar experiences to members of other religions. Their interpretations of these experiences, however, will often be different and such interpretations will sometimes lead to different experiences. Religious experiences notoriously confirm the veracity of whatever beliefs a person holds. Those who pray receive answers. Those who fast for visions see visions. Those who go on pilgrimage are spiritually uplifted. Those who sing hymns experience the closeness of their deity or spiritual helper. Miracles take place in many religions and effective healing is unique to none.

Pagans assert that they have experiences which confirm their understandings of the world. They might, for example, assert that sitting on hillsides, gazing into fires and pools and so on are significant religious experiences in their own right. They are not merely recreational, or rather, their being recreational (re-creational) is an important part of their spirituality. The discovery of a pile of firewood immediately after an hour of fruitless searching has culminated in a request to the woodland or deities for help seems a fairly characteristic Pagan experience. Being tripped over by something invisible after failing to ask permission to cut a tree is also far from rare. Owls and eagles seem to delight in flying in circles around Pagan festival fires— as they do around Native American ones. Animals of particular significance to an individual are more often encountered in the company of that person that otherwise. Someone who is enacting the role of Odin or another deity often appears to be transformed into the likeness of that deity—which is particularly startling when the deity and the actor are of different gender, build and demeanour.

In addition to experiences of this kind, which appear to confirm the validity and effectiveness of Paganism if not the veracity of its interpretations, another sort of experience is formative of Pagan identity. Paganism takes into consideration people's ordinary lived reality, their embodied experience and spatiality. It does not require a valuable "religious experience" to be "numinous" or revelatory of the supernatural, un-human world.[29] What is significant to women and men is significant in Paganism and not only what is desired or rejected by deities. Sexuality, ageing, menstruation, laughter, anger and other

[29] Cf. Raphael (1994).

aspects of natural life-cycles are incorporated into Pagan spirituality and not separated from it into less valuable or less spiritual domains.

Paganism encourages an experimental approach to life, tending to treat beliefs and interpretations as changeable and secondary—and sometimes ignoring the extent to which they affect the experiences and actions which it values. Treating an explanation "as if" it were true unless or until a better story is offered is perhaps a more postmodern version of "belief" than fundamentalist or theological assertions of certainty based on claimed revelation. What seems to be important is that something happens, some action results.

Alongside experience Pagans value intuition. An interpretation of an ancient site or artefact, a way of speaking to or about a deity may be said to "feel right". The character and purpose of a place can be intuited from moods evoked in visitors. Sometimes individuals will celebrate festivals, especially the ones at quarter-days marking the beginning of seasons, both when they feel attuned to its resonances and also in communal gatherings timed according to traditional dates. Pagans experiment with ways of addressing deities and can assert that their intuition provides them with appropriate words or gestures.

Intuition is enhanced by meditation and by study, both of which might be thought of as offering possibilities for consideration. Participation in groups might be thought of as a means of gathering insights to feed Imagination and encourage effective intuition. Knowing the attributes and typical activities of particular deities might, for example, enable greater engagement with a place which seems to be named after that deity, such as Baldersby or Grims Ditch. Discovering that there are others who share one's seemingly eccentric attachment to places incites greater attention to what happens there. Groups can also be valuable contexts for developing skills of meditation and contemplation, of energy recognition, raising, focusing and harnessing.

Beyond the Enlightenment

The anthropologist Howard Eilberg-Schwartz has noted the common features of the "ideology and rhetoric" of Paganism and the discourses of the Enlightenment, modernity and postmodernity.[30] He argues that Paganism arose from the intellectual programme of the Enlightenment and offers a critique of modernity that points towards post-modernity. Having noted that both Pagans and Enlightenment philosophers appeal to pagan antiquity and criticise Christianity and Judaism (as they understand them), he explores further similarities. Both encourage the celebration of nature, and although they view nature very differently,

[30] Eilberg-Schwartz (1989).

those differences arise from the Enlightenment itself. The problems of modernity are rooted in human alienation from nature and are particularly expressed in hierarchical, power-over social structures which disempower both individuals and communities. Both traditions perceive divine revelation and scriptures as further abuses of power, denying human autonomy and self-worth. The Enlightenment offered Reason as a means of empowering individuals, who all had equal access to "the truth". Pagans do not share this veneration of reason— certainly not to the detriment of other ways of knowing and being—but do share similar ideological aversion to the power structures they see as inherent in monotheism. Eilberg-Schwartz suggests:

> The turn to ancient paganism as a source of inspiration is itself one of the moves that made the modern world possible.

He argues that the use of the word "Witch" as a self-designation is also dependent on the Enlightenment's "dismantling of differences and the interiorization of Otherness": the process by which we discover that the "Other" is in reality much like ourselves. The "savage" is little different from the cultured urbanite, the "witch" is a fearful victim rather than a fearful villain. Pagans are like anthropologists in being inspired to study others by the belief that doing so leads to self-understanding. Eilberg-Schwartz says that they take anthropological rhetoric more seriously in that they are willing to "go native" rather than simply return from "the field" to the study unchanged.

If Paganism arose from the Enlightenment it also offers a critique of modernity. It says that it is not enough to dethrone a dominating deity and his authoritarian priests only to replace them with Reason and equally lofty intellectuals. It offers polytheism with its pluralist and tolerant diversity as a more complete criticism of dogmatic religion and authority. Nor does Reason function very well in liberating humanity; rather it alienates people from other ways of knowing such as imagination, spirituality, emotion, subjectivity and sensuality. Reason elevates one form of narrative above myth, poetry, ritual and fiction. In disenchanting the world, the Enlightenment alienated humanity from itself, its communities and its place in nature. Experimentation and exploration, not certainty, are closer to the heart of the Pagan enterprise. Those Pagans who continue to assert that they have a long, unbroken lineage which legitimises their spirituality continue, at least partly, to inhabit an Enlightenment world. The increasing trend, however, is to accept these myths as empowering but not historical, or to jettison them if they cease to be empowering. Pagan spirituality can then be legitimised according to whether it works or feels right. The criteria by which a ceremony or story can be judged to "work" vary in ways which lead beyond the Enlightenment into postmodern validation of intuition, experience, diversity, subjectivity and pluralism.

Experimentation and pragmatism are hallmarks of this spirituality. All people are authors of their own lives, authoritative in their own experience. They do not require priests or priestesses—or their secular counterparts, scientists and doctors—to tell them the truth about everything. Pagans can draw on such people, just as they can draw from many other deep and satisfying wells. Eilberg-Schwartz fails to note something fundamental to Paganism, which is that it requires a definition of "person" far wider than the human-centred semantics of modernity. Animals and trees are encountered as persons, autonomous and communicative beings, as are deities and other inhabitants of myth and folklore. Selena Fox's introduction to Circle Sanctuary includes slides of trees and glades, not as mere scene-setting but as integral members of the community which forms the place.[31] Humans are only part of the Pagan community and, equally important, they are part of the environment they inhabit.

Howard Eilberg-Schwartz concludes his argument:

neopaganism represents an attempt to create a religious form for a post-modern world... They experiment with life forms that science has decried as primitive and nonsensical. They suggest that metaphors are truth and that science fiction can be the basis for religious life. Like post-modernism, they have only one form of intolerance: other forms of life that are intolerant and authoritarian.

Old Religion or New Religion?

Some Pagans continue to consider their religion an "Old Religion" or even "*the* Old Religion". Others are happy to acknowledge that Paganism is a new religion with some ancient roots.

The Odinic Rite has questioned the legitimacy of Wicca on the grounds that Margaret Murray's work has been torn to shreds by Jacqueline Simpson.[32] However, many Wiccans had already questioned the Murray version of witchcraft without doubting the effectiveness or legitimacy of their spirituality.[33] Similarly, whether or not Gerald Gardner built on Murray's shaky foundations, using materials borrowed from nineteenth-century Masonic and Kabbalistic sources, Wiccans correctly argue that what was built was strong and sound. Gardner remains important because of the effectiveness of the techniques he disseminated, e.g. "raising energy", casting spells and creating a sense of belonging.[34] Ancient Pagans may have done nothing

---

[31] Presentation at Lancaster University Conference on Nature Religions, 1996.
[32] Simpson (1994).
[33] Adler (1986): 87.
[34] Lamond (1993): 34.

like Wiccans—for example, they did not celebrate eight annual seasonal festivals—but this does not negate the effectiveness of what Wiccans do today.

The Odinic Rite's argument, of course, is that historical accuracy is important. Its practitioners can certainly draw on better-documented understandings and excavated evidence of the ancestral religions of Britain than Murray's fictitious witchcraft does. Their polytheism is more closely related to these religions than the "Goddess and God" of Wicca. Nonetheless, the sources they use and the things they do relate more to contemporary life than to the past. They are explicit that their religion is a "revived faith". A small example: if Valhalla was once the after-death destination for male heroes, specifically those killed in battle, it is now democratised in the Odinic Rite's Bael (funeral) ceremony. All who die in the faith might expect to be greeted there. More significantly, the Odinic Rite does not attempt to be merely of historical or antiquarian interest, it is not a battle re-enactment or cultural movement trying to live like seventh-century Anglian settlers or tenth-century Vikings. It is a spiritual tradition of value in today's fragmented urban world. It is a tradition open to individual membership and individual practice in a way that ancient religions were not. In this it is more like the ancient Mystery religions and therefore similar to Wicca. It is also able to speak to the contemporary world about the threat of ecological disaster in a way that ancient sources do not. Finally, these sources may be better than those for other traditions, but they do not enable complete certainty about many aspects of the real "Old Religion". These arguments about the "Old Religion" function well as part of a call for clarity of thought in contemporary Pagan self-definition. However, they are not necessary to the legitimation of Paganism. Paganism is a new religion, albeit one which draws on ancient sources in addition to its contemporary inspirations.

Coming Home and Coming Out

Most Pagans say that the question "What led you to become a Pagan?" is inappropriate. People do not convert to Paganism and thus do not "become" Pagan. Perhaps something reminds them of childhood awareness of the aliveness of the world. Perhaps a walk in the woods or by the sea evokes wonder or pleasure that requires life changes. Maybe an intuition that trees communicate grows towards a certainty that demands expression. Perhaps other-than-human people are encountered in ways that require different stories to those available in other religions. Perhaps people consciously seek a spirituality to match the political and ecological imperatives of their lives. Then an apparently fortuitous meeting with a friend, a casual conversation on a train or a book picked up while browsing in a library or bookshop reveal that these intuitions, desires, hints, visions and upheavals are not unique and lonely eccentricities. Others are celebrating the Earth's life, meeting with the faerie-folk, protecting trees, creating women-centred, non-hierarchical or communitarian tradition, or are honouring deities first encountered in books of myth and legend. These people call themselves Pagans and make it possible to "come home" to oneself and one's own way of celebrating. They also permit a "coming out", an acceptance or a celebration of having a name, a place and a voice for the imaginings. As Prudence Jones and Caitlín Matthews say,

> Paganism has re-emerged within Western twentieth-century society for a good reason, for though it draws upon the past, it is designed for living in the present. Its reappearance at this time is a spiritual corrective to what many see as the head-long hurtle towards planetary destruction.[35]

---

[35] Jones and Matthews (1990): 13.

12

RITES OF PASSAGE

"What happened to... you know... changing the fate of one individual means changing the world?"
SOMETIMES THE WORLD NEEDS CHANGING.[1]

Every year Pagans celebrate seasonal festivals. These festivals honour the natural cycles of the Earth and her relationship with the Sun and the Moon. They also embrace common experiences of ordinary human people. In celebrating the seasons of the year, with their beginnings, middles and ends, Pagans celebrate the seasons of their lives.

This chapter explores some Rites of Passage: more or less public or communal celebrations of some natural events of human life-cycles. The seasonal festivals that Pagans celebrate are not unrelated to these rites of passage and are referred to often in the course of this exploration. Not all events and transitions in life are pleasant or welcome; many are deeply traumatic and call for deep healing, and a key section of this chapter discusses some of the therapeutic rites of passage aiding people who have suffered abuse. Another section explores the idea that part of the attraction of Paganism itself is as a much-needed journey towards wholeness. Some notes on rites of passage and human life-cycles set the scene for that discussion.

From room to room

If for a moment we consider that life begins with conception and ends in death, we can then draw a straight line between these two events. Between them human life progresses: the individual grows from fertilised egg to foetus, baby, child, adolescent, adult and elder, and eventually dies. Disease and untimely death can interrupt this cycle, but let us assume, for the present, a complete progress from a happy conception to a peaceful death.

The transitions between these phases are not often abrupt and immediate. People do not go to sleep as children and wake in the morning as adults. Nor do the changes take place at the same speed for every individual. Most cultures have found ways of marking the changes in more or less public ways. For example, a girl's first menstruation may be taken to mark her move from childhood to adulthood. Before she can enter the full responsibilities, benefits and

[1] Terry Pratchett, *Soul Music*. (1994): 281. (*1995b): 373.

restrictions her new status brings, she undergoes a rite of passage: a guided move through a passage from one room, childhood, to another, adulthood. In western society this particular event is not celebrated, and is rarely honoured as a positive experience and initiates neither parties nor pleasure. This is in part due to the patriarchal devaluing of women's experience, women's bodies and indeed women in any sense. It is also part of the wider ignoring of the passage into adulthood—in our individualistic society we are expected to "make it" on our own.

The transition from "single person" to "wife", "husband" or "partner" is a rite of passage that is celebrated with a series of increasingly public celebrations: proposal, engagement, stag or hen parties, wedding. Our society then allows the couple a return to privacy for their "first night". In some other societies the couple's first sexual intercourse is a fairly public event, especially where it is necessary for the bride to "show proofs of her virginity". The degree to which a culture stresses the relative value of the individual or the community strongly affects its celebrations of marriage, as it does other rites of passage. In Anglo-Saxon society marriage is generally seen exclusively as a relationship between two people. However, many people experience their wedding day almost passively while family and friends control and direct what, when and how things happen. Only rarely do people get married with only the minimal requirement of a state-recognised official (priest or registrar) and witnesses. A wedding in some religions emphasises the relation between marriage and procreation, family, lineage and descent; the couple being married are at the centre of a web of relationships involving their parents and families (sometimes including distant ancestors) and they are expected to provide that family, clan or nation with children who will themselves continue this complex process of human living. All of these understandings (of the couple's role in their society, of sexuality, family, power relationships between the genders and so on) are reflected in some way in the ceremony that marks the passage into married life.

In short, human societies often express their complex understandings of life in the context of ceremonies marking the times at which people, as individuals or groups, move from one state or status to another.

Anthropologists studying rites of passage in many societies have noticed that they typically follow a similar pattern which includes three stages: separation, transition and re-incorporation.[2] For example, children moving through the passage to adulthood are separated from those things most associated with childhood, such as mother, home and

[2] Especially see Gennep (1960); Turner (1967); Bloch (1992).

village. They are taken out of their normal environment, sometimes without warning and in frightening ways, and removed elsewhere—physically, emotionally, spiritually—to undergo the central phase of the rite. Here a ceremony takes place, perhaps including an ordeal and the learning of new understandings, responsibilities and stories. That is, those who were once children are taught what their society expects adults to be and do. The rite of passage then has to reincorporate the new adults into normal everyday life. They cannot return to the things of childhood or expect the kind of comfort they might have received as children. They are, almost literally, new and different people, strangers to their people and to themselves. They must practise, fully engage with and experience what they have been told or shown in their rite of passage. Their people must learn to treat them differently also.

Not only does much of Western society not put people through ordeals in this way, but it almost completely ignores rites of passage, along with many calendar and seasonal festivals. Perhaps the rebirth of Paganism is assisting a re-enchantment of life and therefore of such celebrations.

Life cycles

Typical events in many people's journeys between birth and death include the following events (not quite in random order): naming, weaning, teething, first word, potty training, birthdays, first awareness of self, first school day, first experience of death or funerals, first awareness of world, first menstruation, voice breaking, first love, first drink or drugs, first sexual experience, first disappointment, first responsibility, leaving school, "coming out", first experience of violence, first job or dole, first disenchantment, joining group or club, first car, first accident or major illness, legal maturity, marriage, anniversaries, moving house, child-birth, parenting, divorce, grandparenting, retirement, croning or becoming elderly.

Naming, marriage, retirement and death, as well as significant birthdays and anniversaries, are often marked in some way in contemporary Western society by a group larger than the individual's immediate family. There are clubs and associations (Cubs, Guides, Freemasons, Churches, Bardic Orders, Covens and so on) which have ceremonies to mark an individual's joining and perhaps progressing. Such groups and some jobs or careers, such as the military are also likely to have symbols or regalia marking the person's position within the group. Otherwise status is rarely marked with outer symbolism. Perhaps the wedding ring is the most common, if not the only, such symbol of a person's status outside of club or career associations. Westerners no longer cut or grow their hair to mark transitions into different age groups. Jewish and Islamic circumcision is one of the few instances which take place in the West (as well as elsewhere) of marking the body as a sign of identity or affiliation. Not everyone in mourning follows the tradition of wearing sombre clothes for an extended period. Menstruating women are not expected to withdraw themselves from their normal occupations (except in some religions) nor do they outwardly and publicly mark these periods.

Not only are these significant events not marked with symbols, but they are rarely marked with celebrations or rituals, which have become the preserve of religious groups or other associations voluntarily participated in, rather than part of normal day-to-day living. Before discussing particular ceremonies, it is necessary to note that the above list contains events which some people consider negative and certainly not something "respectable" people, religious or otherwise, would celebrate. Among these events, especially those that can be labelled "natural", are ones to which Paganism might be expected to have a very different attitude. Conversely, there are negative events not in the list but which certainly count as major experiences in many people's lives and must also be taken into account in thinking of rites of passage today. Sexuality is a useful context for illustrating both these points. Some religions would insist that a first sexual experience should follow a marriage ceremony and only be acceptable within heterosexual monogamous marriage. Conversely, many people's first sexual experience is abusive. Both these points will be expanded upon below.

Paganism and Rites of Passage

In giving honour to ordinary, physical, mundane reality Paganism is different from many other religions—although perhaps no more different from them than they are from each other. It is also a growing tradition in which diversity and pluralism are themselves seen as natural and positive. This celebration of Nature and diversity gives Pagans the opportunity to rethink, recreate and re-enchant their life-cycles. Certain events in ordinary life which are celebrated by non-Pagans, whether religious or secular, can be seen in new ways. Other events ignored or denigrated by non-Pagans, perhaps especially religious ones, can be rescued and celebrated as good and even sacred, and events which Pagans consider unnatural or wrong can also be responded to in ceremonial ways.

Pagans have developed distinctive ways of honouring birth, naming, first menstruation, sexuality, adulthood, marriage, giving birth, honouring the dead and receiving death. It is no accident that these are related to the seasonal festivals. In at least one of these festivals and often in several of them, in different ways, the events of ordinary human and other-than-human life are incorporated into a response to the whole of Life. "The Sacred" and "the Profane" are not polar opposites which can and must never meet. In the words of William Blake, "Everything that lives is holy".[3] Everything is both profane and sacred, ordinary and special, mundane and spiritual. (This is part of the meaning of the name chosen by the Secular Order of Druids.)

There are also Pagan ceremonies that aim to enable people to deal in some way with abuse, rape and other violence inflicted on them. Paganism is not alone in developing responses to these events, but does have advantages over some other spiritualities and secular therapies. Seeing what is natural as good enables the celebration of the body and does not denigrate "the flesh" as something opposed to deity, perfection, health and well-being. Clearly it will take a long time for survivors of abuse to be able to enjoy their sexuality—they often blame and punish themselves for their abuse. But not being encouraged to deny the body's moods, desires, fears, dislikes and needs may be considerably more enabling than such self-denial.

It also needs to be said that while Paganism may encourage people to honour Nature, it does not demand that you like or accept everything. It does not demand that you like mosquitoes: you can honour them without letting them drink your blood. Death is a fact of life, part of the cycle of life that Pagans celebrate, particularly in the harvest festivals of Lughnasad/Lammas and Autumn Equinox, and also at Samhain and other winter festivals. However natural AIDS and malaria may be, they do not have to be enjoyed or celebrated, but they can be seen as part of Nature and dealt with in that light. People kill to eat (even vegans are life-takers in this sense) and find ways to cope with their daily violence against other living beings. Similarly, ways can be found to cope with things that are disliked or things which endanger life.

If killing is necessary to living, then certainly anger is sometimes necessary. In order to survive the passage from victim of abuse or survivor of rape into secure, independent, growing, whole person, it may be necessary to express anger, bitterness, hatred, fear and sorrow.[4] Conversely, in such cases some evangelical Christians advise people that they must first forgive and love their abuser or attacker before God or God's people can or will help, heal and forgive the *victim*. Pagans have produced rites of passage helpful in the process of living beyond survival. They have also faced AIDS, cancer and other invasive forms of death with ceremonies.

Rather than describe ceremonies for every rite of passage, the following sections are devoted to examples which permit greater clarity about Paganism in the contemporary world. Apart from further

---

[3] Blake (1795): 2.366.
[4] The most powerful "ritual" narrative I have found is not Pagan, but should be heard: Rushing (1993).

illustrating the diversities of Pagan traditions, beliefs and practices, the examples chosen—child blessing, marriage and funerals—are central to the attempt by certain groups to gain legal recognition. Discussion of initiations into specific traditions such as Wiccan covens, Bardic groves or Odinic hearths lead to discussion of the "male mysteries" which are important to some Pagans. This will be followed by an exploration of healing rites, especially the ways in which some Pagans have responded to rape and abuse. This leads to a final section in which the idea of Paganism itself as a healing movement is considered.

Child Blessing

Pagans reject the Christian notion that children enter this world bearing the burden of "original sin". There is no place in their worldview for the denigration of the body, especially that of the life-giving body of mothers. They also agree that naming or blessing ceremonies are not the time to bring babies into the "true faith" or to proselytise among non-Pagan relatives. Free from these temptations to sermonise and proselytise, Pagan naming ceremonies tend to be happy occasions in which babies or children are welcomed into the world and given signs that they are loved. Their birth has already been a rite of passage (for the mother too) which can be celebrated as re-enacting the birth of all things, and the naming celebrates this creativity and beauty. The deities of parents and friends may be asked to further bless and guard the child—but children are permitted to find their own relationships with the deities as they grow. They are welcome in many Pagan gatherings, though this has been made difficult in recent years by false accusations of Satanism and abuse.[5] Adolescence is usually the earliest time at which Pagan groups accept and welcome an avowal of Pagan identity, which may then lead to a different sort of naming or initiation rite.

As in other Pagan ceremonies, child-blessings or namings usually take place in a circle. Often the actual naming of the child is not a central part of the ceremony—old taboos against speaking the child's name until its official naming are rarely honoured these days so babies are named even before birth. More central are various blessings of children, who may be carried around the circle by a parent or guardian ("god-parent" is not entirely appropriate in this context) so that they can be introduced to, and welcomed and blessed by the quarters, elements or other significant people such as deities, the Norns or ancestors. Ceremonial washing, sprinkling or signing the child with water should not be seen as a borrowing from Christian ritual, or as purification from sin, as it is common throughout the world and carries

[5] Harvey (1995b) and (1995c).

various meanings, especially as a symbol of the gift of the waters of life. In Norse tradition a newly-born baby was laid on the ground by the midwife, *jordemoder* (literally Earth-mother) to reverence the source of life, and then handed to the father if he intended to keep the child. In a Druid ceremony at Avebury a child was lifted into the air to be seen and blessed by the life-giving sun. Vivianne Crowley provides a suggestion for the anointing of the child's feet, hands, heart, lips and brow with "non-toxic oil" and suitable blessings such as "I anoint thy feet which have brought thee in our ways".[6] Symbolic gifts are given to the child—some which will be kept in reserve until s/he is much older. The Ring of Troth's ceremony includes the gift of a *taufr* (talisman or piece of shiny jewellery with runic symbols)[7] accompanied by blessings recited by the mother and dipped in spring water,

> I lay this sign in laguz-depths
> it sinks, to shine from roots.
> As ringing and bright when rinsed with this stream
> be thou, stemmed from our stock,
> be thou, beloved bairn.[8]

Many Pagans share the understanding that a child's conception is not the beginning of its life, and nor will death be its end. The ritual circle replicates the circle of life, without beginning or end. Birth is the coming again into this world of one who has previously been here. Some believe that children are reborn in the same family line, others that they might have existed previously in a completely different, not necessarily human, physical form. Reincarnation is an increasingly popular belief in Western countries and is as prevalent among Pagans as in the rest of the population—though there are a remarkable number of Merlins in Pagan groups.

In child-blessing ceremonies there is thus a balance between the individuality of children who must make their own choices later in life and the community of life of which they are an integral part. Such rites of passage basically welcome children into the Earth, home from their travels, and introduce them to "all our relations".

Marriage

Every May Day (Beltain) many Pagans celebrate the beginning of summer in the northern hemisphere. Some in the southern hemisphere do so too, rather than adapting the festival cycle to their seasons. Pagans tend to blend traditions from English, Welsh, Irish and Scottish

---

[6] Crowley (1989): 141.
[7] See chapter 4.
[8] Gundarsson (1993): 500.

folklore with understandings gained from the surviving literatures of these lands. To this they add the recently-born understanding that the festival is one of eight in an annual seasonal cycle. Out of this potent cauldron comes a celebration of vitality, fecundity and sensuality, which includes garlanding lovers and homes, dancing and sexuality, music, drinking and laughter. This expresses the intimation that everything alive is holy and that all of life is holy, and simultaneously asserts that holiness does not preclude either sensuality or humour. "Summer is a-coming in": it is brought in by those who go maying. For some the festival celebrates the marriage of the vigorous Sun and the bountiful Earth and is thus an appropriate time for rites of love and marriage.

Although Beltain is both an appropriate time for marriage ceremonies and provides abundant festive symbolism, other festivals also yield appropriate contexts for such occasions. The Summer Solstice and Lughnasad continue the themes of vitality and fertility. A wedding incorporated into these festivals of summer's beginning, middle and end can, for example, include the participation of personifications of summer: perhaps summer kings and queens, oak kings and May queens or Sun God and Earth Goddess. The couple being married can play these roles themselves or can complement others, evoking powerful resonances and establishing rich harmonies.

As well as being included in the celebration of these summer festivals, Pagan weddings can also take place as discrete events. Some Pagans prefer to call a wedding by the name handfasting; it has been suggested that this is different from a wedding in that it is not necessarily intended to be permanent. It might be a sort of trial marriage of "a year and a day" after which the couple may either reaffirm their love and commit themselves to each other for life, or separate (ideally) without prejudice. However, usually people getting handfasted are no less committed to the hope of a lifelong relationship than people getting married. The name is preferred only because it is different—new to most people and bearing rumours of those (mythical) more romantic days of Merrie England. It also stresses a central symbol of the ceremony: the binding of the hands of the happy couple. Some Pagans follow their handfasting with a legal civil marriage at a registry office—others are happy to keep the state separate from this part of their lives.

Weddings or handfastings usually follow a pattern similar to other Pagan ceremonies, especially when they occur during other ceremonies. A circle is formed—the cardinal directions, elements, ancestors and/or deities are greeted or offered gifts or libations (especially among Ásatrúar)—the handfasting takes place, then the proceedings end with a farewell to the quarters and a formal announcement that the ceremony is over. The threefold pattern of separation, transition and re-incorporation recognisable here is no accident but seems to arise naturally from something deep and deeply shared in humanity.

Weddings are popular in the context of the inter-Druid (and increasingly inter-faith) Gorsedd of the Bards of Caer Abiri (Avebury). In these the couple represent Lleu and Blodeuedd, described as "Sun God" and "Earth Goddess". The Order of Bards, Ovates and Druids gives a more active role to the four elements: four people represent them and the four Quarters. They ask the couple questions recognising that marriage is not always an easy relationship and expect the couple to face the difficulties of "the clear light of day", "the harsh fires of change", "the ebb and flow of feeling" and "the times of stillness and restriction". On hearing affirmations of loving commitment from the couple they also offer the blessing of their element and its associated season. East, for example, offers the

> blessing of the Element of Air in this place of Spring. May your marriage be blessed by the Light of every new Dawn.[9]

Similar blessings are offered in other Pagan traditions.

Rings are widespread symbols of marriage and resonate harmoniously with other symbols of significance to Pagans such as stone circles and the horizon where Earth touches sky. Exchanges of rings and kisses are central moments in most weddings. The ceremonial binding together of the couple's hands, symbolic of their unity, is stressed in handfastings (probably drawn from Christian ceremony). In Craft handfastings the couple leap together over a broomstick which symbolises male and female in sexual union, "the rod which penetrates the bush", and the threshold between past and present.[10] In other words, the broomstick symbolises what is only verbal in Christian rituals: the initiation of a new life "forsaking all others" and "becoming one flesh".

In much of what has been said here about weddings it might be assumed that the happy couple are heterosexual. Some Pagans seem obsessed with matching the gender and sexuality of divinities and those who represent them in ceremonies. Some are certainly homophobic. However, many Pagans have no difficulty in celebrating the loving commitment of any couple wishing to affirm it publicly and there have been gay and lesbian Pagan marriage celebrations. Paganism does not devalue the body in favour of something more "spiritual"; gender and sexuality are not peripheral to the celebration of marriage and they are clearly central to the experience of embodied life.

---

[9] Carr-Gomm (1993): 151-5.
[10] Crowley (1989): 71. Traditional besom broomsticks are commonly found near the entrance of Witches' homes and form the threshold of some circles.

Funerals and Remembrance of the Dead

Death is a rite of passage for both those who die and for the family and friends "left behind". This rite enables the mourners to express their loss and to begin finding new ways to relate to the one who has departed. Inability to do these things can be damaging and shocking. As a rite of passage for the dead, some funerals address the deceased helping them journey to their new place in the scheme of things.

Paganism does not demand a particular method of disposing of the body, although the generally accepted choices in the West are burial or cremation. A *Newsletter* of the Pagan Funeral and Hospice Trust enthusiastically reports the use of fireworks to take one man's ashes high into the atmosphere. Funeral directors now deal with most of the necessary preparation of the body, perhaps lessening the trauma but still distancing people from the greatest fact of life: death. The increasing trend towards the beautification of the dead in French and American style contradicts the Pagan acceptance of death and decay as a natural if not always welcome part of our life-cycle. The keynote of Pagan dealings with the dead is the attempt to accept what is natural. Hopes and beliefs about some sort of life continuing beyond death do not entirely overwhelm these concerns.

Summer celebrations express a kinship between the bonds of human affection—sexuality, love, marriage, fertility—and the increasing vitality and fecundity of the land. Similarly, autumn and winter celebrations explicitly refer to death in various manifestations. At Lughnasad the cutting of grain is honoured. John Barleycorn is cut down in his prime, sacrificially feeding people and animals. (Things that are otherwise impossible can take place in mythology and rituals: Christians can drink blood in the eucharist, Pagans can sacrifice the corn king). The Autumn Equinox balances growth with decay, vitality with decline. At Winter Solstice, before rejoicing in the rebirth of the sun and her turning northwards once again, Pagans wait in the cold dark and acknowledge that sleep and death are part of Nature's life-cycle in midwinter. Winter teaches that death is not always a complete end in Nature. Trees shed their leaves which provide life for myriad teeming lifeforms. In spring new leaves form. Even when a tree does die it continues to provide life to others. Life continues.

Samhain, however, is the festival most closely associated with human mortality. At this beginning of winter feast (often also considered to be the beginning of the year) Pagans honour their dead, both "the ancestors" and recently deceased loved-ones, and are given the opportunity to contemplate their own death. In *Reaper Man* Terry Pratchett powerfully links Beltain and Samhain.[11] A Morris dance at the

---

[11] Pratchett (1991a).

beginning of summer is not unusual, at least in literature, but here it has an equally important counterpart in a dance at the beginning of winter. The dancers remove the clappers of their bells and wear sombre clothes: honouring death does not encourage exuberance in the way that celebrating sexuality does, but on the other hand, wakes and bell-ringing might remind us that making a lot of noise is not alien to mourning and can be central to human dealings with death. Both the dance of death and that of life should be performed to honour the whole cycle of the year and of Life. Beginnings and endings, summer and winter, birth and death, growth and decline—all unite in the cycle. Such dances can incorporate ideas into physical experiences and people can return to ordinary daily life with renewed understanding.

More commonly in Pagan celebrations of Samhain, the presence of the dead is acknowledged in various ways. A bottle of beer may be opened for a loved grandparent or cake left on a plate for a lost child. Given the cold of this time of year, some Pagans choose to celebrate indoors and may then open the door to bid the dead welcome. "Why should I be afraid when my own dead are among them?" is a frequent response to fears raised by Hollywood horror films and Evangelical Christian misrepresentations of honouring the dead as evil. Pagans honour the dead because they are thought to maintain a relationship with the living, and vice versa. Whether the dead return at that time or are in fact "dead and gone", celebrating their gifts to their descendants is a powerful experience. Such gifts include life itself—and their own death, without which life on this planet would be difficult if not impossible.[12]

At Samhain death can also be ritually or meditatively enacted as a boat journey to the Otherworld, or encountered in the form of someone acting the role of Lord of Death.[13] Contrary to the pervasive taboo against talking about death, which suggests some sort of unusual, unlikely or esoteric idea, these ritual-dramas present it as an ordinary part of the life-cycle but also as a profound transformation. Traditional folk customs and party games are significant in the serious fun of the festival, especially as a way of including the children in what might otherwise become an overly solemn occasion.[14] Ducking for apples, hands dipped into bags of pealed grapes or cold spaghetti ("dead people's eyes and entrails"), trick or treating, and fancy dress combine with trying to see the future in a bowl of water. Honouring death and the dead, acknowledging the changing seasons of the year and one's life-cycle and having a party are not considered contradictory.

---

[12] See Harvey (1994).
[13] Starhawk (1989): 193-6; Luhrmann (1989): 258-60; Edwards (1996).
[14] See Edwards (1996).

If the eight festivals provide resources for understanding death more than purely intellectually, the test comes in the actual experiencing of it or of dying. It is hoped that facing death at Samhain is a valid preparation for an individual's own dying. What is clear is that Pagan approaches to death are productive of valuable ways of honouring the dead.

Ancient Celts and Gauls are said to have believed in the transmigration of souls: when people died their souls (some separable continuing essential part of them) took up residence in another physical form.[15] Other ancient and medieval sources intimate an Otherworld of bliss—the land of youth, the summer lands—which can be seen as a permanent paradise or as a temporary rest between incarnations. Arthur's rest in Avalon and Taliesin's initiatory births and transformations provide support for such Pagan beliefs.[16] Another ancient view is that when people die that is the end of them, except for memories and artefacts they have left behind.[17] The body returns its nutrients to the land and life (though not the individual's consciousness or separate existence) continues. All these understandings (and others) are valid options for contemporary Pagans and have indeed played their part in contemporary rites of remembrance of the Dead.

Accounts of actual funeral celebrations and texts for them are to be found in an increasing number of Pagan books. Some of the more organised groups make invaluable suggestions about ways of preparing the body, helping the bereaved, and deciding whether to cremate or bury the body and, in the case of the former, whether to scatter the ashes or bury them in an urn, ways to address deities, the deceased and their friends and relations, how to dress and what symbols and offerings are appropriate in funerals. Some indicate traditional understandings about the afterlife or the current state of the dead.[18] All this is evidence of a creative and growing tradition trying to find ways to root an old/new understanding of the world in the contemporary situation. Although there is considerable diversity in the actions and beliefs represented in this literature and these liturgies, they share a concern with the formation of more close-knit communities, whether of families or of close friends. In other words, the most individual experience people face is also the prime context for the revalidation of social values.

Most Pagans live in the hope of continuing life beyond death, but unlike other religions Paganism does not suggest that the individual's

[15] Julius Caesar, *Gallic War* 6:14. See Caesar (1951): 32-3.
[16] Ford (1977).
[17] The most ancient surviving account of this is the Epic of Gilgamesh, see Sanders (1972).
[18] I note some of these in Harvey (1994).

post-mortem existence in any way depends on beliefs held or deeds performed in this life. There is no "heaven, hell or purgatory", no judge but the self, and no reward or punishment. The afterlife (like death) is democratic in that everyone gets it equally. Whatever deities there are, do not seem particularly concerned with directing human affairs in the afterlife. A generalised belief in *karma*—deeds done now resulting in other deeds later—is held by Pagans as much as it is held in wider society now.

Initiation

Joining a groups can require a rite of passage for which metaphors of death and rebirth may be useful. While some groups, clubs, societies or careers have nothing like initiation, others require a break with past ways of life and the rapid inculcation of new habits and understandings. An increasing number of Pagan groups are completely open, making no demands on members other than active participation, but others require careful preparation before they permit an individual to join. Some Pagan initiation ceremonies, such as those of Bardic groups, are simply more or less public recognitions of ability or competence. Others aim to transmit profound transformative experiences. Wicca, for example, sees itself as an initiatory mystery tradition. Its three degrees reveal the true nature of the world—especially in the interweaving of male and female characteristics, energies or essences—and transform the initiate into one able to perceive and use these energies "for the good of all and the harm of none". Some Odinists also insist on the expression of a difference from wider society. What is central in this context is not sex but race. Obviously it is not that the gender or race of the initiate changes, but that they affirm their agreement with the tradition's teaching that sex or race are central to the way things are. This is at least part of the foundation for the explicit rejection of Christianity in some Odinist initiations.

Male Mysteries

It is a mystery to many women that there are men who feel that history has denied them a chance to be spiritual, to express themselves fully, to be aware of their true manhood. Recognition of the dominance of men and male deities throughout most of recorded human history and in the archaeological record seems rather to prove that men have had ample opportunities to express themselves and their spirituality. The resulting aggression is hardly mysterious.

The men's movement, however, presents itself as a much-needed way for men to explore new ways of being male while using archaic initiatory forms.[19] It is asserted that boys need to be initiated into being men by other men, and that men need male companionship to develop into whole men. These are not "new men", able to wash the dishes and cry in public provided that they receive credit for doing so. They are strong men bonding with other men dancing in the wilderness. They aim is not to conquer the wilderness but to find its resonance within: the wildman, the true initiator. They wish to leave behind dogma, hierarchy, the separation of humanity from the world and the privileging of "male rationality" over "female spirituality and materialism". They struggle against both the gender stereotypes of patriarchy (male breadwinner and aggressor) and those they associate with feminism (soft, guilt-ridden men). They assert that men are as much victims of patriarchy as women and that only if men find new ways to be men will the future be better. They point out that patriarchy encourages men to be suspicious and aggressive towards one another and rewards them for acting out that aggression—or alternatively permits them only to redirect it against women and children. Brotherhood between men is required before men can be proper lovers, fathers, sons and brothers to women. Men need to learn how to be warriors, poets, prophets, priests and kings as well as workers, brothers, meditators, heroes, pupils, teachers and devotees of the wild man/forest God and Great Mother Goddess.

This is too young a movement to say whether it will make any significant impact in other Pagan traditions or in wider society. While there is no doubt that men need to change to a more respectful way of living and may require careful teaching and encouragement to that end, it is not clear that the old role-models are available for this new vision. Wiccans might offer their Horned God, who combines explicit sexuality with more cultured attributes, as a better role-model encouraging men to situate the revisioning of masculinity within wider, more global and communal transformations.[20] Although the warriors, kings, poets, lovers, farmers and smiths of Norse and Celtic mythology offer very different models of leadership and manhood to the Horned God, they too provide resources for men struggling with patriarchy.

Passages to Health

Pagans are adept at creating safe spaces for each other to deal with problems, however personal, emotional or traumatic. Gatherings of established groups often begin by affirming that whatever happens in the circle goes no further, particularly when the purpose of the

[19] See Stewart (1991) and John Matthews (1991b).
[20] Oakley (1996): 274-9.

gathering is to deal with problems. It also happens because these meetings allow people to ask for help in dealing with a specific situation. Energy raised in a Craft circle may be directed for the healing of a member's problem. Individuals may be chanted over until they feel empowered to express their need or deal with whatever concerns them.[21] Some groups, particularly in North America and among the peace and protest camps, have adopted the convention of the "talking stick". Only the person holding the stick speaks, the others listen respectfully. Sometimes the talking stick is passed around the circle, everyone speaking in turn (traditionally without repeating what anyone else has said and certainly without correcting, negating or pointedly disagreeing with another), in others it is taken up by anyone who wishes to address an issue. The building up of trust and a safe atmosphere is necessary to each person being empowered.

Explicit healing or therapeutic rituals also take place. Extreme but not uncommon examples are the ceremonies which aim to help victims of rape or abuse journey along the dark passage beyond being a survivor towards a more whole life. Contrary to Siân Reid's assertion that magic "assigns a positive value to the pain they have experienced", and that "to learn, you must suffer" is a common phrase in the Witchcraft,[22] most Pagans have no difficulty in recognising the wrongness and harm of abuse and rape. They do not attempt to give them meaning or learn from them, but do face their darkness and attempt to find healing, hope and life. Sometimes this requires the expression of anger and fear as well as facing the dark self-loathing and pain of being a survivor.

Rituals for women survivors only rarely include men. Otherwise they vary depending on the group, the survivor, her needs and the insight of those facilitating the ceremony. At the heart of several such ceremonies is the provision of a womb-like space in the centre of the circle, an attempt to find ways to affirm the goodness of the body, and awareness that complete wholeness is rarely if ever achieved instantaneously. The affirmation "You are the Goddess" or, more simply, "You are good" is borrowed from other rituals which recognise, express and encourage awareness of divine being manifested or of significance and autonomy in all things.

Cancer, AIDS and other life-threatening diseases have also been the focus of healing rituals, as have less extreme conditions for which herbs, massage or peer-counselling may be effective. However, in addition to these healing rituals, Paganism itself and its various forms can be experienced as a passage to health.

---

[21] For clear examples see Luhrmann (1989): 225-6; Greenwood (1996).
[22] Reid (1996): 156.

Paganism as therapy

Shelley Rabinovitch has argued convincingly that Paganism itself is therapeutic.[23] In her research among Canadian Pagans she was startled to discover that a high percentage were survivors of abuse and/or rape. She identifies a number of aspects of Paganism which attract people who have been badly mistreated and have internalised a very low opinion of themselves.

Paganism affirms the sacredness of all life, and celebrates the physical and the mundane as integral parts of the sacred whole. It rejects dualistic concepts of good and evil, encouraging responsibility and permitting- emotional, rational, spiritual, intuitive and other responses to the world. It encourages each individual to find a healthy place for themselves within the web of life. It permits individuals to affirm their intuitions, likes, dislikes, desires, visions, hopes and fears. It refuses to privilege one person's or one group's beliefs or practices above another's. It encourages the building of close-knit groups in which trust, mutuality and care are developed. At its centre is a metaphor of transformation and growth: magic. It not only asserts that magic can change things or situations—anything, any situation—but also celebrates the use of magic as a means of self-discovery and personal growth. Magic not only permits but also requires the expression of Will: all individuals can "have their way" without being blamed, belittled or punished. This is experienced in circles which inspire mutuality rather than hierarchy, completeness rather than subservience, continuity rather than fixity or finality, friendship rather than abuse, safety rather than fear.

Human beings are, of course, adept at manipulating situations to their benefit, so some Pagan circles are dominated by those who seek power over others, men continue to expect precedence for themselves and the nudity which is meant to express freedom can be far from liberating.[24] These human failings can be damaging, but Pagans are not unaware of them and the increasing openness and awareness of alternative ways of working and celebrating make it increasingly difficult for the power-hungry to gain control. The essence of the tradition is therefore one which answers a deep need in many people for a context in which they can grow towards self-assurance, self-affirmation and wholeness. It is important to note with Rabinovitch that Pagans are not "driven to this religion solely or even primarily to heal inner wounds".[25] They recognise Pagans as people like themselves and

---

[23] Rabinovitch (1992) and (1996).

[24] See Bennett (1996), Magliocco (1996): 107, Pike (1996) and Greenwood (1996).

[25] Rabinovitch (1992) and (1996): section entitled "Dysfunctional 'Chickens' or Religio-Philosophical 'Eggs'?"

Paganism as a tradition that feels like "home"—for survivors this is a very different sort of home from those in which they were abused.[26]

While the last two sections have focused on survivors of rape or abuse, a similar discussion of those diagnosed as schizophrenic or ostracised as eccentric might produce similar ideas. Would Opal Whiteley (childhood author of a profound nature-diary) have been incarcerated in a mental hospital for most of her life if she had found a Pagan community to celebrate her easy conversation with the plants and animals of her Singing Creek?[27]

Rounding off

Life is not a straight line, nor does it always progress smoothly. An individual's conception is preceded by generations of life with considerable significance for this new beginning, and with death the individual is relocated in a longer history and a wider ecology of human and other-than-human relationships. Seasonal festivals enable Pagans to locate their individual, ordinary experience in the wider spirals of seasonal and annual growth and decay. Paganism continues to explore ways of marking rites of passage which move people into new phases of their current lives: it also faces those traumatic abrupt interruptions into the circle of life, and recognises that these are part of the experience of being human. Paganism honours ordinary physical existence because everything that lives is holy and all of life is holy. It provides resources for the healing and health of individuals through rites of passage, initiations and explicit healing ceremonies. It also recognises that the world needs to be changed and that part of the required change is provided by a movement which honours the natural life of the human body and the Earth itself.

[26] See chapter 11 for discussion of "coming home".
[27] Hoff and Whiteley (1994).

13

PAGANISM AND OTHER RELIGIONS

"It's hard to explain," said Brutha. "But I think it's got something to do with how people should behave. I think... you should do things because they're right. Not because gods say so. They might say something different another time".[1]

Pagan rituals and festivals tell a story in which it is important to recognise who comes—and to offer the proper greeting. This is true of the elements and elementals, the Goddesses and Gods, the ancestors and animals, all the human and other-than-human people. This is a tradition in which relationships are central. There is power in meeting others and there is a danger. Many Pagans have experienced religions in which power is vested in dominating leaders, scriptures and deities, and the power of their own imagination, will, desires, fears, memories, experiences, pleasures and intuitions has been denied, ridiculed and suppressed. Repentance or renunciation, not celebration, has been required. This is "power-over".[2] Pagans know too that some who set themselves up—and gain some acceptance—as Pagan leaders, teachers or representatives are power-hungry.[3] The Pagan tradition, however, encourages "power with" and "power within". The growing number of "solitary" Pagans illustrates this: they develop and use the power that is within them "for the good of all and the harm of none". They also celebrate power with those from whom they learn and those for whom they "work", however quietly. If these tensions between different experiences of power pull Pagans and Paganism in different directions, they are also significant in the various encounters between Pagans and members of other religions.

This final chapter explores such encounters. It discusses Pagan views of other religions and other people's views of Paganism, both positive and negative, and investigates Pagan participation in Inter-Faith Dialogue and its attempts to end defamation and discrimination. The chapter's generative impulse is the observation that Paganism is a religion among the many others of the world, to which it is both similar and dissimilar. It is sometimes confused, perhaps deliberately, with two other traditions that Pagans consider distinct and even alien to their own: Satanism and New Age. On the other hand, Pagans have very

---

[1] Terry Pratchett, *Small Gods*. (1992): 249. (*1994): 249.
[2] Starhawk (1990).
[3] Bennett (1996).

different reactions to the various other religious traditions around them. Discussion of these complex views and interactions begins with an exploration of sources of authority in Paganism.

Authority

One way to explore the place of Paganism among the religions is by comparing sources of authority.[4] Many things that are central to other religions are not in the least authoritative in Paganism. What is distinctive about Paganism is made clear in its sources of authority.

The most commonly claimed sources of religious authority are deities, especially in the monotheistic traditions of Islam, Baha'i, Judaism and Christianity. Although most Pagans are theists—usually polytheists—their spirituality, even in its demonstrably ancient parts, is not derived from divine self-revelation, For example, many Heathens draw on a poem called *Hávamál* which contains much of Odin's wisdom and from which much can be learnt about his character. There are some profound thoughts about it being better to be alive than dead, and some references to deities, elves, giants and other non-human beings. However, the majority of Odin's wisdom, even in the final rune songs, concerns advice on guests, fools, strangers, politeness, bravery, sadness, passion, love, generosity, asking questions, not eating or drinking to excess, and so on. Similarly, in the Craft the Charge of the Goddess which also contains divine self-revelation has as its climax the affirmation that "if that which you seek you find not within yourself, you will never find it without". Pagan deities say more about life than about themselves. Imagine if Jesus's thoughts on helping neighbours who receive unexpected visitors (Luke 11:58) were the centre of Christianity.

As a corollary to this, Pagans are intimate with the divine, but they are not asked to imitate divine lives. Celtic and Teutonic myths present some deities as hedonists or, to be explicit, as greedy drunks on the rampage. Even "good" deities do things which human people are not permitted or expected to do. Myth and ritual are good places to explore anti-social actions, desires and possibilities. People do not have to spend their lives like Thor or the Morrigan; indeed they would be ostracised if they did so.

Authority in Paganism does not come from a canon of scripture although there are books which are important to Pagans. Neither the above-mentioned Charge of the Goddess or *Hávamál* is venerated or taken as an infallible guide to life or belief. Pagans celebrate diversity,

---

[4] Harvey (1995d).

individual experience and intuition. They do not bow to creeds or dogmas—or to those who assert them.

Although many Pagan traditions have priests and priestesses, their role is unlike that of hierarchical religions. Pagans tend to see themselves more as a "priesthood of all believers" than as sacerdotal communities. Pagan priestesses and priests are not clerics but people recognised by their group and by themselves as capable of conducting ceremonies or simply as being capable of participating in ceremonies— almost as if all who were ever called up to read Torah in a synagogue thereby gained permission to call themselves Cohen. Pagan priestesses and priests have no inherent authority to decree what others should do, or to determine the direction of the religion or even the group. They are not licensed to act on behalf of anyone else (whether Pagan or not). Some Pagan groups in North America have gained legal recognition to the degree to which the state recognises religion. For most Pagans, this entails limited recognition of some Pagan leaders as representatives. Sometimes it allows Pagan weddings, funerals and other ceremonies to be legally recognised, but it does not mean that these designated representatives stand above other Pagans.

Pagans join groups because they discover an affinity with what they perceive them to be doing or intending to do. Sometimes groups form or divide around strong personalities, but generally leaders only maintain groups while they have something to teach, something to show. Pagans are intolerant, sceptical or even cynical about leaders. They do not gather around "Guru" figures and are not asked to imitate the lifestyle of leaders of whatever undoubted knowledge or magical abilities. Paganism encourages each individual and group to form their own identity in relation to their environment.

Some religions derive their authority from "the supernatural", that which is above and beyond the "natural", the human, the physical, the ordinary.[5] Paganism is closer to those religions in which everything is related and in which humanity is part of the "web of life". In these relationship-oriented traditions, deities too are among "all our relatives" and do not inhabit some supernatural un-worldly place. They too are affected by their relationships and their participation in Nature: they are not all-knowing, omni-competent denizens of supernature.

Antiquity and continuity are sometimes asserted as legitimations of a religion ("we have been around for *x* thousand years, therefore we must be right/our deity must care for us"). To some Pagans it is important that their tradition is directly continuous from some "Old Religion", whether that be Witchcraft or Ásatrú. However, while such

[5] Morrison (1992a) and (1992b).

claims are historically inaccurate, they are certainly not the primary foundation for Pagan identities.

If these things which are fundamental to the authority of other religions are not central to Paganism, "intimacy" indicates what is most significant. The practice of contemporary Paganism encourages intimacy with Nature—inclusive of the Earth and its constituent seasons, lands and inhabitants, and the embodied human person. Such intimacy constitutes an obligation on all individuals to find their place in the web of relationships and to play their part in the re-balancing of human life and all other life on Earth. Embodied, physical life integrates us into the world in which we live and inculcates respectful celebration of the Earth as "home". In Paganism the intimate relationships which form us are the prime sources of authority.

At the root of the difference between Paganism and many other religions is a very different way of relating to the Earth and the body. Pagans say Earth is home and are finding ways to *be* at home in Earth and in bodies. Other religions say Earth is not home and the body is not the true person. Various more important—more holy, more pure, more spiritual or more ultimate—destinations are advertised, such as heaven, nirvana or enlightenment. Various other parts of the person are more essential, e.g. the spirit, soul or Buddha nature. These locations of virtue and hope define much of what religious people do, say and believe. Someone on the way to heaven and trying to keep bodily desires under the control of the spirit is likely to be detached from the problems of living in the world today. Warfare, ecological devastation, famine, sexual and racial discrimination and the inequalities of wealth and class are firmly based in physical concerns which can too easily be dismissed as illusory or merely temporal or temporary.

This is not to assert that Pagans are more moral or more compassionate that other religionists. An honest observer must see that all religions encourage respect and concern for neighbours—but might wonder whether this is in spite of their various belief systems. The following discussion of Pagan participation in and contributions to the exercise of Inter-Faith Dialogue further explores the relationship between Pagans and their religious neighbours.

Inter-Faith Dialogue

Following increasing interest of religious groups in environmental issues Pagans are increasingly invited to participate in Inter-Faith Dialogue. They obviously have strong views on ecology, but this is not the only contribution they could make to these encounters between religious people. They might offer considerable insight in discussions about pluralism: balancing the development of personal spirituality with respect for other people's spirituality. Another problem for some religious people, especially parents, is finding appropriate ways of introducing children to religions without trying to force them to accept a particular view. Pagans could make valuable contributions to dialogue about a wide range of ethical and social issues, and have considerable experience of issues of religious freedom, land rights, freedom to disseminate ideas and freedom to protest against perceived injustice.

The concern here is in understandings of dialogue rather than in these specific issues. According to William Blake, religion is the attempt to reconcile enemies which, if successful, would destroy existence.[6] This explains his proverb "Opposition is true friendship". The reconciliation he warns against is that in which one side is kept in chains or becomes so convinced of its own error that it joins the other side. Instead the two "enemies" should honestly oppose each other and live in dynamic balance, remaining "good neighbours". Existence depends on this dialogue of creativity and destruction, of acceptance and rejection, just as life depends on diversity and difference. Uniformity and conformity are expressions of death, prefiguring the final entropy of the universe. Some would assert that such entropic and dualistic aggression is typical of Patriarchy.

Dialogue is an encounter which aims to improve understanding and mutual respect between two or more parties. It does not require agreement but it does require honesty. Without at least some level of initial understanding and respect there would be no dialogue, and the desire to improve understanding and respect would be severely hampered. There are other sorts of encounter: e.g. hostility, fear, evangelism and propaganda. Failure to distinguish between these things and dialogue has permitted some people to claim to be engaged in dialogue when their real intention is to convert others. Perhaps dialogue is marked by listening where other sorts of encounter are marked by talking; "conversation" is an apt synonym for it.[7] Nelle Morton's "hearing into speech" is also evocative.[8]

Some theologians understand dialogue differently, asserting that all religions have *some* correct understandings of ultimate or divine reality and that dialogue is a dialectical means of getting closer to a shared knowledge of that reality.[9] The role of the expert is to produce the methodology by which people can sift out the nuggets of Truth from the murky confusions that make up the diverse particularities of each

[6] Blake (1793).
[7] Berling (1993).
[8] Morton (1985).
[9] Especially see Hick (1977, 1985).

Faith. It is questionable whether these ideas are part of the motivations and interests of most "ordinary people" of different Faiths who participate in dialogue.

Dialogue is easier for Pagans than for many religionists because they are not obsessed by proving the truthfulness or universal applicability of their tradition. People do not convert to Paganism, but rather discover in its name and traditions what they have been feeling towards or even doing already. There is no repentance, but often a sense of "coming out" and discovery that there is a word for the experience. There is no "truth" to assent to that is not already held. There is a sense that the individual's perception of "beauty" is honoured. Keats was correct: "Beauty is truth, truth beauty, this is all you know on earth and all you need to know."[10] Everyone has preferences, some people celebrate them, Paganism grows from them. To talk of "Truth" is to invite conflict—this much at least is clear in all Christian involvement in Inter-Faith Dialogue. Discussions of "beauty" are rarely deadly; one can point to her favourite colour and say "Isn't that shade of green beautiful?", and another might reply "Yes, but I prefer indigo". Then the two might gain a greater appreciation of those colours; they do not have to change the preferences but they will be enriched by the encounter. No one who has read Alice Walker's *The Color Purple* will see the colour purple in the same way again.

The Pagans' intimation is that religion—especially their own—is a matter of "beauty" rather than of "truth". This in no way belittles the serious business of religion or of Inter-Faith Dialogue, but it is considerably easier to engage in dialogue if participants do not believe that the end-result must be a triumph of one side's truth over the other side's error. Pagans are pluralist and generally tolerant of diversity among themselves—the level of disagreement is rarely as hostile as in other religions, though even this generally low-level unpleasantness is disappointing and can grow quite fierce[11]—and are frequently open to friendly discussions with other religions. Dialogues in which Pagans have participated are becoming increasingly common, although they have rarely moved beyond discussions of specific issues into joint celebrations or festivals. Part of the problem of such encounters would be Pagan views of other religions, about which more is said below.

Some Inter-Faith Dialogue has been made difficult by misconceptions of the need to reach unity which usually result in spurious attempts to include the "other" within one's own tradition. For example, Christians frequently treat members of other religions as "anonymous Christians",[12] claiming that the Christian deity has a hand

[10] Keats (1819).
[11] See Bennett (1996).
[12] A term coined by Karl Rahner (1966).

in all the "good" parts of that tradition. It has often been asserted that when Christianity arrived in Britain it was received favourably by Druids, who easily converted. This unhelpful fantasy is at last being jettisoned by Pagans now that its sources have been explored more carefully and academic discussion considered more carefully.[13] There have been "dialogues" in which Pagans have been invited to consider the place of Jesus in their worldviews. In others it has been suggested that Pagans and Christians are really approaching the same deity, one seeing "him" (clearly the Christian deity) as immanent and the other as transcendent, but both being correct. These concerns may further theological reflection but make no contribution to mutual understanding or to facing the real problems and delights of the contemporary world.[14] Two further misconceptions about Paganism deserve more detailed notice.

Paganism Misunderstood

Evangelical Christians and the media frequently confuse Paganism with Satanism or evil-doing. Some do this out of ignorance but others do it deliberately, believing either that the devil is behind everything other than Evangelicalism, or that Paganism is a stepping-stone towards devil-worship. Meanwhile, others assert that Paganism is an aspect of (the) New Age. Distinguishing between Paganism and either New Age or Satanism is made difficult by a refusal to take seriously what "insiders" say.

Satanism. It has been alleged that 10 per cent of the population of Britain are Satanists who conspire, perhaps influenced by a real devil, to corrupt and blaspheme against everything godly, good or socially valued. The same is said of many other countries around the world.

The truth is that there are less than 100 self-identified Satanists in Britain.[15] The percentages in populations elsewhere will be no higher. For these people Satanism is a series of techniques for allowing individuals to affirm, develop and express themselves and to do what they wish to do in the context of an individualistic spirituality. It does not require belief in the Satan of the Christian pantheon, although it thrives on the sinister image and hostility it tends to evoke in Christians and the media. Satanism is an adversarial form of self-religion which is well documented and does not have the force or the capability of spearheading a conspiracy. This is not a simplistic dismissal of other claims about Satanism, but is based on evidence available to anyone

[13] See Hutton (1996c): 28-30 and Oakley (1996).
[14] These are also common problems in dialogue between other religions.
[15] Harvey (1995a).

willing to do the research. The only reason that exaggerated claims about the prevalence of Satanism continue is that Evangelical Christians present beliefs as if they were evidence. They feel justified in this by the fact that the Bible appears to demand belief in both a devil and wicked "Witches". That these texts about "Witches" are not specific has been a major part of their power throughout Christian history: any accusation can be supported by a text that does not say what "Witches" are, do or believe.[16]

If this were merely an aspect of the tensions between two religious traditions it would be interesting, but because people have been arrested and accused of "Satanic Abuse" or "Ritual Abuse" in many countries around the world this has become a very important issue. Few of the accused have been Pagans or even Satanists. The only pattern to many of the accusations has been the involvement of a "therapist" or "counsellor" with a history of identifying "survivors" of such alleged abuse and of promoting claims about "Ritual Abuse". There is now a considerable body of literature about these issues, but our concern here is to note this aspect of Pagan relationships with others. There is also a broader shadow cast by these "incitements to religious hatred".[17] Twice a year the media phone their contacts in the academic world or among Pagan representatives: around Summer Solstice they want "silly season" stories about Druids for light-hearted mockery of eccentrics, and at Halloween they seem desperate for sinister tales of wickedness in the woods, nude dancing around bonfires, orgies and human sacrifice. Meanwhile, the Witchcraft Act has still not been repealed in Queensland,[18] and there are those who would have it reinstituted in Britain. In many rural communities in North America it is still dangerous to identify oneself as a Witch. In South Africa the Witchcraft Act, which largely targets traditional Sangoma witchcraft, can also be applied to Pagans, especially the Craft. In various countries bookshops and market stalls selling "occult" materials have been forced to move or close.

Rational argument is not an effective counter to scares such as this.[19] By now, however, it should be possible simply to state that Paganism is not Satanism, it has no place for a devil or for belief in ontological evil. Its cosmology has no room for a battle between forces of "good" and "evil" fought over the "souls" of humans who might be enticed towards heaven or hell. Most Pagans consider Satanism to be a branch of Christianity. A few Satanists do name themselves Pagans. Some consider themselves to be close kin to Left Hand Path ritual magicians.

[16] Harvey (1995c).
[17] See Harvey (1995b).
[18] Hume (1995).
[19] Richardson, Best and Bromley (1991).

Others assert that the Satanic belief that "everyone is their own God" makes them polytheistic and therefore, according to some dictionaries, "Pagan". As a self-religion, Satanism fits uneasily with either Christianity or Paganism for all that it might draw on the stereotypical Hollywood inversions of the former, but such arguments are unlikely to persuade Evangelical exorcists that Pagan deities, elements, genii loci and faery-folk are not demonic spirits.

New Age. If Satanism is confused with Paganism because of assertions of their "dark" interests, New Age is distinguishable from Paganism by its obsession with "light". There are similarities between Paganism and New Age—but no more than there are (different ones) between Christianity and New Age.

Margot Adler says:

> There is a funny saying in the Pagan movement: "the difference between Pagan and 'new age' is one decimal point". In other words, a two-day workshop in meditation by a "new age" practitioner might cost $300, while the same course given by a Pagan might cost $30.[20]

Pagans claim that this "one decimal point" is emblematic of the New Age as a predominantly white middle-class phenomenon in which health and wealth are prime indicators of spirituality. New Age celebrates modernity but tries to imbue it with a suitable spirituality.[21] Pagans frequently associate New Age with a "fluffy bunnies" vision of the world: their cosmos is a generous, self-sacrificing and loving place, "all sweetness and light, the lions don't bite and the thorns don't scratch".[22] Being poor or unwell is a result of spiritual wrong or failure to think positively. Humanity is being "allowed" to pollute the world and destroy species as part of a learning process—and the animals and plants are giving up their lives for this great and cosmic good. Cosmic, global and human evolution depend on humanity thinking positively, embracing the "light" and abandoning the darkness, looking to spirit rather than earthiness. While many New Agers celebrate the seasonal festivals which Pagans identify as their own, they combine this with a redemptive and millennial metaphor or agenda that is alien to Paganism. The Earth may be described by New Agers as Mother, but this enshrines the old dualisms of male as active, rational and higher as against the female as passive, receptive and lower. Channelling of alleged wisdom from exalted masters, angels, devas and others is typical of New Age and causes considerable cynicism among Pagans, who feel that if New Agers faced their darkness honestly, they could

[20] Adler (1986): 420.
[21] Heelas (1996).
[22] Quoted by York (1995): 160.

admit that the "airy-fairy, wishy-washy" messages about being nicer people with more positive thoughts come from their own egos. Spirituality is far more important in New Age than the ultimately illusory material world or existence. Ability to meet the exorbitant and prohibitive cost of New Age events enables its beneficiaries the degree of leisure necessary to indulge in continual self-absorption.

Whether or not these Pagan views of New Age are entirely accurate, they indicate a rejection of the placing of Paganism under the New Age umbrella. The two broad movements appear similar because they celebrate similar festivals, name some similar other-than-human beings (e.g. elves and faeries), use visualisation and meditation, eclectically draw on South Asian, Native American and Shamanic ideas and technology (e.g. chakras and sweat lodges) and read widely in astrology, geomancy, anthropology and Celtic mythology. But the exact mix of these elements produces atmospheres and actions which are distinguishable. The devas of Findhorn (a New Age community in Scotland) are much "nicer" and more "cosmic" than the localised, trickster faeries of many Pagans' experience. Paganism rejects the gnostic denigration of matter and darkness prevalent in New Age, and celebrates the world as real and as given. It does not equate healing with either positive thinking or problem-solving. Certainly its magic asserts that the world can be changed and that what is done affects everything else, but it rejects the "'blame the victim' syndrome as well as a rationalized neglect of social-justice issues"[23] that it identifies as endemic in New Age.

As Michael York says:

> Among the further contrasts between the two, we find a theatrical and ritualistic side to Neo-Paganism which is largely absent in New Age. Neo-paganism also embraces the idea or practice of ritual/symbolic or sacred sex. Within New Age, we find little if any use of the sexual metaphor.[24]

Sexuality has little place in New Age for at least two reasons: it would, first, require a more Pagan celebration of embodiedness and, secondly, diminish New Age's respectable image. Even though Druidry and Ásatrú court mainstream attention more than the Craft, which makes much of its antithetical status,[25] they share a concern to challenge the *status quo* of late capitalism in ways completely alien to New Age. Alongside theatricality and sexuality, York might have noted the humour of many Pagan gatherings, in contrast to the seriousness of New Age events.

---

[23] York (1995): 162. Also see Sjöö (1992).
[24] York (1996): 164.
[25] See Oakley (1996).

New Age perhaps constitutes the gnostic temptation of postmodern spirituality. Its influence on Paganism certainly tends in this direction. Paganism might just constitute

the this-worldly grounding of New Age—one which counterbalances the tendency otherwise to drift off into the airy-fairy realms of "pure" and transcendent spirit.[26]

To the extent that this is true, it suggests only that two different traditions run parallel for part of their journey. New Age disseminates the perennial wisdom of theosophy in which nature's meaning is to be found in spiritual realities and there is only a passing concern for life's social and political realities.[27] Paganism engages with nature sensually and derives from a critique of modernity answering the needs of post-modernity. All branches of Paganism have been influenced by feminism while New Age offers women typically patriarchal subordination to male leaders or voices. The centre of attention for Paganism is Nature. While Pagan festivals can be escapist, they encourage deeper engagement with "green" concerns and even with direct action against what assaults the Earth. Paganism's aim—if such a thing can be distilled without doing violence to the multiplicity of Pagan experience and experimentation—is to find more life-affirming ways for human people to live with their other-than-human neighbours. The centre of New Age attention is humanity, some would say Man. Its program is to facilitate a leap forward in human evolution engineered through self-spirituality.

Dealing with Defamation

Since the 1970s Pagans have become confident enough to be open about their worldviews and experiences. Some events and ceremonies remain private, but there are more and more occasions where "outsiders" are welcome. In most British cities there are monthly gatherings in pubs—some to hear presentations, others for purely social purposes. In London it is possible to find something happening every week. In North America the festival circuit is probably as well established as the First Nations' pow wow circuit. Throughout the summer it is at least theoretically possible to go from one such gathering to another. There are innumerable Pagan publications and World-Wide-Web sites which exchange information, ideas, rituals, recipes, news, views, gossip, stories, book reviews, traditional or new lore about animals, plants, rocks and birds, and more. Not all Pagans make their beliefs and practices public; for some people in some places

[26] York (1996): 164.
[27] See Sellon and Weber (1992).

this remains unwise or unsafe. However, Paganism responds to the misconceptions, misinformation and defamation by being as open as any other religious tradition.

There are specific groups such as the British "Sub-culture Alternatives Freedom Foundation" (SAFF) which monitors the media and responds vigorously to anything seen as wrong, insulting, misinformed or prejudiced by fundamentalist Christian propaganda. The "Pagan Educational Network" (PEN) is establishing semi-autonomous groups across the US whose educational aims include proactive campaigns to gain First Amendment rights of religious freedom for everyone. Many national networking groups facilitate similar groups. Their efforts sometimes result in apologies from offending newspapers, but their pre-emptive provision of information and news items are probably more effective, at least in having "both sides" of a story told. For example, every year Evangelicals try to persuade everyone that Halloween is a celebration of evil. Pagans respond, somewhat more soberly, that Halloween is a festival in which Christians used to honour their dead and Pagans still do. The quantity and quality of Pagan responses to the media vary, which is as it should be in a tradition that celebrates pluralism, diversity and active participation by as many people as possible. Michael York has argued that organisationally Paganism fits the SPIN model: it is a "Segmented Polycentric Integrated Network".[28] The applicability of such a construct is illustrated by the diversity and only partly co-ordinated responses to negative or false media representations of Pagans or Paganism. It also makes writing definitively about what Pagans do and believe difficult. This will again be illustrated in the following section concerning Pagan views of other religions.

Among the Religions

Pagans understand themselves to be members of a religious movement manifest in different traditions. Although it is a spirituality distinguishable from others, it is also in some ways similar to them. Pagans vary greatly in their views about other religions and over whether they relate positively or negatively to them.

For some Pagans Christianity is total anathema, with its hierarchy, patriarchy, demonisation of the physical and long history of persecution. Others believe that "Celtic Christianity" forms some sort of bridge between the two religions. Few Pagans privilege their own tradition as the sole truth and are willing to accept that deity is bigger than any one interpretation or vision, and that there is some good in all.

[28] York (1995): 324-9.

A number of Christians have participated in Pagan festivities with apparent pleasure. Nonetheless, in dialogue with Christians, however "liberal", it is usually clear that bridges are illusory. Christians tend to think that their claim that Jesus is the only saviour is the stumbling-block for non-Christians, but salvation is simply not an issue in Paganism and most other religions. The singularity central to Christian claims about the incarnation can have no place in a tradition centred on Nature—or influenced by feminism.[29] This indicates the real problem: even the most "Green" of Christians has at some point to deal with biblical and traditional assertions that Nature needs redemption. Earth remains at best a school preparing humanity for somewhere else: a place where lions do not eat lambs, where there is neither sun, moon, plate tectonics nor sexuality and where nothing dies.[30] There is nothing like this in nature or in Pagan hopes for the afterlife. There is a world of difference between Christianity, which encourages a radical disjunction from nature as experienced now, and Paganism which is at home in nature—and recognising this has the advantage of permitting a real dialogue.

There are anti-Semitic Pagans but "Jewish Pagans" or "Jewitches" are not uncommon, especially in the USA.[31] Asphodel Long discusses the anti-semitism underlying the (increasingly infrequent) accusations that "the Jews" are responsible for the patriarchal destruction of matriarchy and denial of the Goddess.[32] That such language replicates two millennia of Christian anti-Judaism, especially its "deicide" charge, should have made its proponents realise they were dealing with an abhorrent stereotype. On the other hand, many Pagans are aware of more substantial bridges between Judaism and Paganism. Neither tradition engages in proselytism, offers salvation or believes that it holds the whole truth for the whole world. The experience of being a misunderstood and misrepresented minority can be productive of similar mentalities among Jews and Pagans. Again, however, it is nature which is the major area of common ground. The most common experience in both religions is the celebration of seasonal festivals with evocative rituals which reveal the cyclical nature of time ("We were there", this ancient history is our present situation and our hope arises from our past). Real foods play a major role in these meals, e.g. wine can be celebrated as "the fruit of the vine" and not merely as a symbol of something spiritual or redemptive. Starhawk's Witchcraft has been

---

[29] Cp. Hampson (1990).
[30] I am grateful to Stephen Hollinghurst whose unpublished dissertation (1996) led me to reconsider these ideas.
[31] Kelly (1992): 145-6 summarises and discusses figures from Adler and Melton.
[32] Long (1991).

deeply influenced by "regular Jewish tradition" (rather than by what some imagine Israelite religion was like in pre-patriarchal times),

> I'm sure there's a lot of aspects of my work that are very Jewish in a real gut-level and intuitive way. Especially the idea of the spiritual and the political. The spirituality not being removed from the world, but being part of the world, lived in the world.[33]

The monotheism of Judaism is a problem for Pagans, although it might be noted that Jews say "Our God is one" much as love songs say "My lover is the only one". As the nature-honouring, world-affirming tradition of one people, Judaism might be conceived of as a particular type of Paganism.

By way of contrast, Islam is rarely seen positively by Pagans or other Westerners. Some, however, celebrate its mystical traditions— more accurately, the *techniques* employed by Sufi mystics abstracted from their Islamic context. While Pagans might consider the perambulation of the Ka'bah and the kissing of its rock as close to Pagan celebration of similar places, this is far removed from the intention, understanding or vision of Muslims engaged in *tawaf*.

Some Pagans consider particular types of Buddhism to be excellent teachers of mindfulness and respect, while others are vehement that its world denial is incompatible with Pagan affirmation of the Earth and the body. Its refusal to give central space or consuming attention to deities is attractive to many Pagans for whom spirituality is just as human and worldly a concern as ecology. Those who walk both the Buddhist way and the Pagan path do not blend them into a third tradition but see them as providing different imperatives. Buddhism insists on a disciplined seeking of the individual's true nature, the discovery of which is enlightenment for everyone, while in Paganism personal growth is part of a less intense discovery of humanity's place in the world. The difference might be exemplified when one observes Buddhists and Pagans actually walking. A Buddhist might walk around a circular mountain path a thousand times, honouring special places by the way. While mindful of their walking and breathing and their surroundings, Buddhists basically seek to achieve mystical union with the true "Ground of Being" beyond the illusion of material form. A Pagan walk in the woods will be more like a nature ramble. Different plants and rocks may be touched, water drunk from a pool, a fire lit in a clearing and all the senses engaged in relating to the place and its inhabitants. Buddhism is a path, Paganism a sitting among the trees. Some consider these activities (as metaphors or physical engagements) compatible while others do not.

[33] Starhawk (1989b): 126.

It is not uncommon to hear Pagans assert kinship with the polytheistic traditions of Hinduism. While stressing their understanding that Odinism is a tradition particularly suited to people of North European descent, some Ásatrúar view Hinduism as a cognate religion. Many Pagans explore Hindu ways of expressing reverence for the divine— as *both* the all-embracing and underlying All and the Many of immediate experience. The role of powerful Goddesses and of an underlying power, Shakti, inspire Pagans who view them as cognate with their own Goddesses or with the Druidic Awen. At the same time, Hinduism also provokes consideration of the possibility of powerful Goddesses co-existing with patriarchal social conditions. The etiquette of *Darshan*—seeing and being seen by deities—is of interest to those seeking ways to express their polytheistic intimations. While most Pagans still accept the Enlightenment dualism of "head" versus "heart" or "thinking" versus "feeling", a slow move towards more traditional understandings of ritual is beginning. That is, most Pagans continue to assert, in harmony with the prevailing culture, that it is important to engage in ritual "from the heart" rather than merely repeating words and gestures "by habit" or "from the head". Perhaps because Pagan ceremonies are becoming increasingly open and therefore have to attempt to encourage greater participation by those without active roles (who are thus in danger of being mere spectators), they are discovering that this dualism is a bankrupt imposition on a richer experience. Ritual is something to do—thinking and feeling are neither prerequisites nor primary techniques. Pagans are now beginning to learn from experience and from those whose understanding has not been so radically shaped by the Enlightenment that ritual is conducted or acted. The elementals, the deities and the Earth are always "there", and the festivals take place whether they are "felt" or "thought", so rituals are a means of paying attention to what is happening, an engagement with wider concerns and relationships.[34]

Many Pagans consider the Japanese Shinto (or *kami*) tradition to have many affinities with Paganism. As a way of relating to nature deities or spirits and to the landscapes in which they are manifest, Shinto offers some obvious common ground. Its blend of priests and shamans seems an attractive possibility to Pagans seeking to create a more public form of Paganism, with buildings and personnel trained to minister to a wider clientele. Shinto is not an exclusivist religion but is practised alongside Buddhism, Taoism and Confucianism. This too is attractive to Pagans who rarely negate all other traditions—although they do have problems with the exclusive claims of some religions. However, there are Japanese Pagans who were brought up in the

[34] Smith (1987).

thoroughly modernist context of contemporary Japan and therefore find Wicca and Druidry more attractive and appropriate than Shinto or other indigenous traditions; this is especially because the current form of Shinto is a male-centred and emperor-centred tradition at least as much as it is a nature-spirituality. They also point out that Japanese religiosity is thoroughly eclectic, and so it is natural to include Western Paganism in the blend.[35]

The indigenous traditions of the First Nations, aboriginal or native peoples, have frequently been labelled "Pagan". Hence, the label "Neo-Pagan" is often applied to those discussed in this book to distinguish them both from ancient Pagans and from these other contemporary polytheistic Nature-respecting spiritualities.[36] Anthropological writings about such peoples stimulated earlier Pagans in their construction of ways of considering, describing and manifesting their developing tradition. Now it is increasingly common for Pagans to be in touch with indigenous peoples themselves—although they have also not stopped reading and studying, and one result of these contacts and studies has been a deepening understanding and widening experience of shamanism and animism. Pagans are not immune from the temptation to reanimate "Noble Savage" stereotypes and to participate in the disrespectful appropriation of elements abstracted from these cultures. However, genuine contact with people living real and complex lives enables a more mutually beneficial relationship, especially with those First Nations who are attempting to re-establish their own traditions in ways appropriate to their contemporary contexts. For example, those who are finding the sweat lodge or stone-people lodge tradition helpful in revitalising communities—and in combating alcoholism—have much to teach Pagans who can be tempted to abstract the practice as one more "spiritual experience" or as a "technique of ecstasy". Here, dialogue might lead to radical changes in the consumerism of the West and its turning even spirituality into a commodity.

These notes on Pagan understanding and encounters with other religions are intended not to be exhaustive but merely suggestive. Such encounters and the character of Pagan relationships with people of other religions vary greatly because religions are not monolithic and their adherents have widely differing experiences, even in the more dogmatic traditions.

It is often suggested by those who engage in Inter-Faith Dialogue that "religious" people should work together to tackle the problems of the world and of their own society. In practice it rarely takes proponents long to discover that differences between religions are at

---

[35] I am grateful to Ikari Segawa for informative correspondence and discussion.

[36] For an excellent discussion of "American Indian Land Wisdom" see Callicott (1989): 177-219.

least as great as their differences from "secular" people. Joint actions often get bogged down or side-tracked by differences of motivation, approach or aim that should have been obvious from the start. This is especially true of attempts to co-ordinate multi-faith spiritual experiences and to hold joint services which tend to highlight differences between religions far more quickly than joint charitable work would do. Circumventing the difficulties by not mentioning deities—often a major source of contention—might be simple for Pagans whose ceremonies are not primarily for the benefit of divinities. There are still conventions to each tradition which can only be bent so far without confusing everybody and satisfying none.

Despite the "Greening" of religions, many central concerns of Pagans are articulated more in secular than in religious discourses. Pagans might find a closer kinship or a better expression of their spirituality in ecology and folklore than in many more "religious" writings.

All Our Relations

The interests of other religions, philosophies and ways of life intersect with those of Paganism at a number of points. Paganism is not a dogmatic or doctrine-centred religion, and has little time for the discipline of theology as Christians understand it. It does invite people to change their lives, but "coming out" or "coming home" are more common metaphors than "conversion"; it does not encourage people to convert but to discover what is already inherent in them—even if that is not Paganism but an entirely different way of being human. Like New Age, Paganism encourages personal growth, but unlike New Age or Satanism, it has not developed into a self-religion. The changes Paganism encourages are similar to the more relational spiritualities of many First Nations. Human activity, creativity and expressiveness participate in these religious systems far more profoundly than domineering divinities. In the realm of Inter-Faith Dialogue and of understanding "religion" as a category, Paganism contributes to the understanding that the relationships of expressive human people with other persons—not objects—are significant and creative.[37] It claims, by its rituals and festivals rather than by sermonising or pontificating, that people have to find better ways to relate to the world around them, ways that honour "all our relations". The criticism that polytheistic deities are capricious misses the paradox that this is acceptable in traditions in which deities are neither the sole authority nor the prime focus of attention. In the end and also paradoxically, Paganism might

[37] See Morrison (1992a) and his discussion of Berger (1967).

be summed up as a poly-theophany in which the big and small Gods of Pratchett's Discworld declare an end to religious wars:

> What the gods said was heard by each combatant in his own language, and according to his own understanding. It boiled down to:
> I. This is Not a Game.
> II. Here and Now, You are Alive.[38]

(Pagan deities could be expected to speak to women too.)

[38] Pratchett (1992): 272.

BIBLIOGRAPHY

Abram, David. 1985. "The Perceptual Implications of Gaia". *The Ecologist* 15.3: 96-103.

Adler, Margot. 1986. *Drawing Down the Moon: Witches, Druids, Goddess-Worshippers and Other Pagans in America Today*. Boston: Beacon.

——. 1989. "The juice and the mystery" in Judith Plant (ed.): 151-4.

Allen, Paula G. 1990. *Spider Woman's Granddaughters*. London: Women's Press.

Anderson, Richard. 1993. "Geomancy" in Swan (ed.): 191-200.

Apuleius, Lucius. 1950. *The Golden Ass*. Harmondsworth: Penguin.

Ash. 1992. "No Compromise in Defence of Mother Earth". *Deosil Dance* 34: 3-4.

Ashe, Geoffrey. 1990. *Mythology of the British Isles*. London: Methuen.

Aswynn, Freya. 1990. *Leaves of Yggdrasil*. St. Paul, MN: Llewellyn.

Atkinson, Clarissa, Margaret Miles and Constance Buchanan, (eds) *Shaping New Vision: Gender and Values in American Culture*. Ann Arbor: University of Michigan Research.

Aziz, Peter. 1992. Advertising fliers for his Shamanic Healing Courses.

Baker, James W. 1996. "White Witches: Historic Fact and Romantic Fantasy" in James Lewis (ed.): 171-92.

Barstow, Anne L. 1988. "On Studying Witchcraft as Women's History: A historiography of the European Witch Persecutions". *Journal of Feminist Studies in Religion* 4.2: 7-19.

Bates, Brian. 1983. *The Way of Wyrd*. London: Century.

——. 1996. *The Wisdom of the Wyrd*. London: Rider.

Bell, Shannon, 1992. "Tomb of the sacred prostitute: the Symposium" in Philippa Berry and Andrew Wernick (eds): 198-207.

Bender, Barbara. 1993. *Landscape: Politics and Perspectives*. London: Berg.

Bennett, Jim. 1996. "Profile". *Pagan Dawn* 120: 19,22.

Berger, Peter. 1967. *The Sacred Canopy: Elements of a Sociological Theory of Religion*. New York: Doubleday.

Berling, Judith A. 1993. "Is Conversation between Religions Possible?" *Journal of the American Academy of Religion* 61: 1-22.

Berry, Philippa and Wernick, Andrew (eds). 1992. *Shadow of Spirit: Postmodernism and Religion*. London: Routledge.

Beth, Rae. 1990. *Hedge Witch: A Guide to Solitary Witchcraft*. London: Robert Hale.

Blake, William. 1793. "The Marriage of Heaven and Hell" in Geoffrey Keynes (ed.): 148-60.

——. 1795. "Vala or the Four Zoas" in Geoffrey Keynes (ed.): 263-382.

Bloch, Maurice. 1992. *Prey into Hunter: The Politics of Religious Experience*. Cambridge University Press.

Bonds, Diane S. 1992. "The Language of Nature in the Poetry of Mary Oliver". *Women's Studies* 21: 1-15.

Bonewits, Philip E.I. 1974. *Real Magic: An Introductory Treatise on the basic Principles of Yellow Magic*. London: Sphere.

——. 1996. "The Druid Revival in Modern America" in Philip Carr-Gomm (ed.): 73-88.

Bordo, Jonathan. 1992. "Ecological peril, modern technology and the postmodern sublime" in Philippa Berry and Andrew Wernick (eds): 165-80.

Bowes, Pratima. 1977. *The Hindu Religious Tradition: A Philosophical Approach*. London: Routledge and Kegan Paul.

Bowman, Marion. 1994. "The Commodification of the Celt: New Age / Neo-Pagan Consumerism". *Folklore in Use* 2: 143-52.

——. 1996. "Cardiac Celts: Images of the Celts in Contemporary Paganism" in Graham Harvey and Charlotte Hardman (eds): 242-51.

Bradley, Marion. 1984. *The Mists of Avalon*. London: Sphere.

Buckland, Raymond. 1971. *Witchcraft from the Inside*. St. Paul, MN: Llewellyn.

——. 1974. *The Tree*. York Beach: Weiser.

Budapest, Zsuzsanna E. 1979. *The Holy Book of Women's Mysteries*. 2 vols. Oakland, CA: Susan B. Anthony Coven 1.

Butcher, G.D. nd. *Stav: An Introduction*. Hull: Stav.

Butler, W. Ernest. 1991. *Magic: its Ritual, Power and Purpose* and *The Magician: His training and work*. London: Aquarian (first published separately in 1952 and 1959).

Buttimer, Anne. 1993. *Geography and the Human Spirit*. Baltimore: Johns Hopkins University Press.

Caesar, Julius. 1951. *The Gallic War*. Harmondsworth: Penguin.

Cal. 1995. Letter. *Pagan Voice* 43: 9-10.

Caldecot, Leonie and Stephanie Leland, (eds). 1983. *Reclaim the Earth: Women Speak Out for Life on Earth*. London: Women's Press.

Calder, George (ed.). 1917. *Auraicept na n-Éces: The Scholars Primer*. Edinburgh: John Grant.

Callicott, J. Baird. 1989. *In Defense of the Land Ethic: essays in Environmental Philosophy*. Albany, NY: State University of New York Press.

Cameron, Anne. 1984. *Daughters of Copper Woman*. London: Women's Press.

——. 1989. "First Mother and the Rainbow Children" in Judith Plant (ed.): 54-66.

Carpenter, Dennis. 1996. "Emergent Nature Spirituality" in James Lewis (ed.): 35-72.

Carr-Gomm, Philip. 1991. *The Elements of the Druid Tradition*. Shaftesbury: Element.

——. 1993. *The Druid Way*. Shaftesbury: Element.

—— (ed.). 1996a. *The Druid Renaissance*. London: Thorsons.

——. 1996b. "Returning to the Source" in John Matthews (ed.): 5-6.

Carroll, Lewis. 1872. *Through the Looking Glass*. Published in a combined volume in 1962 with *Alice's Adventures in Wonderland*. London: Puffin.

Chagnon, Napoleon A. 1992. *Yanomamö*. London: Harcourt Brace College.

Cheney, Jim. 1989a. "Postmodern Environmental Ethics: Ethics as Bioregional Narrative". *Environmental Ethics* 11: 117-34.

——. 1989b. "The Neo-Stoicism of Radical Environmentalism". *Environmental Ethics* 11: 293-325.

Chippindale, Christopher and Peter Fowler,. 1990. "Stonehenge Tomorrow" in Christopher Chippindale, Paul Devereux, Peter Fowler, Rhys Jones and

Tim Sebastian (eds). 1990. *Who Owns Stonehenge?* London: Batsford: 160-73.

Christ, Carol. 1979. "Why Women Need the Goddess: Phenomenological, Psychological and Political Reflections" in Christ and Plaskow (eds): 273-87.

——. 1985. "Roundtable Discussion: What are the Sources of My Theology?" *Journal of Feminist Studies in Religion* 1: 123.

——. 1987. *The Laughter of Aphrodite.* San Francisco: Harper & Row.

Christ, Carol and Plaskow, Judith (eds). 1979. *Womanspirit Rising.* New York: Harper & Row.

Churchill, Ward. 1992. *Fantasies of the Master Race; Literature, Cinema and the Colonization of American Indians.* Monroe: Common Courage.

Clifton, Chas (ed.). 1992. *Witchcraft Today* 1: *the Modern Craft Movement.* St. Paul, MN: Llewellyn.

——. 1994. *Witchcraft Today* 3: *Shamanism and Witchcraft.* St. Paul, MN: Llewellyn.

Collins, Martin. 1995. *Pagan Atheism: a Personal View.* Wallsend: Pagan Atheist Synthesis.

Conkey, Margaret and Tringham, Ruth E. 1995. "Archaeology and the Goddess: Exploring the Contours of Feminist Archaeology". In Donna C. Stanton and Abigail J Stewart (eds). *Feminisms in the Academy.* Ann Arbor: University of Michigan: 199-247.

Crowley, Aleister. 1973. *Magick.* ed. John Symonds and Kenneth Grant; London: Routledge and Kegan Paul.

——. 1976. *Magick in Theory and Practice.* New York: Dover.

——. 1983. *The Holy Books of Thelema.* York Beach: Samuel Weiser.

Crowley, Vivianne. 1989. *Wicca: the Old Religion in the New Age.* London: Aquarian.

——. 1990. "The Initiation" in Prudence Jones and Caitlín Matthews (eds): 65-82.

——. 1993. "Women and Power in Paganism" in Elizabeth Puttick and Peter B. Clarke (eds) *Women as Teachers and Disciples in Traditional and New Religions.* Lampeter: Edwin Mellen: 125-40.

——. 1994. *Phoenix from the Flame.* London: Aquarian.

——. 1996. "Wicca as Modern Day Mystery Religion" in Graham Harvey and Charlotte Hardman (eds): 81-93.

Crowther, Patricia. 1992. *Lid of the Cauldron.* York Beach: Weiser.

Culpepper, Emily E. 1987. "Contemporary Goddess Thealogy: a Sympathetic Critique" in Clarissa Atkinson, Margaret Miles and Constance Buchanan (eds): 51-71.

——. 1989. In "Roundtable Discussion: If God Is God She is Not Nice". *Journal of Feminist Studies in Religion* 5.1: 106-9.

Cunningham, Scott. 1993. *Wicca for the Solo Practitioner.* St. Paul, MN: Llewellyn.

Daly, Mary. 1987. *Websters' First New Intergalactic Wickedary of the English Language.* London: Women's Press.

Dames, Michael. 1992. *Mythic Ireland.* London: Thames and Hudson.

Davidson, Hilda R.E. 1964. *Gods and Myths of Northern Europe.* Harmondsworth: Penguin.

——. 1988. *Myths and Symbols in Pagan Europe*. Manchester University Press.
——. 1989. "Hooded Men in Celtic and Germanic Tradition" in Glenys Davies (ed.): 105-24.
——. 1993. "Mythical Geography in the Edda Poems" in Gavin Flood (ed.): 95-106.
Davies, Glenys. 1989. *Polytheistic Systems*. Edinburgh University Press.
Deane-Drummond, Celia. 1992. "Moltmann's Ecological Theology: A Manifesto for the Greens?" *Theology in Green* 1: 21-7.
Detwiler, Fritz. 1992. "'All my Relatives': Persons in Oglala Religion". *Religion* 22: 235-46.
Devereux, Paul. 1991. *Earth Memory*. London: Quantum.
——. 1992a. *Shamanism and the Mystery Lines*. London: Quantum.
——. 1992b. *Secrets of Ancient and Sacred Places*. London: Blandford.
Diamond, Irene and Orenstein, Gloria (eds). 1990. *Reweaving the Web: the Emergence of Ecofeminism*. San Francisco: Sierra Club.
Dickens, Peter. 1992. *Society and Nature: Towards a Green Social Theory*. London: Harvester Wheatsheaf.
Dillard, Annie. 1976. *Pilgrim at Tinker Creek*. London: Picador.
Douglas, Mary. 1990 *Implicit Meanings*. London: Routledge.
Drury, Neville. 1989. *The Elements of Shamanism*. Shaftesbury: Element.
Dumézil, Georges. 1973. *The Destiny of a King*. Chicago University Press.
——. 1988. *Gods of the Ancient Northmen, Mitra-Varuna: an Essay on Two IndoEuropean Representations of Sovereignty*. New York: Zone.
Dundas, Paul. 1992. *The Jains*. London: Routledge.
Düerr, Hans-Peter. 1987. *Dreamtime: Concerning the Boundary between Wilderness and Civilization*. Oxford: Blackwell.
Edwards, Leila. 1996. "Tradition and Ritual: Halloween in Contemporary Paganism" in Graham Harvey and Charlotte Hardman (eds): 224-41.
Eilberg-Schwartz, Howard. 1989. "Witches of the West: Neopaganism and Goddess Worship as Enlightenment Religions", *Journal of Feminist Studies in Religion* 5.1: 77-95.
Eisler, Riane. 1987. *The Chalice and the Blade: Our Story, Our Future*. San Francisco: Harper & Row.
Eliade, Mircea. 1974. *Shamanism: Archaic Techniques of Ecstasy*. Princeton: Princeton University Press.
Eller, Cynthia. 1991. "Relativizing the Patriarchy: the Sacred History of the Feminist Spirituality Movement". *History of Religions* 30: 279-95.
——. 1993. *Living in the Lap of the Goddess: the Feminist Spirituality Movement in America*. Boston: Beacon.
Ellis, Peter B. 1994. *The Druids*. London: Constable.
Fairport Convention. 1978. *Tippler's Tales*. Vertigo.
Faivre, Antoine and Jacob Needleman, (eds). 1992. *Modern Esoteric Spirituality*. London: SCM.
Farrar, Janet and Stewart Farrar,. 1981. *Eight Sabbats for Witches*. London: Robert Hale.
——. 1984. *The Witches' Way*. London: Robert Hale.
Feyerabend, Paul. 1985. *Science in a Free Society*. London: Verso.
Finn, Geraldine. 1992. "The politics of spirituality: the spirituality of politics" in Philippa Berry and Andrew Wernick (eds): 111-21.

Flaherty, Robert P. 1991. "T.M.Luhrmann and the Anthropologist's Craft: Differential Identity and the Ethnography of Britain's Magical Subculture". *Anthropological Quarterly* 64: 152-5.

Flood, Gavin (ed.). 1993. *Mapping Invisible Worlds*. Edinburgh University Press.

Foley, Helene P. 1994. "A Question of Origins: Goddess Cults Greek and Modern". *Women's Studies* 23: 193-215.

Ford, Patrick K. 1977. *The Mabinogi and Other Medieval Welsh Tales*. Berkeley: University of California.

Foreman, David. 1987. *Ecodefence: a Field Guide to Monkeywrenching*. Tucson: Ned Ludd.

Fries, Jan. 1992. *Visual Magick*. Oxford: Mandrake Press.

———. 1993. *Helrunar: a manual of rune magick*. Oxford: Mandrake Press.

Gadon, Elinor W. 1990. *The Once and Future Goddess*. London: Aquarian.

Gamman, Lorraine and Margaret Marshment (eds). 1988. *The Female Gaze*. London: Women's Press.

Gantz, Jeffrey (transl.). 1976. *The Mabinogion*. Harmondsworth: Penguin.

Gardner, Gerald. 1949. *High Magick's Aid*. London: Atlantis Bookshop.

———. 1954. *Witchcraft Today*. London: Rider.

———. 1959. *The Meaning of Witchcraft*. Wellingborough: Aquarian.

Geertz, Armin W. 1993. "Archaic Ontology and White Shamanism". *Religion* 23: 369-72.

Gennep, Arnold van. 1960. *The Rites of Passage*. University of Chicago Press.

Gibson, William. 1995. *Neuromancer*. London: HarperCollins.

Gimbutas, Marija. 1982. *The Goddesses and Gods of Old Europe: Myths and Cult Objects*. Berkeley: University of California.

———. 1989. *The Language of the Goddess*. San Francisco: Harper & Row.

Gittings, Robert. 1966. *Selected Poems and Letters of Keats*. London: Heinemann.

Goldenberg, Naomi. 1979. *Changing of the Gods: Feminism and the End of Traditional Religions*. Boston: Beacon.

Goodman, Felicitas D. 1990. *Where the Spirits Ride the Wind: Trance Journeys and Other Ecstatic Experiences*. Bloomington: Indiana University Press.

Göttner-Abendroth, Heide. 1987. *Matriarchal Mythology in Former Times and Today*. Freedom CA: Crossing.

Grace, Patricia. 1995. *The Sky People*. London: Women's Press.

Grahn, Judy. 1984. *Another Mother Tongue: Gay Words, Gay Worlds*. Boston: Beacon.

Grant, Kenneth. 1991. *The Magical Revival*. London: Skoob.

Graves, Robert. 1948. *The White Goddess*. London: Faber and Faber.

Green, Deirdre. 1989. "Towards a reappraisal of Polytheism" in Glenys Davies (ed.): 3-11.

Green, Marian. 1971. *Magic in Principle and Practice*. London: Quest.

———. 1989. *Elements of Natural Magic*. Shaftesbury: Element.

———. 1991. *A Witch Alone*. London: Element.

———. 1992. "Magic, Nature and the Old Path". *The Occult Observer* 2: 8-11.

Green, Miranda. 1989. *Symbol and Image in Celtic Religious Art*. London: Routledge.

Greenwood, Susan. 1996. "The Magical Will, Gender and Power in Magical Practices" in Graham Harvey and Charlotte Hardman (eds): 191-203.
Grey, Mary. 1991. "Claiming Power-in-Relation: Exploring the Ethics of Connection". *Journal of Feminist Studies in Religion* 7.1: 7-18.
——. 1992. "The Dark Knowing of Morgan Le Fay: Women, Evil and Theodicy" in Teresa Elwes (ed.). *Women's Voices: Essays in Contemporary Feminist Theology*. London: Marshall Pickering: 111-30.
Griffin, Susan. 1984. *Woman and Nature: the Roaring Inside Her*. London: Women's Press.
Grigg, Richard. 1995. *When God Becomes Goddess*. New York: Continuum.
Grundy, Stephan. 1994. "Interface with Stephan Grundy". *Pagan Voice* 32: 11.
Gundarsson, KveldúlfR H. (ed.) 1993. *Our Troth*. Tempe: Ring of Troth.
Hackett, Jo Ann. 1989. "Can a Sexist Model Liberate Us? Ancient Near Eastern 'Fertility' Goddesses". *Journal of Feminist Studies in Religion* 5.1: 65-76.
Halifax, Joan. 1991. *Shaman Voices: a Survey of Visionary Narratives*. London: Arkana.
Hallowell, A. Irving. 1960. "Objibwa ontology, behavior and world view" in Stanley Diamond (ed.) *Culture in History: Essays in Honour of Paul Radin*. New York: Columbia University Press: 19-52.
Hampson, Daphne. 1990. *Theology and Feminism*. Oxford: Blackwell.
Harding, M. Esther. 1971. *Woman's Mysteries Ancient and Modern*. New York: Harper & Row.
Harner, Michael. 1972. *The Jívaro: People of the Sacred Waterfalls*. Berkeley: University of California Press.
——. 1990. *The Way of the Shaman*. San Francisco: Harper & Row.
Harris, Adrian. 1996. "Sacred Ecology" in Graham Harvey and Charlotte Hardman (eds): 149-56.
Harvey, Graham. 1993. "Avalon from the Mists: the Contemporary Teaching of Goddess Spirituality". *Religion Today* 8: 10-13.
——. 1994b. "Death and Remembrance in Modern Paganism" in Jon Davies (ed.). *Ritual and Remembrance: Responses to Death in Human Societies*. Sheffield Academic Press: 103-22.
——. 1995a. "Satanism in Contemporary Britain". *Journal of Contemporary Religion* 10: 353-66.
——. 1995b. "Ritual Abuse Allegations, Incitement to Religious Hatred: Pagans and Christians in Court" in Robert Towler (ed.). *New Religions and the New Europe* Aarhus: Aarhus University Press: 154-70.
——. 1995c. "The Suffering of Witches and Children: Uses of the Witchcraft Passages in the Bible" in Jon Davies, Graham Harvey and Wilfred Watson (eds). *Words Remembered, Texts Renewed: Festschrift for Prof. John F.A. Sawyer*. Sheffield Academic Press: 113-34.
——. 1995d. "The Authority of¸ Intimacy in Paganism and Goddess Spirituality". *Diskus* 4.1: 34-48.
——. 1996. "Heathenism: a North European Pagan Tradition" in Graham Harvey and Charlotte Hardman (eds): 49-64.
—— and Charlotte Hardman, (eds). 1996. *Paganism Today*. London: Thorsons.
Heaney, Marie. 1994. *Over Nine Waves: a book of Irish Legends*. London: Faber and Faber.

Heelas, Paul. 1996. *The New Age Movement: Religion, Culture and Society in the Age of Postmodernity*. Oxford: Blackwell.
Heinlein, Robert. 1961. *Stranger in a Strange Land*. New York: G.P.Putnam's Sons.
Hick, John. 1977. *God and the Universe of Faiths*. London, Macmillan.
——. 1985. *Problems in Religious Pluralism*. London: Macmillan.
Hoff, Benjamin and Opal Whiteley. 1994. *The Singing Creek where the Willows Grow*. New York: Penguin.
Holdstock, Robert. 1984. *Mythago Wood*. London: Gollancz.
Hollinghurst, Stephen. 1996. "Christ and Post-Christian Spirituality". Unpublished dissertation, Trinity College, Bristol.
Hopman, Ellen E. and Lawrence Bond. 1996. *People of the Earth: The New Pagans Speak Out*. Rochester, VT: Destiny.
Horwatt, Karin. 1988. "The shamanic complex in the Pentecostal Church". *Ethos* 16.2: 128-45.
Hughes, Charles, J. 1985. "Gaia: a Natural Scientist's Ethic for the Future". *The Ecologist* 15.3: 92-5.
Hume, Lynne. 1994. *Compendium Beneficiorum: Beliefs and Practices of Modern Witchcraft in Australia*. Adelaide: Charles Strong Memorial Trust.
——. 1995. "Witchcraft and the Law in Australia". *Journal of Church and State* 37: 135-50.
Hutton, Ronald. 1991. *The Pagan Religions of the Ancient British Isles* London: Blackwell.
——. 1993. *The Shamans of Siberia*. Glastonbury: Isle of Avalon Press.
——, 1994. "Neo-Paganism, Paganism and Christianity". *Religion Today* 9.3: 29-32.
——. 1995. "The Shamans of Siberia". *Druids' Voice* 5: 4-8.
——. 1996a. "The Roots of Modern Paganism" in Graham Harvey and Charlotte Hardman (eds): 3-15.
——. 1996b. *The Stations of the Sun: a History of the Ritual Year in Britain*. Oxford University Press.
——. 1996c. "Who Possesses the Past?" in Carr-Gomm (ed.): 17-34.
James, Stanlie M. and Abena P.A. Busia (eds). 1993. *Theorizing Black Feminisms: The Visionary Pragmatism of Black Women*. London: Routledge.
Jayran, Shan. 1994. *Circlework*. London: House of the Goddess.
——. 1996. "Darklight Philosophy: A Ritual Praxis" in Graham Harvey and Charlotte Hardman (eds): 204-23.
Johnson, Paul C. 1995. "Shamanism from Ecuador to Chicago: A Case Study in New Age Ritual Appropriation". *Religion* 25: 163-78.
Jones, Leslie. 1994. "The Emergence of the Druid as Shaman". *Folklore in Use* 2: 131-42.
Jones, Prudence. 1996. "Pagan Theologies" in Graham Harvey and Charlotte Hardman (eds): 32-46.
Jones, Prudence and Caitlín Matthews. 1990. *Voices from the Circle: The Heritage of Western Paganism*. London: Aquarian.
Jones, Prudence and Nigel Pennick. 1995. *A History of Pagan Europe*. London: Routledge.
Jung, Carl G. 1953. *Psychology and Alchemy*. London: Routledge & Kegan Paul.

Jung, L. Shannon. 1988. "Feminism and Spatiality: Ethics and the Recovery of a Hidden Dimension". *Journal of Feminist Studies in Religion* 4.1: 55-71.

Kaplan, Jeffrey. 1996. "The Reconstruction of the Ásatrú and Odinist Traditions" in James Lewis (ed.): 193-236.

Keats, John. 1819. "Ode on a Grecian Urn" in Gittings (1966): 124-8.

Keller, Catherine. 1988. "Goddess, Ear, and Metaphor: On the Journey of Nelle Morton", *Journal of Feminist Studies in Religion* 4.2: 51-67.

Kelly, Aidan. 1991. *Crafting the Art of Magic.* Book 1: *A History of Modern Witchcraft, 1939-1964.* St.Paul: Llewellyn.

——. 1992. "An Update on Neopagan Witchcraft in America" in James Lewis and Gordon Melton (eds): 136-51.

Kelly, Michael. 1995. "The Power in Polarities". *Hoblink* 32: 2.

Keynes, Geoffrey (ed.). 1972. *Blake: Complete Writings.* Oxford University Press.

King, Ursula. 1989. *Women and Spirituality.* Basingstoke: Macmillan.

Kohák, Erazim. 1991. "Speaking of Persons". *Personalist Forum* 7: 41-58.

——. 1993. "Speaking to Trees". *Critical Review* 6: 371-88.

——. 1994. "Transitions: Ploughman, Pilgrim, Conqueror". *Psychoanalytic Review* 81: 101-24.

Koppana, Kati-ma. 1990. *The Finnish Gods.* Helsinki: Mandragora Dimensions.

LaChapelle, Dolores. 1989. "Sacred Land, Sacred Sex" in Judith Plant (ed.): 155-67.

Lake, Bobby (Medicine Grizzlybear). 1993. "Power Centers" in James Swan (ed.): 48-59.

Lamb, Christopher. 1996. "Faiths and the Environment: Introduction", *Faiths and the Environment: conference papers* 1 (1996): 5-8.

Lamond, Fred. 1993. "Magicking the Art of the Craft". *Deosil Dance* 34: 33-4.

Lefkowitz, Mary R. 1993. "The New Cults of the Goddess". *The American Scholar* 62 : 261-8.

Le Guin, Ursula K. 1986. *Always Coming Home.* London: Gollancz.

——. 1992. *Dancing at the Edge of the World.* London: Paladin.

——. 1993. *The Earthsea Quartet.* London: Puffin.

Leonard, Joan. 1990. "Teaching Introductory Feminist Spirituality, Tracing the Trajectory through Women Writers". *Journal of Feminist Studies in Religion* 6.2: 121-35.

Lerner, Berel D. 1995. "Understanding a (Secular) Primitive Society". *Religious Studies* 31: 303-9.

Lerner, Gerda. 1986. *The Creation of Patriarchy.* Oxford University Press.

Letcher, Andy. 1996. "So you wanna be a Bard?" in Philip Shallcrass (ed.): 38-41.

Leviton, Richard. 1993. "The Ley Hunters" in James Swan (ed.): 245-56.

Lewis, Charles S. 1943. *The Case for Christianity.* New York: Macmillan.

Lewis, Ioan M. 1989. *Ecstatic Religion: a study of Shamanism and Spirit Possession.* London: Routledge.

Lewis, James R. (ed.). 1996. *Magical Religion and Modern Witchcraft.* Albany, NY: State University of New York Press.

Lewis, James R. and J. Gordon Melton (eds). 1992. *Perspectives on the New Age.* Albany, NY: State University of New York Press.

Long, Asphodel. 1981. Review of Monica Sjöö and Barbara Mor (1981). *Women Speaking* July-December: 17-18.

———. 1991. "Anti-Judaism in Britain". *Journal of Feminist Studies in Religion* 7.2: 125-33.

———. 1992. *In a Chariot Drawn by Lions*. London: Women's Press.

———. 1994. "The Goddess Movement in Britain Today". *Feminist Theology* 5: 11-39.

———. 1996. "Ways of Knowing: The One or the Many—the Great Goddess Revisited". Unpublished paper, Britain and Ireland School of Feminist Theology Annual Conference, Dublin.

Lovelock, James E. 1982. *Gaia: A New Look at Life on Earth*. Oxford University Press.

———. 1985. Reply. *The Ecologist* 15.3: 95.

Luck, Georg. 1987. *Arcana Mundi: Magic and the Occult in the Greek and Roman Worlds*. London: Crucible.

Luhrmann, Tanya M. 1986. "Witchcraft, morality and Magic in Contemporary London", *International Journal of Moral and Social Studies* 1: 77-94.

———. 1989. *Persuasions of the Witch's Craft; Ritual Magic in Contemporary England*. Oxford: Blackwell.

———. 1993. "The resurgence of romanticism: contemporary neopaganism, feminist spirituality and the divinity of nature" in Kay Milton (ed.): 219-32.

MacLellan, Gordon. 1996. "Dancing on the Edge: Shamanism in Modern Britain" in Graham Harvey and Charlotte Hardman (eds): 138-48.

Madsen, Catherine. 1989. "If God Is God She Is Not Nice". *Journal of Feminist Studies in Religion* 5.1: 103-5.

Magliocco, Sabina. 1996. "Ritual is my Chosen Art Form: The Creation of Ritual as Folk Art among Contemporary Pagans" in James Lewis (ed.): 93-119.

Maltwood, Katherine. 1964. *A Guide to Glastonbury's Temple of the Stars*. London: Clarke.

Martin, James M. 1994. "Gay and Bisexual Archetypes in Classical Mythology". *Chaos International* 16: 25-9.

Matthews, Caitlín. 1986. *Mabon and the Mysteries of Britain: An exploration of the Mabinogion*. London: Arkana.

———. 1992. "Shamanism in Britain". *Quest* 92: 15-18.

———. 1995. *Singing the Soul Back Home: Shamanism in Daily Life*. Shaftesbury: Element.

Matthews, John. 1991a. *Taliesin: Shamanism and the Bardic Mysteries in Britain and Ireland*. London: Aquarian.

———. 1991b. *Choirs of God: Revisioning Masculinity*. London: Unwin Hyman.

———. 1992. *The Celtic Shaman: a Handbook*. Shaftesbury: Element.

——— (ed.). 1996. A *Druid Source Book*. London: Cassell.

Matthews, John and Caitlín. 1987. *The Western Way: A practical guide to the Western Mystery Tradition*. Vol.1. *The Native Tradition*. London: Arkana.

McCrickard, Janet E. 1991. "Born-Again Moon: Fundamentalism in Christianity and the Feminist Spirituality Movement", *Feminist Review* 37: 59-67.

McKay, Nellie. 1993. "Acknowledging the Differences: can women find unity through diversity?" in Stanlie M. James and Abena P.A. Busia (eds): 267-82.

McKenna, Terence. 1992. *Food of the Gods: The Search for the Original Tree of Knowledge: A radical history of plants, drugs and human evolution.* New York: Bantam.

McKenna, Terence with Zuvuya. 1993. *Dream Matrix Telemetry.* Delec CD 2012. Gerrards Cross: Delerium.

Meadows, Kenneth. 1989. *Earth Medicine: A Shamanic Way to Self Discovery.* Shaftesbury: Element.

——. 1990. *The Medicine Way: A Shamanic Path to Self Mastery.* Shaftesbury: Element.

——. 1991. *Shamanic Experience: A practical guide to contemporary Shamanism.* Shaftesbury: Element.

Medicine Eagle, Brooke. 1991. "Brooke Medicine Eagle" in Joan Halifax (ed.): 86-91.

Melia, Daniel F. 1983. "The Irish Saint as Shaman". *Pacific Coast Philology* 18: 37-42.

Meskell, Lynne. 1995. "Goddesses, Gimbutas and New Age Archaeology". *Antiquity* 69: 74-86.

Metzner, Ralph. 1994. *The Well of Remembrance: Rediscovering the Earth Wisdom Myths of Northern Europe.* London: Shambhala.

Michell, John. 1974. *The Old Stone's of Land's End.* London: Garnstone.

——. 1988. *The Dimensions of Paradise.* London: Thames & Hudson.

Miller, David L., 1974. *The New Polytheism: Rebirth of the Gods and Goddesses.* New York: Harper and Row.

Mills, Jane. 1991. *Womanwords.* London: Virago.

Milton, Kay (ed.). 1993. *Environmentalism: The View from Anthropology.* London: Routledge.

Morgan, Keith. 1991. *Alternative Wicca.* Doncaster: Deosil Dance.

Morgan, Lynne. 1996. "Women and the Goddess Today" in Graham Harvey and Charlotte Hardman (eds): 94-108.

Morton, Nelle. 1985. *The Journey is Home.* Boston: Beacon.

Morrison, Kenneth, M. 1992a. "Beyond the Supernatural: Language and Religious Action". *Religion* 22: 201-5.

——. 1992b. "Sharing the Flower: A Non-Supernaturalistic Theory of Grace". *Religion* 22: 207-19.

Murray, Margaret. 1921. *The Witch-Cult in Western Europe: a Study in Anthropology.* Oxford University Press.

——. 1933. *The God of the Witches.* Oxford University Press.

Naddair, Kaledon. 1986. *Ogham, Koelbren and Runic.* Edinburgh: Keltia.

——. 1987. *Keltic Folk and Faerie Tales.* London: Century.

Needleman, Jacob. 1975. *A Sense of the Cosmos: The Encounter of Modern Science and Ancient Truth.* New York: Doubleday.

Ó hÓgáin, Dáithí. 1990. *Myth, Legend and Romance: An encyclopaedia of Irish Folk Tradition.* London: Ryan.

Oakley, Christina. 1996. "Druids and Witches: History, Archetype and Identity" in Carr-Gomm (ed.): 260-82.

Oliver, Martin. 1992. "Putting the EARTH FIRST!". *Pagan Voice* 7: 3.

Oliver, Mary. 1986. *Dream Work.* Boston: Atlantic Monthly Press.

Olson, Carl. 1983. *Book of the Goddess Past and Present: An Introduction to Her Religion.* New York: Crossroads.

Orenstein, Gloria. 1990. *The Reflowering of the Goddess.* Oxford: Pergamon.

Paper, Jordan. 1988. "Cosmological Implications of Pan-Indian Sacred Pipe Ritual". *Amerindian Cosmology:* Special Joint Issue of the *Canadian Journal of Native Studies* 7.2 and *Cosmos* 4. (edited by Don McCaskill): 297-306.

Patterson, Barry. 1991. *Finding your Way in the Woods: the Art of Conversation with the Genius Loci.* Coventry: Berkana!

——. 1993. *A Statement of Intent is not Enough.* Coventry: Berkana!

Pennick, Nigel. 1994. *Sacred Geometry: Symbolism and Purpose in Religious Structures.* Chieveley: Capall Bann.

Pennick, Nigel and Paul Devereux. 1989. *Lines on the Landscape.* London: Robert Hale.

Perera, Sylvia B. 1981. *Descent to the Goddess: A Way of Initiation for Women.* Toronto: Inner City Books.

Pike, Sarah M. 1996. "Forging Magical Selves: Gendered Bodies and Ritual Fires at Neo-Pagan Festivals" in James Lewis (ed.): 121-40.

Plant, Judith. 1989. *Healing the Wounds: The Promise of Ecofeminism.* London: Green Print.

Plaskow, Judith and Carol P. Christ. 1989. *Weaving the Visions: New Patterns in Feminist Spirituality.* San Francisco: Harper & Row.

Plumwood, Val. 1993. *Feminism and the Mastery of Nature.* London: Routledge.

Pratchett, Terry.[1] 1983. *The Colour of Magic.* Gerrards Cross: Smythe. New York: St.Martin's.

——. 1986. *The Light Fantastic.* Gerrards Cross: Smythe. *1988. New York: Signet.

——. 1987. *Equal Rites.* London: Gollancz. *1988. New York: Signet.

——. 1988. *Wyrd Sisters.* London: Gollancz. *1990. New York: Roc.

——. 1990. *Moving Pictures.* London: Gollancz. *1992a. New York: Roc.

——. 1991a. *Reaper Man.* London: Gollancz. *1992b. New York: Roc.

——. 1991b. *Witches Abroad.* London: Gollancz. *1993. New York: Roc.

——. 1992. *Small Gods.* London: Gollancz. *1994. New York: HarperCollins.

——. 1993. *Lords and Ladies.* London: Gollancz. *1995a. New York: HarperCollins.

——. 1994. *Soul Music.* London: Gollancz. *1995b. New York: HarperCollins.

Pratchett, Terry and Stephen Briggs. 1994. *The Discworld Companion.* London: Gollancz.

Rabinovitch, Shelley. 1992. "'An' Ye Harm None, Do What Ye Will': Neo-Pagans and Witches in Canada". Unpublished M.A. Thesis, Carleton University, Ottawa.

——. 1996. "Heal the Universe and Heal the Self: Bateson's Double-Bind and North American Wiccan Practice". Unpublished conference paper for "Nature Religion Today: Western Paganism, Shamanism and Esotericism in the 1990s" Lancaster University.

Rahner, Karl. 1966. "Christianity and the Non-Christian Religions". *Theological Investigations* 5: 115-34.

Rainbird, Karin. 1994. "Progressive Wicca" in *Talking Stick Magical Directory.* London: Talking Stick. p.8.

---

[1] US editions are indicated by *.

Raoult, Michel. 1992. *Les Druides. Les sociétés initiatiques celtiques contemporaines.* Monaco: Editions du Rocher.
——. 1996. "The Druid Revival in Brittany, France and Europe" in Philip Carr-Gomm (ed.): 100-22.
Raphael, Melissa. 1994. "Feminism, Constructivism and Numinous Experience". *Religious Studies* 30: 511-26.
——. 1996. *Thealogy and Embodiment.* Sheffield Academic Press.
Rees, Kenneth. 1996. "The Tangled Skein: the role of myth in Paganism" in Graham Harvey and Charlotte Hardman (eds): 16-31.
Reid, Siân. 1996. "As I do Will, so Mote it Be: Magic as Metaphor in Neo-Pagan Witchcraft" in James Lewis (ed.): 141-67.
Return to the Source. 1995. *The Chakra Journey.* London: Return to the Source. RTTS CD2.
Richardson, James T., Joel Best and David G. Bromley (eds). 1991. *The Satanism Scare.* New York: de Gruyter.
Roberts, Peter. 1991. "Is there a Future for the Goddess? Obstacles to the Evolution of Goddess-Spirituality in the New Age". *Religion Today* 6.3: 8-13.
Rufus. 1992. "Unity and Diversity". *Pandora's Jar* 3: 1-2.
Rushing, Andrea B. 1993. "Surviving Rape: a morning/mourning ritual" in Stanlie M. James and Abena P.A. Busia (eds): 127-40.
Rushkoff, Douglas. 1994. *Cyberia: Life in the Trenches of Hyperspace.* London: HarperCollins.
Sachs, Wolfgang. 1994. "The Blue Planet: An Ambiguous Modern Icon". *The Ecologist* 24: 170-5.
Saiving, Valerie. 1976. "Androcentrism in Religious Studies". *Journal of Religion* 56: 177-97.
Sanders, Nancy K. 1972. *The Epic of Gilgamesh.* London: Penguin.
Sellon, Emily B. and Weber, Renée. 1992. "Theosophy and the Theosophical Society" in Antoine Faivre and Jacob Needleman (eds): 311-29.
Sered, Susan S. 1993. "Religious Rituals and Secular Rituals: Interpenetrating Models of Childbirth in a Modern, Israeli Context". *Sociology of Religion* 54.1: 101-14.
——. 1994. *Priestess, Mother, Sacred Sister.* Oxford University Press.
Seymour-Smith, Martin. 1982. *Robert Graves: His life and work.* London: Hutchinson.
Shamen with Terence McKenna. 1993. *Re: Evolution.* 118TP7CD. London: One Little Indian.
Shallcrass, Philip. 1995. Editorial Comment in *The Druids' Voice* 5: 25.
—— (ed.). 1996. *Druidry: Native Spirituality in Britain.* St.Leonards-on-Sea: The British Druid Order.
Shual, Katon. 1993. The Demon Doctrine". *Nuit Isis* 10: 2-5.
——. 1994. *Sexual Magick.* Oxford: Mandrake.
Sidhe, Wren. 1991. "Drawing Down the Moon". *From the Flames* 1: 6-7.
Simes, Amy. 1996. "Mercian Movements: Group Transformation and Individual Choices amongst East Midlands Pagans" in Graham Harvey and Charlotte Hardman (eds): 170-90.
Simpson, Jacqueline. 1994. "Margaret Murray: Who Believed Her, and Why?". *Folklore* 105: 89-96.

Sjöö, Monica. 1992. *New Age and Armageddon: The Goddess or the gurus? Towards a feminist vision of the future.* London: Women's Press.

Sjöö, Monica and Barbara Mor. 1981. *The Ancient Religion of the Great Cosmic Mother of All.* Trondheim: Rainbow.

———. 1987. *The Great Cosmic Mother: Rediscovering the Religion of the Earth.* San Francisco: Harper & Row.

Slade, Paddy. 1990. *Natural Magic.* London: Hamlyn

Smart, Ninian. 1993. "The formation rather than the origin of a tradition". *Diskus* 1.1: 1.

Smith, Jonathan Z. 1987. *To Take Place: Toward Theory in Ritual.* University of Chicago Press.

Spivak, Gayatri C. 1987. *In Other Worlds: Essays in Cultural Politics.* London: Routledge.

Spretnak, Charlene. 1978. *Lost Goddesses of early Greece.* Boston: Beacon.

——— (ed.). 1982. *The Politics of Women's Spirituality.* Garden City: Doubleday.

———. 1989. "Towards an Ecofeminist spirituality" in Judith Plant (ed.): 127-32.

Stafford, Greg. 1990. "The Medicine Circle of Turtle Island" in Jones and Matthews (eds): 83-92.

Starhawk. 1982. *Dreaming the Dark.* Boston: Beacon Press.

———. 1989a. *The Spiral Dance.* San Francisco: Harper & Row.

———. 1989b. In "Roundtable Discussion: If God Is God She is Not Nice". *Journal of Feminist Studies in Religion* 5.1: 105-6.

———. 1990. *Truth or Dare.* New York: Harper & Row.

Stewart, Robert, J. 1991. *Celebrating the Male Mysteries.* Bath: Arcania.

Stone, Alby. 1989. *Wyrd: Fate and Destiny in North European Paganism.* Loughborough: Heart of Albion.

Stone, Merlin. 1976. *When God was a Woman.* New York: Harcourt Brace Jovanovich.

Sutcliffe, Richard. 1996. "Left-Hand Path Ritual Magick: an Historical and Philosophical Overview" in Graham Harvey and Charlotte Hardman (eds): 109-37.

Swan, James. 1993. *The Power of Place and Human Environments.* Bath: Gateway.

Tawhai, Te Pakaka. 1988. "Maori Religion" in Stewart Sutherland, Leslie Houlden, Peter Clarke, Friedhelm Hardy (eds). *The World's Religions.* London: Routledge: 854-63.

Thorpe, Lewis. 1978. *Gerald of Wales.* Harmondsworth: Penguin.

Thorsson, Edred. 1991. *The Nine Doors of Midgard.* St. Paul, MN: Llewellyn.

Tolkien, John R.R. 1937. *The Hobbit.* London: Allen & Unwin.

———. 1954-5. *The Lord of the Rings.* London: Allen & Unwin.

Turner, Victor. 1967. *The Forest of Symbols.* Ithaca: Cornell University Press.

Valiente, Doreen. 1975. *Natural Magic.* London: Robert Hale.

———. 1978. *Witchcraft for Tomorrow.* London: Robert Hale.

Vayne, Julian. 1995. "The Invisible Pagans". *Pagan Voice* 40: 9-11.

Voigt, Valerie. 1992. "Sex Magic" in Chas Clifton (ed.): 85-108.

Walker, Alice. 1983. *The Color Purple.* London: Women's Press.

———. 1984. *In Search of Our Mothers' Gardens: Womanist Prose.* London: Women's Press.

Weaver, Mary Jo. 1989. "Who is the Goddess and Where Does She Get Us?" *Journal of Feminist Studies in Religion* 5.1: 49-64.

Wittig, Monique. 1985. *Les Guérillères*. Boston: Beacon.

Wolff, Virginia. 1929. *A Room of One's Own*. London: Hogarth.

Wolkstein, Diane and Samuel N. Kramer. 1983. *Inanna, Queen of Heaven and Earth*. New York: Harper & Row.

Wood, Harold W. 1985. "Modern Pantheism as an Approach to Environmental Ethics". *Environmental Ethics* 7: 151-64.

Woodhead, Linda. 1993. "Post-Christian Spiritualities". *Religion* 23: 167-81.

York, Michael. 1995. *The Emerging Network: A Sociology of the New Age and Neo-Pagan Networks*. Lanham: Rowman & Littlefield.

——. 1996. "New Age and Paganism" in Graham Harvey and Charlotte Hardman (eds): 157-65.

INDEX

Abred, 28
Abuse, 2, 49, 119, 184, 198, 209
Acupuncture, 147, 149, 156–7
Affirmation, 141, 175
Ageing, 187
Age-ism, 83
Aggressive magic, 121
Agriculture, 140
AIDS, 146, 198, 208
Alchemy, 91, 147
Alexandrian Wicca, 35, 44, 50
Allopathic medicine, 47
Altruism, 145
Anarchy, 103
Ancestors, 5–6, 21, 28, 171, 195, 201
Animals, 139, 171
Animism, 66, 98, 118, 125, 133, 134–5, 139–41, 144, 163, 170–1, 175, 226
Annwn, 28
Anthropology, 107–25, 181, 194–7, 226
Anti-semitism, 66, 84, 223
Appropriation, 108, 181, 226
Apuleius, 166
Archaeology, 17, 151, 179–81
Archetypes, 69, 118, 125, 146, 166
Arthurian legends, 71, 183, 205
Asatrú, 53–68, 71, 161, 167, 179, 180, 191–2, 200, 201, 206, 212
Asatrú Alliance, 53
Asatrú Folk Assembly, 53
Asterix the Gaul, 186
Astrology, 14, 102, 147
Athame, 48
Atheism, 66, 171
Aural tradition, 20
Authority, 212–14
Autumn equinox, 13, 198, 203
Avalon, 72, 205
Awen, 20–2

Bagpipes, 22
Balance, 10

Bananas, 163
Bards, 20–5, 60, 116, 206
Beauty, 216
Becoming Pagan, 192
Belief, 37, 100, 156, 161, 171, 174, 189
Beltain, 10–11, 200
Berserkers, 113
Bindrunes, 63, 102
Birth, 39, 199
Bisexuals, 99
Black magic, 35, 93, 97
Blake, William, 132, 166, 198, 215
Blasphemy, 134, 175, 185
Blood, 121
Bloom County, 184
Bodhrans, 22
Book of Shadows, 46
Book of the Law, 98
Branwen Daughter of Llyr, 25
Brittany, 18
Buddhism, 129, 161, 224
Burial, 203

Cakes and wine, 48–9
Calendar customs, 2–13, 46, 126, 189
Cancer, 187
Cannibalism, 49
Carroll, Lewis, 107
Celtic Christianity, 217, 222
Celtic mythology, 28
Ceremonial magic, 94–100
Ceugant, 28
Chakras, 40, 124, 147
Channelling, 39, 219
Chanting, 21, 30, 61, 95, 110, 183
Chaos butterfly, 91
Chaos magick, 99–100, 124
Charge of the Goddess, 36–8, 212
Child blessing, 199–200
Children, 5, 133, 137, 163, 170, 199–200
Christian anti-semitism, 66

243

Christianity, 74, 174, 179, 198, 222–3
Church of All Worlds, 182
Circle Sanctuary, 172, 191
Circles, 43, 70, 95, 103, 150, 199, 201, 207
Cities, 120
City farms, 120
City parks, 137, 150
Clarsach, 22
Classism, 83
Clergy, 31, 44
Coelbren, 26, 101
Color Purple, The, 216
Coming home, 193, 210
Coming out, 193
Commodification, 110, 226
Communion, 48
Computers, 120
Cone of power, 47, 116
Conjuring tricks, 87
Consumerism, 22, 142, 151, 181, 226
Conversion, 192
Correspondence courses, 20, 109
Correspondences, 90
Cosmology, 28–9, 54–7, 114, 143–59, 160–76, 218
Craft, 35–52, 134, 166, 178, 191–2, 200, 202, 207, 212, 218
Creator, 71, 145
Cremation, 203
Criminal Justice Act, 130
Crowley, Aleister, 88, 98, 104, 174
Cucumber dance, 10, 23
Cyberia, 23–4, 122–4

Dabbling, 185
Dark, 7, 208
Darwin, 131
Death, 5, 39, 64, 187, 203–6
Deconditioning, 98
Deep Ecology, 136
Defamation, 217–19, 221–2
Deforestation, 137
Deists, 29
Deities, 9, 36–43, 54, 65, 66–8, 69, 71, 75–7, 84, 114, 121, 132, 133, 144–6, 155, 161,

165–70, 174–6, 185, 188, 192, 199, 201, 207, 212, 227
Demonology, 88, 166, 173
Dianic Craft, 35, 50, 84
Didgeridoos, 22
Dillard, Annie, 187
Direct Action, 22, 31, 32, 48, 63, 102, 113, 120, 130–1, 185
Discworld, 50–1, 185–6
Dísitrú, 67, 71, 85
Divination, 61, 154
Dongas, 130
Dragon Environmental Group, 63, 102, 123, 129
Dragon lines, 148–50
Dragons, 9, 156–7, 183
Drawing Down the Moon, 39–40, 41
Druid Time, 33
Druid's Prayer, 30
Druids, 10, 17–34, 71, 128, 161, 166, 186, 200, 202, 218
Dualism, 73, 97, 153, 173, 182, 218, 219, 225
Dumézil, Georges, 55
Dwarves, 54

Earth First!, 121, 128
Earth Liberation Front, 128
Earth Mysteries, 143–59
Earth People, 27
Earthing, 48
Easter, 9
Eco-drama, 31, 63, 130
Eco-fascism, 129
Ecofeminism, 136, 141
Ecology, 1, 27, 64–5, 71, 102, 126–42, 176, 186–8
Eco-magic, 102, 118
Ecotage, 121, 130
Ecstasy, 38, 108
Eight Festivals, 2–13, 43, 57, 192, 205
Eliade, Mircea, 82, 108
Elves, 54, 58, 114, 172–3
Emotions, 118
Empowerment, 74, 79, 112, 169, 208
Enchantment, 94, 164, 172, 181
End of Patriarchy, 78

Endangered Earth, 131–2
Energy, 9, 47–8
Enlightenment, 90, 96, 189–91, 225
Entropy, 57, 59, 215
Environmental education, 120, 129
Environmental ethics, 104
Equality, 70
Escapism, 158, 184
Esotericism, 90
Essentialism, 42
Ethics, 104–5
Evangelism, 1, 23, 215, 223
Evil, 7, 92, 204
Evolution, 145
Excalibur, 183
Experience, 129, 188–9
Experimentation, 105, 124, 185, 189

Faery, 2, 12, 116, 140, 163, 172–73
Faivre, Antoine, 90
Fantasy literature, 71, 181–6
Fatalism, 55
Fellowship of Isis, 78, 85
Feminism, 69, 72, 79, 193
Feminist Wicca, 50
Feng Shui, 148, 153, 155
Fertility, 42, 76, 178, 201
Festivals, 33, 49, 128, 161, 181, 184, 194, 221
Fetch, 115
Finland, 167
Fionn mac Cumhaill, 159
First Amendment, 222
First Nations, 27, 81, 83, 89, 107, 111, 115, 118, 135, 149, 161, 174, 181, 185, 188, 221, 226
Fluffy bunnies, 12, 219
Folklore, 5, 10–13, 23, 102, 172–4, 178–79, 201
Folkvang Horg, 67
Food, 12, 38, 118, 125, 134–5
Fool, 23
Football, 47, 161
Fortune telling, 61
Fortune, Dion, 184

Four directions, 5, 20, 21, 44, 95, 201
Four elements, 5, 43, 167, 201
Four seasons, 43
Four winds, 5, 44
Fox hunting, 13
Frazer, James, 178
Free Festivals, 49
Freemasonry, 18, 49, 166, 178, 191
Free-will, 55
Freud, Sigmund, 110, 118
Friends of the Earth, 127
Fundamentalism, 82
Funerals, 192, 203–6
Future Fiction, 182
Fylgia, 115

Gaia, 24, 90, 103, 123, 131, 133, 144–6, 171
Galdor, 61, 110
Gardner, Gerald, 52, 117, 184, 191
Gardnerian Wicca, 35, 50
Garner, Alan, 182
Gays, 40–3, 99, 202
Gendered metaphors, 141
Geomancy, 143–59
Geometry, 152–3
Gerald of Wales, 21
Ghosts, 21
Giants, 54, 133
Gibson, William, 184
Gimbutas, Marija, 73, 180
Global warming, 11
Gnosis, 92
Gnosticism, 88, 92, 138–9, 153, 221
Goddess Spirituality, 69–86, 166, 180
Golden Ages, 22, 72, 82
Golden Dawn, 96
Gothar, 60
Grail, 116
Granny Weatherwax, 51
Graves, Robert, 26, 69, 184
Great Work, 99
Green products, 127
Greenpeace, 48, 127

Greenwood, 6, 153, 157, 162–5, 183
Groking, 92, 182
Grounding, 48
Group formation, 49
Guided meditation, 95, 113, 115, 127, 138, 165
Gwynvid, 28

Halloween, 3–6, 93, 218
Halloween Gathering, 49
Hallucinogens, 108–12
Hamingja, 55
Hammarens Ordens Sällskap, 53, 128
Hammers, 58–9, 63, 180
Handfasting, 11, 119, 200–2
Harner, Michael, 111
Harps, 22
Hávamál, 66, 212
Healing, 26, 102, 112, 117, 118–20, 185, 207–10
Heathens, 53–68, 71, 161, 167, 179, 180, 191–2, 200, 201, 206, 212
Hedge Witchcraft, 35, 178
Hedgehogs, 139–41, 166, 174
Hedonism, 123
Heinlein, Robert, 92, 182
Hengest and Horsa, 14
Herbalism, 26, 47, 62, 102, 119, 147, 156, 208
Hereditary Craft, 35, 179
Heritage Industry, 151
Hermeticism, 88, 91, 139
Heroes, 58, 157
Her-story, 72–75, 80, 180
Heterosexuals, 40–3, 99, 202
High Priestesses, 36, 39
High Priests, 36, 39
Hinduism, 38, 168–9, 225
History, 17–19, 72–5, 82, 177–81
Hobby Horse, 10
Holdstock, Robert, 183
Holy Guardian Angel, 96
Homeopathy, 26, 47, 119, 156
Homophobia, 66, 202
Homosexuals, 40–3, 99, 202
Hooded men, 56
House of the Goddess, 8, 49

Human sacrifice, 17, 49, 218
Humour, 10, 23, 38, 51, 184, 185–6, 201
Humpty Dumpty, 107
Hunting, 140
Hunt-saboteurs, 13
Hurricanes, 171

Iceland, 53
Icon, 39
Images, 9, 175
Imagination, 21, 47, 80, 90–1, 96, 99, 127, 175, 181–86
Imbolc, 8–9
Immanence, 37, 39, 43, 134, 175
Immortality, 139
Improvisation, 95
Incense, 95
Indians, 120
Individualism, 96, 101, 110, 142
Initiation, 27, 32, 44–5, 91, 108, 199, 206–7
Inner-worlds, 113, 115
Inspiration, 20–2
Intention, 21
Interconnectedness, 127
Inter-Faith Dialogue, 31, 214–17
Internet, 103, 122, 221
Intimacy, 138, 186, 214
Intuition, 70, 92, 175, 189
Invention, 85
Invocation, 36–8, 105, 167
Iolo Morganwg, 25, 30
Iron Age, 17, 22
Islam, 196, 224

Jack in the Green, 10
Japanese Pagans, 225
Jester, 23
Jewish Pagans/Jewitches, 223
John Barleycorn, 12–13, 24, 203
Journey metaphor, 142, 171, 224
Judaism, 96, 161, 196, 213
Julius Caesar, 179
Jung, Carl, 110, 118
Jungians, 57, 114, 116
Justice, 27

Kabbalah, 95, 113, 191

Karma, 55, 206
Keats, John, 216
Kibbo Kift, 59, 179
Kipling, Rudyard, 184
Kitchen magic, 101–2

Lammas, 12–13, 198
Land rights, 33, 130, 150–2
Land-spirits/Landvættir, 56, 65
Le Guin, Ursula, 182
Left-Hand Path magick, 97–9
Legitimation, 177, 190–2, 213
Lesbians, 99, 202
Lewis, C.S., 187
Ley lines, 117, 148–50, 157, 162
Liberation theology, 85
Libertarianism, 182
Life after death, 205–6
Lothlorien, 184
Lovers Blessing, 41
Lowerworld, 111
Lughnasad, 12–13, 198, 201, 203
Lunar cycle, 14, 39, 57, 132

Mabinogion, 22, 115, 180
Macrocosm, 96, 146–8, 186
Magic, 48, 57, 63, 87–106, 118,
    127, 135, 147, 154, 182, 184,
    208, 209
Magick, 97–9
Magrat Garlick, 51
Male gaze, 80
Male mysteries, 102, 206–7
Marriage, 11, 119, 195, 200–2
Maternity, 69
Mathematicians, 100
Matriarchal Study Group, 75
Matriarchy, 72–5, 180
May Day, 10–11, 157, 200
Media, 11, 31, 35, 119, 120, 128,
    181, 218
Meditation, 9, 20, 95, 127, 189
Mediums, 108
Megatripolis, 24, 123
Men's movement, 206–7
Menstruation, 39, 69, 121, 187,
    194
Metempsychosis, 28
Microcosm, 96, 146–8, 186
Middle Earth, 54, 64

Midgard, 54, 64
Midsummer, 11–12, 20, 58
Midwinter, 6–8, 14, 20, 58
Mimesis, 103
Miracles, 175, 188
Misrule, 23
Mists of Avalon, The, 183
Mithraists, 7, 71
Mjölnir, 58–9, 63, 180
Modernity, 142, 156, 158, 182,
    189–91, 195
Modranacht, 6
Monotheism, 77, 83, 167–70
Moon, 37
Morton, Nelle, 215
Mother Earth, 71, 76, 127, 155
Mother Night, 6
Mourning, 203–6
Multi-culturalism, 65
Murray, Margaret, 42, 178–9,
    191–2
Mutuality, 136, 181, 187, 209
Mystery Religions, 7, 35, 44, 192
Mysticism, 96, 122, 138
Mythago Wood, 183
Mythology, 57, 124, 166, 172–4

Naming, 199–200
Nanny Ogg, 51
National Parks, 163
Native Americans, 27, 81, 83, 115
Natural history, 25
Natural magic, 101–2
Nature, 186–8
Nature reserves, 163
Nazis, 65, 179
Neighbourliness, 27, 141, 214
Neuromancer, 184
New Age, 12, 27, 71, 81, 111,
    115, 121, 131, 136, 152, 158,
    219–21
New Age travellers, 11
New Religious Movement, 191–2
Nietzsche, 66, 101
Nine worlds, 54–7, 64
Noble Savages, 22, 149, 226
Non-violence, 32, 121
Norns, 55, 61
Nuclear tests, 129
Nudity, 44, 209

Numinous, 70, 92, 138

Occult jewellery, 51
Octarine, 94
Odinic Rite, 53, 191–92
Odinist Fellowship, 53, 64
Odinshof, 53, 128
Ogham, 26, 101
Old Religion, 52, 59, 191–2, 213
Oliver, Mary, 187
Opiates, 132, 176
Oral tradition, 20
Order of Bards, Ovates and
    Druids, 20, 202
Ordnance Survey, 132, 162
Orgies, 218
Otherness, 190
Otherworld, 2, 7, 12, 28, 110–16,
    153, 165, 204
Outback, 164
Outland, 184
Ovates, 25–9

Pacifism, 112, 121
Pagan Animal Rights, 128
Pagan Educational Network, 222
Pagan Funeral and Hospice Trust,
    203
Panentheism, 176
Pantheism, 133, 176, 187
Passover, 9
Pathworking, 95, 113
Patriarchy, 67, 73, 157, 180, 195,
    206, 215
Patterners, 120–2, 135
Peace camps, 79
Peer-counselling, 208
Pentagrams, 95, 121
Personal development, 43, 52, 87–
    106, 112, 182
Persons, 191
Philosophy, 122, 137, 170, 191
Pluralism, 72, 216
Polarity, 40–3
Police, 11, 31
Pollution, 43
Polytheism, 38, 55, 67, 77, 83,
    133, 167–70, 175, 192, 225
Possession, 21, 108, 113

Postmodernism, 72, 122, 123,
    189–91
Power, 209
Power, 2, 75, 211
Power animals, 108, 113
Pragmatism, 124
Pratchett, Terry, 35, 50–1, 172,
    185–6, 203
Priestesses, 36, 60, 84, 213
Priests, 36, 60, 213
Profane, 1, 144, 197
Progressive Craft, 35, 50
Protests, 48, 79, 120, 130–1, 185
Psychology, 57, 63, 116, 122
Public Order Act, 130
Pubs, 22, 33, 49, 221

Quantum physics, 100
Quarries, 147
Queensland, 218

Race, 65–6, 79, 206
Racism, 65–6, 83, 179
Ragnar Loðbrók, 14
Raising energy, 47–8, 110, 116,
    191
Rand, Ayn, 182
Rape, 119, 134, 184, 198, 209
Raves, 23–4, 122–24, 130
Rebirth, 39, 200
Reciprocity, 68, 144, 169, 174,
    204
Recreation, 188
Reincarnation, 28, 200
Religion, 161
Remembering, 85
Repression, 97
Responsibility, 27, 104, 129, 182,
    186
Return to the Source, 124
Revelation, 37, 43, 92, 175, 187,
    206, 212
Ring of Troth, 53
Riot squads, 11
Rites of passage, 43, 119, 194–
    210
Ritual, 63, 225
Ritual Abuse accusations, 5, 218
Ritual magic, 94–100
Robin's Greenwood Gang, 128

Romans, 17
Rosicrucianism, 178
Rune Gild, 53
Runes, 25, 61–62, 101, 102, 121

Sacred, 1, 144, 161, 197
Sacred geometry, 152–3
Sacred sites, 11, 31, 33, 71, 98,
    130, 150–2, 155, 158, 200
SAFF, 222
Saints, 74
Salvation, 80, 139, 169, 174, 223
Samadhi, 40
Samhain, 3–6, 171, 198, 203–5
Samye Ling, 129
Satanism, 217–19
Scepticism, 105, 213
Science, 91, 124, 145
Science Fiction, 182
Scriptures, 187, 212
Seax Wicca, 50
Secrecy, 35, 45, 49
Secular Order of Druids, 10, 71,
    123, 130, 198
Seers, 115
Seidr/Seething, 62, 115
Self blessing, 45
Self-sacrifice, 59
Sex magick, 99
Sexism, 2, 66, 83, 209
Sexual imagery, 40–3
Sexuality, 10, 38, 40–3, 62, 69,
    99, 116, 129, 157, 169, 175,
    182, 187, 195, 198, 200–2, 220
Shamanism, 21, 23, 62, 103, 107–
    25, 130, 134–5, 150, 167, 171,
    184, 226
Shinto, 225
Siberia, 107
Sidhe, 116
Sigils, 101
Sigrblot, 58
Sin, 92
Sincerity, 18
Singularities, 134, 176, 223
Skalds, 60
Sociology, 143, 222
Solitary Craft, 50, 211
Somatic ecology, 129–31
Song lines, 149, 183

Sorcery, 37, 112, 121
Soul loss, 108, 118
Soul-retrieval, 108, 119, 125
Souls, 28, 88, 125, 138, 147, 205
South Africa, 218
Spatiality, 186
Spirit, 20
Spirit of the age, 24
Spirits of place, 5, 103, 113
Spirituality, 161
Spring equinox, 9–10
St George, the Princess and the
    Dragon, 9, 156–7
St Valentine's day, 14
Star Trek, 184
State recognition, 53, 201, 213
States of consciousness, 23, 39,
    44, 61, 107–25, 150
Stereotypes, 19, 68, 84, 226
Stewardship, 141
Stonehenge, 33
Stone-people lodges, 27, 120, 181,
    226
Stories, 21
Sufism, 224
Summer camps, 22, 29, 120
Summer solstice, 11–12, 20, 201,
    218
Supermarkets, 1, 79, 140
Supernatural, 213
Sweat lodges, 27, 120, 181, 226
Symbols, 58, 61–4, 101, 102, 121,
    180, 200

Taliesin, 115, 205
Talking Stick, 49
Talking sticks, 208
Tantra, 42, 97, 104
Taoism, 39, 174
Taufr, 63, 200
Technology, 23, 122
Technoshamanism, 122–4
Techno-shamanism, 23–4
Temples, 95, 98, 117
Temporality, 186
Terrestrial zodiacs, 152, 162
Thealogy, 66, 69, 133
Thelema, 98
Theodicy, 83
Theoilogy, 66, 133

Theology, 1, 66–8, 133, 160–76
Therapies, 26–8, 57, 84, 102, 108,
     118–20, 147, 149, 156–7, 185,
     207–10
Tobacco, 112
Tolkien, 54, 67, 100, 172, 181–2
Traditional Craft, 35, 52
Traditional music, 23
Trance, 62
Transcendence, 139, 145, 175
Transmigration of souls, 28, 205
Tree lore, 25, 138
Tree Spirit, 128
Tricksters, 165, 173
Troubadours, 21
True self, 38, 88, 98
Trust, 44, 49

Uccello, Paolo, 157
Universalism, 110
Utilitarianism, 104
Utopias, 72, 145

Valhalla, 64, 192
Vanatrú, 67
Vegans, 140, 198
Vegetarians, 140
Vigils, 11
Vikings, 65, 192
Violence with impunity, 135
Visionaries, 21
Visualisation, 95, 113, 127, 138,
     165
Völva, 115
Voyeurism, 160, 176

Wagner, 66, 184
Wakes, 204

Walker, Alice, 216
Walknot, 58
Wally Hope, 33
Warlocks, 36
Warriors, 121
Way of the Shaman, The, 111
Way of Wyrd, The, 184
Web of Wyrd, 103
Western Mysteries, 115
White Goddess, 184
White magic, 93
White witches, 93
Wicca, 35–52, 138, 166, 178,
     191–2, 200, 202, 206, 207, 212
Wiccan Rede, 38, 135, 174
Will, 88–9, 98, 124, 135, 209
Wind Hags, 49
Winter solstice, 6–8, 20, 203
Winternights, 58
Witch trials, 178
Wittig, Monique, 85
Wizards, 36
Womanism, 83
Women's vision, 80
Woodcraft Chivalry, 59, 178
World-Wide-Web, 103, 122, 221
Worship, 55, 57, 71, 139, 166,
     174
Wyrd, 55, 57, 61, 103

Yggdrasil, 54–7, 63, 164
Yule, 6–8, 14, 58, 59

Zodiac, 14, 152